LOTUS BOOKS Start Here Series

Who Should Read This Book

For new spreadsheet users. This book helps you quickly master the most important features of 1-2-3.

What's Inside

- an easy introduction to computers and spreadsheet basics
- short step-by-step lessons that are easy to follow
- practical examples that show how to solve specific business problems quickly
- time-saving tips and tricks to make you instantly productive with 1-2-3

About *LOTUS BOOKS*

LOTUS BOOKS, written in collaboration with Lotus Development Corporation, help you derive the most from Lotus software. There are four series within *LOTUS BOOKS*:

Start Here books introduce beginning users to Lotus software with simple step-by-step instructions.

Pathways to Mastery titles provide the authoritative perspective and expertise from Lotus. Each book is a fast-paced, clear, and concise guide that helps you build on what you know and teaches new product features quickly.

Business Solutions books concentrate on using software to meet your specific business and professional needs. They provide essential tools for working faster and smarter.

Technical Reference titles provide advanced information for experts, programmers and applications developers.

Start Here with 1-2-3

Daniel Gasteiger

Brady Publishing

LOTUS BOOKS

New York London Toronto Sydney Tokyo Singapore

Copyright © 1991 by Daniel Gasteiger
All rights reserved,
including the right of reproduction
in whole or in part in any form.

 Brady Publishing

A Division of Simon & Schuster, Inc.
15 Columbus Circle
New York, NY 10023

Manufactured in the United States of America

10 9 8 7 6 5 4 3 2 1

Library of Congress Cataloging-in-Publication Data

Gasteiger, Daniel
    Start here with Lotus 1-2-3 / Daniel Gasteiger
        p.   cm.
    Includes index.
    1. Lotus 1-2-3 (Computer program) 2. Business—Computer programs.
    3. Electronic spreadsheets.   I. Title.
    HF5548.4.L67G373 1991
    658'.05421—dc20   91-32135
                                                              CIP

Limits of Liability and Disclaimer of Warranty

Trademarks

Contents

Introduction

What Can 1-2-3 (and this Book) Do for You?

Welcome to spreadsheet computing. Perhaps you want nothing to do with computers, but you have to learn about them for your job. Or, you might recognize that a computer can speed your work and have chosen this book to help you through your first sessions with Lotus 1-2-3. Whatever your orientation, there's a lot to learn. Before you begin, you should be convinced it'll be worth the effort.

Millions of people use 1-2-3 each day. Because 1-2-3 is the standard computer spreadsheet product used in businesses today, you'll be able to apply the skill you develop with 1-2-3 almost anywhere you work.

Far more important than the prevalence of 1-2-3 in business is the wealth of problems that the spreadsheet software can solve. At its simplest, 1-2-3 is a powerful desktop calculator. And, with a little study, you can use the spreadsheet to create fairly polished sales reports and financial statements. You can project trends in your business, analyze past performance, track processes in production and manufacturing, and balance accounts.

With 1-2-3's database management tools, you might keep records of your employees, maintain a list of customers, or even store your personal greeting card list on the computer. At its most complex, 1-2-3 is a powerful tool for developing applications. Eventually, you might use the spreadsheet to create involved programs such as inventory managers, mailing address databases, sales tracking systems, and more.

Some Thoughts on Using this Book

Despite 1-2-3's power, the software's design makes it remarkably easy to learn and to use. Even people who have vowed never to use computers can be up and running with little effort. This book presents a sequence of lessons that help you to develop skills with the spreadsheet and with your computer. Each lesson builds on the preceding lessons. Most of the lessons assume that you're working at your computer. None should require more than 20 minutes to complete.

If you've already installed 1-2-3 and you know how to start up the software, begin your study with Part II. You'll be using the software productively in the first lesson. In only four lessons, you'll understand the basics that get many users though every workday with the spreadsheet.

If you've never worked with a computer, it's helpful to have some guidance from an instructor. Still, if you like to explore and experiment on your own, Part I of this book will help you along. Even if you're already running 1-2-3, you might want to work through the first section at some point to gain both a better understanding of how your computer works and some important insights into the Disk Operating System (DOS), the software that lets you run all other software. While many 1-2-3 users never learn the fundamentals of their computers and DOS (you can get by without learning the fundamentals), knowing the basics can reduce any shyness you might feel toward your machine.

In any case, working on a computer with 1-2-3 is quite easy to do. There's little to learn before you can use the software productively, and each tidbit you add to your knowledge over the days, weeks, or months fits naturally with what you've already learned. This book won't turn you into a computer spreadsheet master, but if you work through all of the chapters you'll be more adept than the average 1-2-3 user. With any luck, you might even discover that working with a computer spreadsheet is fun.

Some Thoughts for Rank Beginners

Many beginning users have doubts about using computers. It's common to feel apprehension toward these machines. Even very knowledgeable users don't understand many of the computer's workings—and why should they? Few of us understand the innards of our cars, yet we drive them without trouble.

The best we can do to help allay any doubts is to point out that your computer isn't likely to explode. Jump right in and try things. Short of pounding on the keyboard with a hammer, dropping your computer on the floor, or otherwise deliberately abusing the hardware, there's little you can do that will cause serious trouble. And in almost all your interactions via the keyboard, your computer warns you if you're about to do something that might destroy valuable data.

Pay attention to what appears on the monitor while your work, and think about it. If you don't like what the computer is telling you, don't proceed. Consider your options carefully, and choose the one that leads to the results you really want. The instructions in this book try to anticipate the questions you might ask while working with your computer and 1-2-3. Stick with the exercises and you won't do anything that can damage the computer or your software.

Another common feeling toward computers is one of anger or resentment. Many of us have done our jobs quite nicely without computers—it can be annoying to have to adopt this complex tool later in our careers. Hang tough. Typewriters and adding machines put the world through this torture in their time—as did electric lights, telephones, elevators, and escalators.

While working with computers may be aggravating at first, as you become comfortable with the computer's capabilites, you're likely to find it more efficient than working without a computer. You may finish your work much more quickly than you do now. Unfortunately, it can also mean doing a lot more work. Perhaps if you find the work to be fun, you won't resent the computer quite so much. We try throughout this book to show how what you're learning can help with your job. At the same time, we try to illuminate some of the things that can make computing fun. Even if you don't enjoy your work with 1-2-3, perhaps you'll appreciate the advantanges you gain by working with a computer.

Part I
Before You Start 1-2-3

You don't need to know how a computer works to be able to use one effectively. It's important to be able to set up a computer, plug in the appropriate cables, install software, and the like, but there's no need to understand how a disk drive works, or what each of the silicon chips that make up the computer's "brain" actually does. In fact, setting up and running a computer can be easier than putting together and running the components of a home stereo system.

Many businesses provide a service that sets up the computers for their employees. If you're in such a company, then you're probably ready to run 1-2-3—or you will be soon after you fill out the appropriate paperwork. If you have to set up your own computer, look at the documentation that comes with it. Most manufacturers include fairly straightforward, step-by-step set-up and installation instructions.

What a computer's set-up instructions don't tell you is what the computer's various components actually do. There's no need to know this information to be able to use the machine well, but even a brief explanation can provide a lot of savvy for people who want to know what goes on "under the hood." Should you ever need to call a company's product support line, or should you wish to improve the capabilities of your computer, knowing the basics can help you to talk intelligently with the support or sales person who helps you out.

Part I begins by describing a computer's major components. It then tells you what to expect when you first turn on the computer. This part includes an overview of how to work with the computer immediately after you turn it on and finishes with an explanation of how to prepare 1-2-3 to run on the computer.

Some of the chapters in Part I—particularly the one about DOS—are rather long. Please don't let the lengths of the chapters scare you away. Once you get the basics, other topics require less discussion to be clear. By the time you work through Part I, you should understand what all the pieces of your computer do and have 1-2-3 installed and ready for your first steps into spreadsheet computing.

Brain-in-a-Box

Computer, CPU, microprocessor, microcomputer, terminal, 80286, 80386, 80386/SX, monitor, display, screen, display adapter, display card, video board, VGA, EGA, CGA, monochrome, keyboard, floppy disk, hard disk, fixed disk, disk drive. . . . Computers are a foreign language. Some programmers can talk for hours about computers and programming and rarely utter a word in English. You don't need to become one of them.

In fact, you'll be able install and use 1-2-3 if you understand only a few words in computerese. This chapter explains some of the terms people use when they talk about computers and identifies the components that make up a typical computer system. By the time you work through this chapter, you should be able to speak intelligently about computers and have a sense of what makes up the machine that sits on your desk.

The chapter is a little longer than most, and it's packed with information that you don't need to know to run 1-2-3. You might prefer to skip to Chapter 2 and use Chapter 1 more as a reference should you have questions about your computer at some later time. The information could prove quite useful should you consider buying a computer for your business or home.

The Standard Configuration

While there are many components that can go into a computer, a typical system is made up of only a few of them: the central processing unit (CPU), disk drives, RAM, a video display adapter, a video display, device ports, and a keyboard. Most users start out with such a system, and rarely go beyond it. Let's look at each of the

In this chapter, you'll:

- *Learn the parts of your computer so you can refer to them correctly*

- *Discover what each major component of your computer does*

- *Learn how fast your computer is and how much information it can handle*

- *Understand how clear an image to expect from your monitor and printer*

components in turn so that you understand the roles that they play in your computer system.

The Big Box: Your Central Processing Unit

The box that holds your computer's main circuits is the CPU, or Central Processing Unit. The box of a typical desktop computer looks similar to the one shown in Figure 1.1.

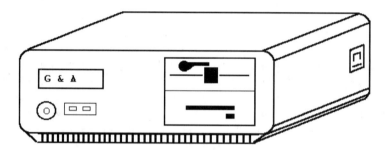

FIGURE 1.1: A box like this one holds most of the circuits of a typical desktop computer.

Chips, Anyone? Microprocessors

The heart of the CPU is a single silicon chip that resides inside the box. You can think of this chip, called a microprocessor, as a sort of crude brain that is etched to follow a basic set of instructions—and has the capacity to follow instructions supplied from an outside agent. The microprocessor brain is intelligent enough to control all of the other components built into and attached to the CPU, and to follow complex instructions fed in as computer programs or software. Figure 1.2 shows a typical microprocessor.

There are several types of microprocessors available in IBM-compatible computers. The first personal computers used 8088 and 8086 chips—numbers assigned by Intel corporation, the company that designed the chips. Later, more "intelligent," and therefore faster, computers used 80286 microprocessors, and still faster computers use 80386 chips. The speed of another chip, the 80386/SX falls between that of the 80286 and the 80386. Yet another microprocessor, the 80486, is the fastest that you typically encounter in today's personal computers.

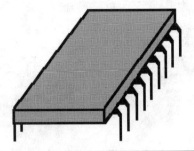

FIGURE 1.2: There are several types of microprocessors, but all of them look like large, flat, rectangular, or square, headless insects.

You usually identify a computer by the type of microprocessor it contains. A machine that contains an 80286 chip is a 286 machine (pronounced "two-eighty-six"). It's also "AT-compatible," meaning that it uses the same chip as the IBM-AT, the first 80286-based machine. A machine that has an 80386 microprocessor is a 386 machine, and an 80486-based computer is a 486 machine.

The microprocessor's clock speed, measured in megahertz (MHz), tells you how quickly the microprocessor follows commands relative to other chips in its class. For example, an 8086 running at 10MHz is slightly less than twice as fast as one running at 6MHz. Likewise, a 386 running at 33MHz is about twice as fast as one running at 16MHz. It's less meaningful to compare the clock

---

Microprocessors: Big Numbers Equal Big Power

There are two numbers associated with your computer's microprocessor: the microprocessor's model number and its speed. In both cases, a higher number, indicates faster performance. The following list shows microprocessor model numbers ordered from least powerful to most powerful:

8088	PC
8086	XT
80286	AT or 286
80386/SX	SX, X, or 386/SX
80386	386
80486	486

The microprocessor's megahertz (MHz) rating tells you how fast the chip runs relative to other chips of its class. A 16MHz 386 computer has about two-thirds of the speed of a 25MHz 386.

How Fast Is Fast Enough?
Many of today's computer programs require at least a 286 machine to run. However, if you're working with Lotus 1-2-3 Release 3.1, or you're planning to use Windows from Microsoft, a 286 machine will slow you down. Consider getting at least a 386/SX machine—but don't expect the software to be snappy until you have a 386 machine running at 25MHz.

speed of an 80286 chip against that of an 80386, as the design of the chips results in speed differences regardless of the clock speeds.

Think Big: RAM and the Mother Board

Your computer's microprocessor chip resides on the "mother board." The mother board is one of several printed circuit boards that you'd find if you removed the cover from your CPU. Mother boards come in all shapes and sizes, but each comes with certain standard features. Most of the features aren't important to know about at this time, but you should be familiar with RAM.

RAM stands for Random Access Memory. It means, "a place to store programming instructions and data electronically while the computer is turned on." The microprocessor moves information into and out of RAM as needed to accomplish whatever tasks you assign it—much in the way that your brain moves information into and out of your memory as you think to solve problems.

The less RAM your computer has, the less it can do at one time: Without memory, the microprocessor can't keep track of what it has done and what it's doing. You measure RAM in bytes.

What's a Byte Anyhow?
A computer's memory consists of thousands of microscopic electrical switches that can be on or off—similar to the way that light switches can be on or off. The patterns made by sequences of on and off switches represent the letters, numbers, and commands that we use when we work with the machine. A single switch is a data "bit." Eight bits together make up one byte, the number of bits that computer designers decided should identify a character. Within a byte there are 256 possible patterns of on and off switches. This means that a computer can recognize and manipulate 256 different characters at one time. Knowing this isn't important to running 1-2-3. What is important is to understand that the more bytes of RAM you have in your computer, the more you're likely to be able to do with the machine.

How Much RAM Do You Have?
There are standard amounts of RAM that you're likely to find in a computer. These days, the least RAM you'll find is 512K—and that's not very likely. 640K is still standard on low-end systems such as XT- and AT-compatibles (see the *Microprocessors: Big Numbers Equal Big Power* box). Many AT-class machines come with 1M of RAM and can expand up to 8M. 386 and 486 machines can go even higher, but you won't need such power to work effectively with 1-2-3.

Historically, a computer with 640 kilobytes (K) of RAM—that is, 640,000 bytes—had a lot of memory. 1-2-3 Releases 2.3 and lower can all run on 640K systems.

These days, a typical computer system running an 80286 or more powerful microprocessor comes with at least one megabyte (M) of RAM—one million bytes—also referred to as "one meg." That may sound like a lot, but programs such as 1-2-3 Release 3.1 and Microsoft Windows need one megabyte to run. They perform rather sluggishly if they don't have four or more megabytes available.

Don't Confuse RAM with Disk Storage

RAM is the computer's short-term memory. Information in RAM goes away when you shut off power to the machine. However, it's possible to move information from RAM into the computer's long-term memory so that the information will be available from one work session to the next. Disks are the computer's long-term memory.

All IBM-compatible CPUs contain at least one disk drive. Except in very special cases, you'll need two drives to run 1-2-3. You need both a floppy disk drive and a hard, or fixed, disk.

A floppy disk, or diskette, is like a cassette tape in the shape of a small record album (see Figure 1.3). On command, the computer can record information from RAM onto the disk, and read the information back into RAM. Depending on the size of the diskette, and on your computer's capabilities, a floppy disk can hold anywhere from 180K of data up to 1.44M.

Floppy disk drives have doors or slots into which you slide the diskettes when you want to record on them or have the computer read from them. Usually, the floppy disk drive or drives are on the front of the CPU so that you can get to them easily. Figure 1.4 shows a CPU with two floppy drives.

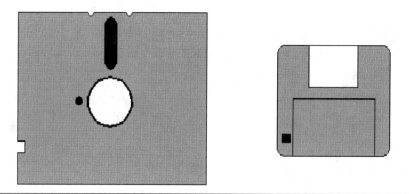

FIGURE 1.3: There are two standard sizes of floppy disks: 5.25" and 3.5". The amount of data that these disks can hold depends in part on your computer's capabilities.

FIGURE 1.4: A typical CPU contains one or two floppy disk drives. This CPU has a 5.25" diskette about to be inserted into one of its drives.

A fixed, or hard, disk usually resides out of sight inside the CPU, but there should be a light on the front of the box that tells you when the microprocessor is moving information onto or off of the disk. You may find a little drawing of a disk or a cylinder next to the drive light.

A fixed disk can hold from 10 megabytes (megs) of data to as many as several hundred megs, depending on the disk's design. The standard hard disk on an XT computer holds 10 megs, and the hard disk of an AT holds 20. In truth,

Fixed Disks: Size Really Matters

Most of the programs you're likely to run on your computer come from the manufacturer on floppy disks, and you must copy them onto your hard disk. Also, any data that you create and wish to store for use from one day to the next should reside on the disk. At first, even a 10-megabyte hard disk will seem very large—it can hold 1-2-3 with plenty of long-term storage to spare. However, if you start to use programs other than 1-2-3, you'll quickly begin to fill the disk.

Programs that take advantage of powerful microprocessors—such as 1-2-3 Release 3.1 and Microsoft Windows—consume a lot of disk space. Also, some computing applications—working with large databases, for example—can fill a disk in a hurry. It's hard to predict how much disk space you'll ultimately fill. But, unless you really catch the computing fever, you're not likely to feel cramped with a 30- or 40-megabyte hard disk.

there's no rule about the size of hard disk that a computer can contain. Powerful 25MHz 80386 systems might have 40-, 60-, 80-, or even 120-megabyte hard disks—and some systems have more than one fixed disk drive. We explore diskettes and hard disks in much greater detail in Chapter 3.

Beyond the CPU: Keyboards, Monitors, and Printers

Obviously, your computer isn't just a box on your desk. For all intents and purposes, that would be no better than a paper weight or a giant bookend. The computer monitor (display), together with the keyboard, provides a way for you to interact with the CPU.

You pass information to the CPU by typing at the keyboard. Most of what you type appears simultaneously on the display, as if the monitor were a piece of paper in a typewriter—though the way information appears can vary greatly depending on the software that you're using.

The CPU passes messages and instructions to you by "typing" them on the display. Again, the appearances of such messages varies depending on the software that you're using. The CPU can also send information to printers, to modems that communicate via telephone with other computers, and to other electronic devices.

There's Nothing Special about Keyboards

Computer manufacturers offer a variety of keyboards with several popular arrangements of keys. All keyboards have the same basic components: keys for the alphabetic and numeric characters and punctuation marks (just like a classic typewriter); the numeric keypad, similar in layout and function to the keypad of a desktop calculator; and a collection of 10 or 12 function keys labeled F1, F2, F3, and so on.

Some keyboards contain an extra collection of keys that have arrows and words such as Home, End, and PageDown stamped on them. These extra keys are cursor-movement keys, the uses of which will become clear in later chapters. Figure 1.5 shows two popular keyboard layouts.

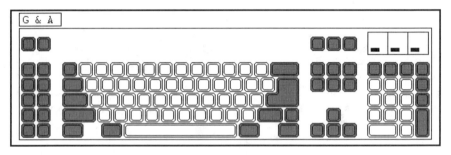

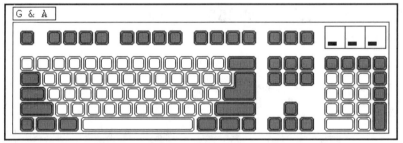

FIGURE 1.5: Two popular keyboard layouts. There is some argument over which layout is better, but you'll probably prefer the one that you use most often in your work. . . . Come to think of it, the upper of the two layouts is definitely the better.

The Computer Speaks: Displays

Your CPU talks to you by displaying information on a monitor. There are several popular types of monitors, varying primarily in the quality of the image they can produce.

The least expensive monitors can show images in only two colors—typically amber, green, or white against a black background. These monitors are "monochrome" because the illuminated part of the display can be only one color. Images on monochrome monitors tend to be very crisp; they don't lead you to create documents that are colorful on-screen but come out looking dull grey when you print them with a black-on-white printer.

Color monitors come in three general standards:

- CGA—the color graphics adapter

- EGA—the enhanced graphics adapter

- VGA—the video graphics array

The image quality of a CGA monitor is the poorest of the three, while the image quality of a VGA display is the sharpest. An EGA monitor's display is fairly crisp and should be adequate for any work you'll do in 1-2-3. Working with a CGA monitor will be exasperating at best for many spreadsheet-related tasks.

Some hardware manufacturers have developed computer displays that don't fit one of the industry standards—or that have become standards in and of themselves. Perhaps the most common is the Hercules graphics display. There is another graphics technology that is unique to Toshiba computers, and still others for AT&T and Grid computers. While knowing the fundamental differences between the various graphics standards isn't important, it is very important to know what standard your computer uses. Software has to be written in a specific way to be able to use a specific type of monitor. When you first put 1-2-3 onto your computer, you must tell the software what type of display the computer has attached so that it will be able to display images.

Displays and Display Adapters

There is a device inside the computer called a display adapter into which you plug the computer's monitor. You need both a display adaptor and a monitor to run the computer, and they must be able to work together; that is, don't get a CGA monitor when your computer contains an EGA display adapter.

Knowing anything about the display adapter isn't so important as knowing that it exists. You might hear it referred to as a "display board," a "display card," or a "display adapter." Sometimes people refer to the display adapter in terms of the type of display that you can plug into it. For example, your computer might have a "monochrome board," meaning that it can accept a monochrome display. Of course, you can call the monochrome board a monochrome adapter or a monochrome card. Likewise, there are VGA boards, CGA cards, and EGA adapters.

Monitors Oversimplified

The computer display is a grid of tiny dots called pixels (for "picture elements"). Each letter, number, or drawing that appears on the display consists of a collection of these pixels. For example, the display might reserve 6 × 11 blocks of pixels in which to display each character. On such a display, the number 8 appears as follows, although reduced significantly in size.

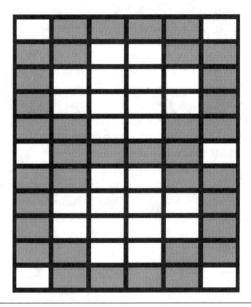

FIGURE 1.6: Magnifying the number 8 reveals which pixels in an 6 × 11 grid the display activates to represent the character.

The number of pixels your monitor can display determines the monitor's resolution. A low resolution monitor (CGA monitors are in this category) can typically display only 320 pixels across and 200 pixels from top to bottom. EGA monitors have higher resolution. They can typically display 640 pixels across and as many as 340 pixels top-to-bottom. VGA and most monochrome monitors have very high resolution, starting at 640 pixels across and 480 pixels down, but going as high as 1,024 × 768 pixels.

A good rule of thumb is that a high resolution monitor is easier to read than a low resolution monitor. With the lowest resolution models, text and graphs can appear very grainy. Some of the displays that will arise as you work with 1-2-3 will be virtually unreadable with a low resolution (CGA) monitor.

Printers

While having a CPU with disk drives, a keyboard, and a monitor are enough to do some serious computing, the culmination of most computing efforts comes when you print a project on paper. To do this, you need some type of a printer plugged into one of the sockets on the back of the CPU. There are so many types of printers available that it's difficult to say anything very meaningful about them.

The most popular type of printer, perhaps because such printers tend to be inexpensive, is the dot-matrix printer. A dot-matrix printer creates printed images in a fashion similar to the way a monitor creates an image: Tiny wires slide forward very rapidly like paper punches and pin an inked ribbon against the paper leaving arrangements of dots on the page. The arrangement of the ink dots on the paper makes up images that we see as letters, numbers, and graphic images.

Inkjet printers actually squirt small amounts of ink through tiny nozzles onto the paper. The images created by inkjet printers are similar in quality to those achieved through professional typesetting services. Inkjet printers tend to be more expensive than dot-matrix printers.

Daisy-wheel printers aren't popular because they take a long time to print in comparison to other types of printers. A daisy-wheel printer has a separate preformed stamp for each character that it can print. To create a character on paper, the printer must rotate the corresponding stamp into position so that a small hammer can drive the stamp against an inked ribbon and press it against the page. Except under rare circumstances, a daisy-wheel printer can print only the characters that appear on a typewriter keyboard. This makes the printers inappropriate for work with 1-2-3 if you plan to take advantage of the software's ability to create dramatic printed presentations. A daisy-wheel printer is a "text printer," meaning that it can print text only. The quality of its printing is very high, but the printer itself isn't versatile.

Laser printers use technology similar to that found in copy machines. They create images by charging paper with static electricity and then run the paper past powdered ink that adheres only where the charge is on the paper. Finally, a heating element melts the powdered ink so that it sticks to the paper permanently. Laser printing tends to be fairly rapid, and the images are close enough in quality to typeset printing that book and magazine publishers sometimes use such printouts along with, and even in place of typeset material. Unfortunately, laser printers are rather expensive when compared with dot-matrix printers.

Once again, this is more than you need to know about printers to be able to use one with your software. The important point is that each printer understands a unique set of instructions to produce alphanumeric characters and drawings. While printers from different manufacturers might recognize the same instructions, generally software must speak a printer's "language" to produce effective output from the printer. When you first put 1-2-3 on your computer, you need to tell the software what type of printer you'll be using. This means that you should be prepared with the printer's make and model name before you start to install the software. The instructions for installing the software that come with 1-2-3 remind you of the need to know what equipment you're using before you begin.

Ready to Go On-line

As promised at the beginning of this chapter, we've covered far more information about your computer than you need to know to be able to run 1-2-3. If you've made it through to this point, you already know more than many people who have been using the spreadsheet software for months.

Being familiar with your computer's components can only help in the long run. Should you need to call a product support person for any reason, knowing about your hardware can help you help the support person track down the cause of your trouble. Also, should you ever wish to add onto your system —to increase its computing power, its storage power, its display quality, or its printing capabilities—you'll make better decisions if you understand the way sales people and computer manufacturers talk about their equipment.

Having completed this chapter, you should:

- *Have a fair understanding of the hardware that makes up a computer*

- *Be able to converse intelligently about your system*

- *Understand the factors that contribute to the performance of your machine*

- *Be prepared to begin working with your computer*

2

When You Switch It On

Understanding what happens when you turn on your computer can save a lot of confusion when you begin installing and using software products like 1-2-3. If you know what goes on in the first two minutes after you turn on the machine, you'll have some sense of how to use the computer before you actually start working in 1-2-3. Knowing what happens when you start the computer isn't crucial to your work with the spreadsheet software, but you might feel more at ease with your computer when you see the continuity from power on to starting 1-2-3.

Much of the documentation that you receive with a computer, or with the software that you'll run on the computer, begins with the assumption that you'll be able to turn on the computer and follow along from there. This is a safe assumption. Unless something is wrong with your computer, there's no trick to what happens when you turn it on. Eventually some numbers and letters appear on the display, and you're ready to go to work.

Actually, a wide variety of things happen when you turn on your computer. Depending on who sold you the machine, who used it before you inherited it, who set it up for you originally, and who has fiddled with it since it first came into your hands, what eventually appears on your display can differ significantly from what appears on someone else's. There is a standard sequence of events that takes place each time you start up the machine. Knowing that sequence helps you to understand how you can customize your system to suit your own tastes. You won't have to be at your computer to follow this discussion. But,

---

In this chapter, you'll:

- Learn what to expect when you turn on your computer

- Get a brief explanation of how your computer uses disks

- Discover files that let you customize your computer system

- Learn what a DOS prompt is

- Become fully prepared to install 1-2-3

15

after you finish, you might wish to watch your machine carefully as it starts up once to see if you recognize the various start-up stages.

Five Steps of the Boot Sequence

When you turn on your computer, the collection of chips and disks proceed through a predetermined sequence of events that make the whole system work in synchrony and that prepare it to follow the instructions you're going to supply to it when it's ready. Most users work successfully without ever knowing what happens as their computers start up—or "boot"—even though they wait through the boot sequence day after day. Here it is in a nutshell.

1. Read the System BIOS

There is a collection of commands called the Basic Input Output System (BIOS) built into your computer's hardware. The BIOS simply tells the various computer components how to work together. It also contains a set of instructions that test the computer's components to make sure they're all working before passing control along to software.

Normally, when you turn on the computer and monitor, a message appears at once telling you what company designed the BIOS that your computer uses. Almost immediately the disk drive lights flash and the disk drives emit a whirring or grinding noise as the BIOS activates them. Your computer beeps once, and numbers appear on the monitor, counting upward rapidly.

The counting represents successful testing of the computer's RAM. The computer determines exactly how much of the installed RAM works before moving ahead with other start-up procedures. If nothing is wrong with the RAM, you can tell during the start-up procedure how much is installed in your system.

2. Read the Hidden Files

After the self-test, the computer looks for a particular type of information stored on a diskette in the computer's A drive. In most cases, the A drive is the uppermost or leftmost of the floppy drives in the front of the CPU. If there is no diskette in the A drive, the computer looks for the necessary information on the computer's hard disk. In almost all cases, you shouldn't have a diskette in the A drive when you start the machine so the computer will find the needed information on the C drive.

The information that the computer looks for resides in a hidden file on the disk—the file's name won't appear when you look at a listing of the disk's contents. Information in the hidden file tells your computer to look for a second hidden file that contains further instructions. That file in turn tells the computer to look for and read a file named CONFIG.SYS.

3. Read CONFIG.SYS

Your computer automatically reads a file named CONFIG.SYS—if the file exists on the disk that contains the DOS files. If CONFIG.SYS doesn't exist, the computer proceeds without incident to the next step in the start-up procedures.

The CONFIG.SYS file contains special information that you establish during your work sessions with the computer. For example, if you use a mouse with your computer, then you've probably created a CONFIG.SYS file that tells the computer how to activate the mouse. Likewise, if you have special equipment such as a scanner or a fax device attached to your computer, then your CONFIG.SYS file most likely contains instructions that tell the computer how to use those devices.

The CONFIG.SYS file lets you customize your computer to some degree. Without the file, the computer starts up, loads DOS, and is ready to do whatever you request of it. However, DOS makes certain assumptions about the

---

What's a Disk File?

As explained in Chapter 1, the computer stores information on the hard disk and on floppy disks. The scheme that the computer uses to store information relies on dividing each disk into discrete storage areas called files. Typically, when your software stores information on disk, you assign a file name that identifies the information so that you can find it easily when you want to work with it later on. When the computer stores information in a file, it "writes" the file. Likewise, when the computer takes information from a file, it "reads" the file.

There are many types of files. Some are the files that contain instructions for the computer to follow—these are computer programs, and their contents can seem unintelligible to the casual reader. Other files contain information that you create when you use a program: These might be word processing documents, spreadsheets, and databases. And, each type of file might have a unique layout and appearance that makes sense only to the program that creates it. We look more closely at disk files in the next chapter.

computer—for example, it doesn't automatically look for a mouse. By entering custom commands in a CONFIG.SYS file, you alert DOS to special circumstances about your equipment. You may never need to be involved with the CONFIG.SYS file. However, it's possible should you ever phone a hardware or software company technical support line, that the specialist who answers might ask you for information about the file.

There are three points to understand:

1. The CONFIG.SYS file may or may not exist on your computer.

2. DOS reads the CONFIG.SYS file automatically at start-up.

3. The file's contents can vary dramatically from one computer to the next.

1-2-3 Release 3.1's installation procedure, as well as the installation procedures for many other commercially available programs (Microsoft Windows included), can automatically create or modify the CONFIG.SYS file so the computer will be able to handle the software properly.

Some of the commands that reside in a CONFIG.SYS file can cause the computer to display messages when DOS follows the commands. Again, the messages vary, but they usually clue you in to what's happening. For example, when the CONFIG.SYS file finds mouse-handling instructions, a message may appear as your computer starts up that tells you a mouse driver is installed and that a mouse exists at a certain port. The exact meaning of the message isn't important, but the gist is that a mouse is available if your software can take advantage of it.

4. Load the DOS Instruction Set

After reading CONFIG.SYS, your computer reads a file named COMMAND.COM. COMMAND.COM contains the set of basic instructions that tell the microprocessor how to read and write disk files; how to interpret instructions that come from the keyboard; and how to interact with the display, printers, and other hardware devices. These instructions are the core of DOS (sounds like "moss"), the Disk Operating System, on which all of your software is based.

DOS must be present on the computer for other applications programs to work. Without DOS, you can't tell the computer to run 1-2-3. 1-2-3 in turn relies on DOS for certain tasks. For example, when you save and retrieve disk files in 1-2-3, DOS really does the work—1-2-3 simply tells DOS to go ahead and save or retrieve. We'll look more closely at DOS in the next chapter.

5. Read the AUTOEXEC.BAT File

After reading the COMMAND.COM file, your computer automatically reads another disk file named AUTOEXEC.BAT. The AUTOEXEC.BAT file can contain commands that you might issue at the keyboard were you working directly with the computer. While a computer needn't have an AUTOEXEC.BAT file, many do, and such a file can dramatically alter the events that take place when your computer first starts running.

For example, without an AUTOEXEC.BAT file, your computer might display messages that ask you to enter the day's date and the current time. Alternatively, your computer automatically reads the date and time from an electronic battery-powered clock built into the CPU. In either case, all action stops, and the very last thing that appears on the monitor—no matter what came before—is a prompt that consists of the letter C followed by a greater than sign (>). Call this the "DOS prompt," the "C prompt," the "command prompt," the "DOS C prompt," or the "system prompt."

If your hard disk does have an AUTOEXEC.BAT file, what happens next depends on the file's contents. That file might have commands that change the look of the DOS prompt, commands that cause a menu of options to appear on the display, commands that automatically start up such programs as 1-2-3 or Windows, and so on. Unfortunately, it's impossible for us to guess whether or not your computer has an AUTOEXEC.BAT file or what's in that file if you have one. The best that we can do is to point out that what ultimately appears on your display after you start up the computer may not match what we're going to assume as we proceed with this book. The trick, then, is to help you to start from the same place that we do.

Get to a DOS Prompt

To be able to install 1-2-3 on your computer, you must get your computer to display a DOS prompt. Usually, the DOS prompt appears as the last item (the lowermost item) on the display after the computer finishes its start-up, or boot, sequence. The prompt can contain any sequence of characters—most likely either *C>* or *C:\>*—and in either case, the prompt is followed by a flashing underline called a "cursor." If that's what finally appears after your machine starts up, you're ready for the next chapters that explain DOS and how to install 1-2-3.

If the last item on your display isn't a DOS prompt, then you need to get to the DOS prompt before you can install 1-2-3. We can't tell you how to

The cursor in almost all computer applications identifies where something will appear on the display when you press a key.

get to the DOS prompt because the fact that it isn't last on the display means that you, or someone else, has customized your system—and we can't guess how. If you don't already know how to get to the DOS prompt, look for a booklet that came with your computer that explains how to get started. It may contain instructions for getting to the prompt.

If you didn't set up your own computer, ask the person who did set it up to show you how to get to DOS. In lieu of a computer technician, a co-worker or a friend who has some experience with computers might be able to guide you to a system prompt. Should none of these people be available (or useful), either phone the company that sold you the computer or contact the computer's original manufacturer for guidance.

Having completed this chapter, you should:

- *Know what to expect when you start up your machine*

- *Understand that the start-up events can vary significantly from one computer to another*

- *Be able to track down the information necessary to get to a DOS prompt if it doesn't appear automatically when you start up*

Basics of the Disk Operating System

U nderstanding what DOS (Disk Operating System) is and how it works for you gives you an edge when you work with 1-2-3. Commands in DOS let you copy information from one disk to another, erase information from disks, determine what information resides on a disk, start programs such as 1-2-3, and perform many other tasks on the computer.

Whether you apply DOS's commands directly, or you learn how DOS performs certain tasks automatically, the Disk Operating System plays into almost everything you do on the computer. Even if you never work with DOS, your software does—and since most computers present you with a DOS prompt when you start them up, you might as well know what DOS is about.

Many computer users, especially those in large companies, can use 1-2-3 and never work directly with the Disk Operating System. If someone else sets up your computer and installs the software for you, your computer might start up with 1-2-3 running, or with some menu system that lets you start up 1-2-3 without ever seeing a DOS C prompt. After you understand a little bit about DOS, you too can set your computer to start up directly in 1-2-3. However, almost all IBM and compatible computers today come with DOS installed so that shortly after you turn them on, you're faced with the DOS C prompt.

In this chapter, you'll:

- *Learn what DOS is*

- *Learn that DOS is important to work with your computer*

- *See how DOS manages the information that you store on disks*

- *Find out how to list the contents of a disk*

- *Understand how DOS organizes information on disks*

- *Learn how to prepare diskettes for use with the computer*

- *Learn the basic commands for working with information on disks*

DOS Essentials

When you see a C prompt on your display, it means that DOS is ready to follow your commands—it prompts you to proceed. While there are many tasks that DOS can perform, a few of those tasks are essential to working with 1-2-3. Let's look at DOS's primary responsibility: managing disks and disk files.

DOS Manages Disks and Disk Files

As the name Disk Operating System implies, DOS manages files on disk. DOS "understands" how to prepare disks for use, move information onto disks, and get information off of them. DOS also offers a clever scheme for you to arrange information on disks so that the information is easy to find. Understanding the scheme that DOS uses to manage disk files is crucial to working with 1-2-3 and your computer.

Disk Files Defined

As explained in Chapter 1, a disk is a piece of magnetic material similar to the material used to make cassette tapes for audio and video systems. The computer stores information as sequences of ones and zeros represented by magnetized points on the surface of the disk—that is, the computer makes digital recordings of the information that you wish to save.

In most cases, the information that you want to record on a disk is a collection of related items, such as all the words in a letter that you just finished writing or all the values and calculations in a loan schedule that you just prepared. Rarely does one set of information take up all of the space on the disk, so the computer has a scheme that lets you store many discrete sets of information on a single disk without jumbling together all of the information. Each collection of recorded information is called a file.

Disk files have a variety of uses. Some hold the software program instructions that determine how your computer behaves. When you tell DOS to read such a file, the instructions in the file take control—suddenly a program such as 1-2-3 or Windows is in charge, rather than DOS. Other disk files hold the documents and information that you create when you use spreadsheet programs or word processors. For example, a word processing program might let you save a copy of a letter that you write. When you save, you assign a name to the letter and the word processor records the letter on disk using the name that you assign. Later, should you want to work further with the letter, you can tell the word processing software to read the letter from the disk file into RAM.

How DOS Stores Files

You don't need to name a file right now. In fact, you won't need to name any files until you've worked several chapters into Part II of this book. Then you'll be saving information that you create while working with 1-2-3. When you reach that point, it will be useful to understand file names and what they mean to DOS.

DOS records information on a disk beginning near the outside edge of the recording surface and working in concentric circles toward the center. The first file on a disk is called the File Allocation Table, or FAT. DOS reserves the FAT for its own use—you can't read the file directly unless you have special software designed for that purpose.

FIGURE 3.1: Each of the shaded arcs represents a file that DOS has stored on the surface of a diskette.

When you save a file, DOS records the file's name in the FAT along with the file's location on the disk. When you retrieve a file, DOS finds the file's name and location in the FAT and copies information into RAM from the appropriate area on the disk.

A file name consists of a sequence of up to eight characters, followed by a period, and then an optional file extension of up to three characters. Any letter or number is valid in a file name, and some other characters are allowed as well. For simplicity, name your files with letters and numbers until you've studied DOS in more depth.

In the previous chapter we talked about three files that might already reside on your computer's hard disk: COMMAND.COM, CONFIG.SYS, and AUTOEXEC.BAT. When you work in 1-2-3, you'll create your own files and add them to the ones already on your disk. Let's find out what files already reside on your hard disk.

A Quick Experiment Introduces DOS Commands   To find out what's on your hard disk, start up your computer and get to the C prompt. Then type the characters *DIR*. As you type, the characters appear on the monitor displacing the cursor to the right of the DOS prompt. Press the Enter key—it probably says "Enter" on it or has a right-angled line with an arrowhead pointing to the left as shown in the margin. Typing *DIR* and pressing the Enter key issues a command to DOS. That command is, "List the names of the files that reside on the disk."

↵

This symbol might identify your keyboard's Enter key.

· · · · · · · · · ·
· · · · · · · · · ·
· · · · · · · · · ·

Peck the Keys, Don't Press Them

One common mistake of beginning users is to press and hold down keys on the computer keyboard. If you hold down a key for too long, the computer responds by repeating whatever character you're typing. To avoid these annoying repetitions, think about tapping keys rather than pressing them. If you do hold down a key too long, press the Backspace key (located above the Enter key) repeatedly to erase the extra characters.

Immediately, DOS responds by typing information on your display. The quantity and specifics of the information will vary considerably from one computer to another. Especially on new machines that have had little or no activity, there may be very little information. Machines that have had some activity, or that have a lot of programs already installed on them, might offer lots of information at this point. Figure 3.2 shows a typical listing, called a "directory listing," that resulted when we issued DOS's DIR command on our computer.

```
C:\dir
      Volume in drive C is DOS400
      Volume Serial Number is 1166-14FF
      Directory of   C:\

      COMMAND   COM      37557 12-19-88   12:00a
      CONFIG    SYS        340 08-17-91    3:37a
      AUTOEXEC  BAT        207 08-18-91    1:41p
      WINDOWS        <DIR>       08-16-91    6:17p
      DOS            <DIR>       08-15-91    1:56p
      R23            <DIR>       08-16-91    6:36p
      SYS            <DIR>       08-16-91    8:05p
      AMI            <DIR>       08-17-91    2:04a
      BAT            <DIR>       08-17-91    3:38a
      GAMES          <DIR>       08-17-91    2:17p
      R23DATA        <DIR>       08-21-91   11:12a
      R22DATA        <DIR>       08-21-91   11:12a
      YOGA           <DIR>       08-27-91   10:01a
           13 File(s)      12371968 bytes free

C:\COLLAGE>
```

FIGURE 3.2: This directory listing resulted when we issued DOS's DIR command on our computer.

Directories Keep Files Organized

When there are only a few files on a disk, you can quickly scan a listing to find the name of a specific file. However, it doesn't take long before there are so many files on your disk that finding any one of them becomes a chore. For example, more than 50 files together make up DOS, and once installed on your hard disk, 1-2-3 consists of more than 40 files. You can find files on your disks most easily if you take advantage of DOS's directory management capabilities.

Directories Defined

DOS provides you with the ability to section a disk into areas called directories. There is a classic analogy for the relationship between files and file directories: Think of a file as a manila folder that contains a select collection of information. To help organize all of your manila folders, you might place them in hanging folders that, in turn, hang in a file drawer. In this analogy, the hanging folder represents a directory, and the file drawer represents the disk.

To help locate information, you first look in the appropriate file drawer— that is, on the appropriate disk. Then you look for the correct hanging folder,

Prepare Diskettes for Use

A diskette fresh from the factory isn't quite ready to hold data and programs that you wish to record with your computer. The surface of the diskette might contain small errors—that is, areas that won't hold a magnetic recording properly. Also, there is no file allocation table (FAT) on a brand new diskette—DOS needs the FAT before it can record the locations of files that you create.

Before you can use a new diskette, you must prepare it by applying the DOS FORMAT command. To format a disk, slide it into the appropriate disk drive. Figure 3.3 shows the proper orientation for inserting diskettes.

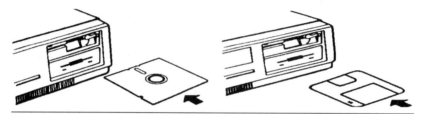

FIGURE 3.3: Orient a 5.25" disk as shown on the left, and a 3.5" disk as shown on the right.

Press the diskette all the way into the drive and, if there is a drive door, make sure the door closes securely. Then enter the command *FORMAT A:* if the diskette is in drive A, and *FORMAT B:* if the diskette is in drive B. Follow the instructions that appear on the display. DOS provides messages to inform you of its progress and eventually asks if you wish to format another disk. Answer with Y for yes, or N for no. Entering N returns you to the DOS prompt.

Be careful with the FORMAT command! Always indicate the drive that contains a floppy disk to format. For example, enter *FORMAT A:* or *FORMAT B:*. The command FORMAT alone prompts DOS to format your hard disk—a procedure that wipes out any files already stored there.

the directory. Finally, you pull out the appropriate manila folder, the file that contains the desired information.

How to Name a Directory

DOS tells you the name of whatever disk is current by displaying the disk's name in the DOS prompt. The prompt C:\> or C> tells you that you're looking at the disk drive named C. If you were looking at the A drive, the DOS prompt would read A:\> or A>.

Change the DOS Prompt

Right out of the factory, the prompt that DOS automatically displays is only the drive letter followed by a greater than sign (and the cursor)—C>, for example. One of DOS's built-in commands—the PROMPT command—lets you customize the prompt to reveal more information about your computer.

Perhaps the most popular customization of the DOS prompt is to tell DOS to display the name of the current disk, along with the name of the current directory. (This will make more sense by the time you complete the chapter.) To do this, at any DOS prompt type the characters *PROMPT PG,* and press Enter. Rather than C>, your prompt should appear as C:\>. If you prefer the extended prompt, remember to issue the PROMPT PG command in DOS at the beginning of each work session.

We've already explored how DOS names files, so the missing information is, "How does DOS name a directory?" Actually, DOS directories have the same naming conventions that files do. A directory can have up to eight alphanumeric characters in its name and up to three characters in its extension. On the other hand, you rarely see directory names that include extensions—omitting that optional part from your directory names helps to make them stand out in directory listings of your disks. The directory names on our hard disk stand out in the listing in Figure 3.2 in part because they lack extensions and also because DOS automatically flags each one with the characters <DIR>.

Directories Grow on Trees

Given the existence of disk names, file names, and directory names, you need to know how all three elements work together to help you store and retrieve files. You'll begin to see these elements work together when you first install 1-2-3, and you'll put the knowledge to use repeatedly as you work with the spreadsheet software.

All disks have a directory called the root directory. On every disk, the root directory's name is "\" (backslash). The root directory can contain both files and other directories. As the directory listing in Figure 3.2 reveals, our hard disk contains four files and ten directories. The directory named DOS contains the files associated with the Disk Operating System software. The directory named R23 contains all of the files associated with the spreadsheet software.

Any directory can contain both files and other directories. So, for example, a directory named LOTUS in the root directory might in turn contain a directory named BUDGET. A structure that involves directories within directories

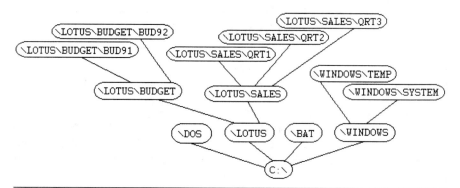

FIGURE 3.4: The arrangement of directories within directories within directories results in a structure that looks something like a tree. The layout of directories on a disk is the disk's directory tree.

within directories is similar to the diagram of a family tree. This organization of directories on a disk is called the directory tree. Figure 3.4 shows a diagram of the directory tree for a typical hard disk.

Paths along the Directory Tree

With a complex directory tree structure, it becomes quite easy to identify a specific file on the disk. The trick is to understand and to describe a file's full path name.

The path name to a file is a list of the directory names, beginning with the root directory, working upward into the tree, and finishing with the name of the desired file. When you write out a path name, you separate each directory name from the preceding name with a backslash (\). For example, the path name to a file named 123.EXE in the LOTUS directory on the C drive is C:\LOTUS\123.EXE. Likewise, the path name to a file named FEB92.WK1 in the BUDGET directory of the LOTUS directory is C:\LOTUS\BUDGET\FEB92.WK1.

Navigate along the Directory Paths

Many of DOS's commands let you manipulate the files and directories on your disks. For example, the DOS COPY command lets you copy a file from one disk or directory to another, or even make a second copy of a file but with a different file name. The RENAME command lets you change the name of a file. The DEL command lets you erase files from a disk. The MD com-

---

Make a Different Drive Current

DOS assumes that the directory you identify in a CD command is on the current disk drive. So, the command CD A:\ won't activate the root directory of the A drive if the C drive is currently active. Before you can change to a directory on a different disk, you must activate that disk drive.

To activate drive A, make sure there's a disk in the drive and then enter *A:*. After a short pause, an A prompt should appear on the display. This indicates that the A drive is active and that you can proceed to activate any directory that might reside on the diskette in the drive. To reactivate the C drive, enter the command *C:*.

---

mand lets you create a new directory on a disk, and the RD command lets you remove a directory from the disk.

When you issue one of these DOS commands, you must identify the file or directory name on which the command should act. For example, to copy a file named TEST.DOC from the root directory of drive C to the root of drive A, you'd enter the command *COPY C:\TEST.DOC A:*. Likewise, to view a listing of all the files in the directory named LOTUS in the root directory of drive C, you'd enter *DIR C:\LOTUS*.

But wait a minute. You don't need to type out the full path name of the "current directory" if you want to include it when you issue a DOS command. DOS automatically assumes you mean "use the current directory" when you issue a command that lacks a path to a specific directory.

Suppose that you wish to list the files and directories that reside in the DOS directory on the C drive. There are two methods:

1. No matter what directory is current enter the DOS command *DIR C:\DOS*.

2. Make the C:\DOS directory current and then issue the DIR command.

Make a Directory Current   You use DOS's CD (for Change Directory) command to make a directory current. Suppose that you want to make the C:\LOTUS directory current. At the DOS C prompt, enter *CD C:\LOTUS*. If your DOS prompt started out reading C:\>, it changes to C:\LOTUS> after you issue the CD command. Try it. Reissue the DIR command (type *DIR* and press Enter) and then pick one of the directories listed on your display. Type *CD* followed by a space and then the path name to the selected directory. Finish by pressing Enter.

With the new directory active, reissue the DIR command. The listing of files should differ from the earlier listing. Return to the root directory by entering the command *CD *.

Throughout this text, the instruction "Enter" means "Type the characters and then press the Enter key."

Have You OverDOSed?

With any luck, you now have a sense of what DOS is and how it relates to your use of the computer. You should be able to format a diskette so that you can use it later to store files. By now you also understand that you can divide disks up into directories to hold files, and you know how to activate a disk drive or a selected directory.

All of this information may be a little intimidating. It probably doesn't seem very important at the moment. However, disks, files, and directories will play an ever increasing role in your work with the computer. We'll see how important DOS really is as we install 1-2-3 and begin working with the spreadsheet software.

Having completed this chapter, you:

- *Know how DOS keeps track of information on disks*

- *Are prepared to assign file names to the work you do in 1-2-3*

- *Understand the nature of disk directories and directory trees*

- *Can navigate among the disks and directories in your computer system*

- *Know how to get a listing of the files and directories within a directory*

- *Have a sense of how to issue commands in DOS*

- *Are ready to deal with software programs that run in DOS*

Install 1-2-3 on Your Computer

This may sound a bit simplistic, but you can't use 1-2-3 until you install it on your computer. The software comes in files stored on several diskettes and includes instructions for transferring files from the diskettes onto your computer's hard disk.

If you're not familiar with computers, disks, and files, the procedure for installing 1-2-3 may seem obtuse. Printed documentation and instructions that your computer displays as you proceed with the installation process make the procedure as simple as possible. However, installation confuses a lot of first-time computer users. This chapter should allay some of the confusion.

We're not suggesting that you use this chapter in place of the installation instructions that come with 1-2-3. Rather, we recommend that you read this chapter and follow the instructions it contains so that you're well prepared when you work through your software's installation instructions.

Four Steps to Installation

Installing 1-2-3 is easiest when you understand the basics of working with a computer and with DOS. Most installation instructions assume that you are familiar with DOS or at least that your system displays a DOS prompt at the completion of its start-up sequence. The DOS prompt is a letter, typically C, followed by a greater than sign or by the characters :\>. Hence, C> and C:\> are the most common of the

In this chapter, you'll:

- *Learn what to expect when you install 1-2-3 on your computer*

- *Gain a sense of the way that your software interacts with your hardware*

- *Receive extra coaching to help when you install 1-2-3*

DOS prompts. If such a prompt isn't the last line that appears on your display after you start up your computer, then skip back to Chapters 2 and 3 for information about starting up the computer and working with DOS.

If a DOS prompt does appear as the last typed line on your display, you should be able to install 1-2-3. The procedure takes less than a half hour and is quite easy to perform. Here are four steps that you should follow to get 1-2-3 up and running.

1. Know Your Computer System

The installation program that comes with 1-2-3 copies many files onto your hard disk. After that, it asks you to describe the hardware that you plan to use with 1-2-3. To be able to respond appropriately, you'll need to know what type of monitor your computer uses, as well as the brand name and the model name of the printer or printers attached to your machine.

If you're not sure what type of monitor your computer uses, or what printer or printers you'll be using, find out before you begin installing 1-2-3. Usually a manufacturer name and a printer's model name appear some place on the casing of a printer. If your printer lacks such markings, find the printer documentation—it's likely to contain the needed information.

Knowing what type of monitor you're using might be more challenging. Some monitors have lettering that identifies their type and resolution. More often than not you'll have to consult the packaging or the documentation that accompanied the monitor to learn what type you have. If there is any doubt as to your monitor type, contact the company that sold you your machine, the technical support person who installed the computer, or the computer's manufacturer so you know before you start what type of monitor you're using.

2. Start Up Your Computer

No tricks here. Make sure the machine is connected as described in the documentation that accompanied it. Cables should run from the appropriate sockets on the back of the machine to the various external devices—monitor, printer, keyboard, and electrical outlet. Make sure there are no diskettes in the drives and then turn the power on both to the CPU and to the monitor.

3. Get to a DOS Prompt

Chances are that after a short time a DOS prompt will appear as the last item on your computer's display. If that isn't the case, you'll need to follow whatever procedure you've learned to get to a DOS prompt. We discussed the possibility that your system might not start up to a DOS prompt and suggested at the end of Chapter 2 where to find help if that is the case.

4. Follow the Installation Instructions

This is the most time-consuming part of installing 1-2-3. Whether you're using Release 3.1 or Release 2.3, it takes a while to get through the necessary procedures. The installation instructions that come with 1-2-3 are quite thorough, and the installation program itself is very easy to use. Still, there are some possible pitfalls. The remainder of this chapter walks quickly through the installation procedures described in your software's documentation and adds a few tidbits to help clarify the process.

The key to installing 1-2-3 successfully is to read everything that appears on the display and follow the instructions.

Some Notes on the Installation Procedure

The procedures for installing 1-2-3 Release 2.3 and Release 3.1 are very similar: Start at the DOS prompt and insert the disk labeled *Disk 1 (Install)* into one of your floppy disk drives. For the sake of this discussion, we'll assume you can use drive A, but if you must use drive B, that's OK. Simply replace the drive designation A: with the designation B: wherever it appears in the text.

Make the A drive current by entering *A:* and then enter the command *INSTALL*. DOS interprets your entry to mean, "Find the program named INSTALL on the disk in drive A and follow the instructions contained in the program." After a lengthy pause, the installation program displays a screen full of information about the installation procedure—read the screen. When you've finished, press Enter to proceed with the installation program as directed by the message at the bottom of the display.

There's nothing useful we can add to the information on the screen that appears next in the install sequence. Read the display and do what it tells you to do. When you've entered your name and your company's name successfully, yet another screen appears.

Choose Your Installation Options

The installation program lets you select what to install on your hard disk. In other words, you don't have to install everything that comes with 1-2-3 to be able to use the spreadsheet. You can choose to install only the spreadsheet software, or the spreadsheet software along with such options as a file translation facility that lets you prepare files created in one spreadsheet program —or in popular database management programs such as dBase III—for use by another spreadsheet program. Other installation options include the Wysiwyg add-in, other add-ins (Viewer and Auditor), and various on-line tutorials—that is, software programs that teach you how to use the spreadsheet software.

Install all the options available if this is the first time you've used 1-2-3.

Follow the instructions carefully to select the options that you wish to install. If this is the first time you've used 1-2-3, elect to install everything. Wysiwyg is an important part of the 1-2-3 package, and leaving it out of your installation will severely limit your spreadsheet's capabilities. Also, the Viewer add-in adds capabilities to 1-2-3 that can significantly ease your work when your hard disk gets crowded with spreadsheet files. These features will make much more sense when we explore them later on in this book.

After you've decided what to install, the Install program asks you to indicate where to put the spreadsheet software. Except in special cases, you'll be installing on drive C. If you're not installing on the C drive, change the letter of the target installation drive offered by the Install program. Likewise, you might as well install 1-2-3 in the directory that the program recommends. If you do use a different directory name for the installation, use one that doesn't already contain files. Better yet, use a directory name that doesn't already exist on the hard disk. The installation program will automatically create a new directory to hold the spreadsheet software.

As explained in the documentation that comes with your software, the Install program copies files from the various 1-2-3 diskettes into the target directory on your hard disk. The procedure is automatic, and the program asks you to place certain diskettes into drive A as needed. When the program has copied all the needed files, it asks you to tell it what equipment your computer has available—that is, what type of display and printers you're using with your CPU.

Specify Your Equipment

Remember that information you recorded before you began the installation procedure? You need it now. The Install program needs you to tell it what type of monitor and printer or printers 1-2-3 will be using so that it can record "device drivers" specific to your hardware.

Device drivers tell 1-2-3 how to talk to the display and the printer. Each type of monitor requires unique instructions to display the clearest possible images. By identifying your monitor type at this point, you tell 1-2-3 what instructions to use to display images on your system. Likewise, printer manufacturers don't seem to agree on how their printers should communicate with computers. Each printer uses its own language, though many manufacturers copy languages of the bigger companies so that their printers are "compatible." In other words, you might be using a dot-matrix printer that's "Epson compatible" or a laser printer that's "HP compatible." While your printer isn't made by Epson or Hewlett Packard, it will work if your software sends it instructions that would work on those respective models.

Follow the instructions on the display to select a display type and a printer or printers. The Install program will do its best to guess what type of monitor your machine is using. If you agree with the selection, follow on-screen instructions to choose that type of monitor—otherwise, select the appropriate monitor type.

1-2-3 can display varying amounts of information on the display, depending on which display driver you install. The standard display for years has had 80 characters across and 25 characters down. With the advent of VGA monitors, you can put 60 or more characters down with little degradation in readability. However, this book assumes throughout that you've installed using one of the 80 by 25 options. Make sure you select one at this point in the install procedure.

Follow the on-screen instructions to identify the manufacturer name and the model of your printer. You need to select each printer twice—once as a "text" printer and a second time as a "graphics" printer. As explained in Chapter 1, some printers can print only text—you won't be able to install them as graphics printers.

You can install more than one printer if you wish. Your choice will depend on whether there is more than one printer attached to your computer—or whether you expect to be switching printers from time to time. Again, the Install program explains on-screen how to install more than one printer.

The first printer that you select while installing is the one that 1-2-3 will use automatically later on when you print.

Save the Driver Set

When you've finished selecting printers, the Install program lets you save the device drivers on disk. You must save the drivers so that 1-2-3 can find the information you've selected when you start up the spreadsheet software. The Install program offers to save the drivers under a preselected file name. Since this is the first time you've installed, accept the name offered. When you become more experienced with spreadsheet computing you may find reasons to create driver sets with different file names, but that's not important now.

Generate Fonts

Generating fonts may make little sense at this point in your computing career, but the installation program asks if you want to do it. By all means do.

Normally, your computer knows how to display text—that is, letters and numbers—without hassle. Such text appears on the monitor when you work in DOS and as you install 1-2-3 to run on your computer. However, when you want to use more than one font, the computer must work a little harder. For more information about text styles, see the *What's a Font?* box.

Before the spreadsheet publishing add-in Wysiwyg will let you work with a font other than the one that DOS uses, the Install program must "draw pictures" of each allowable character of the font and record the pictures on your hard disk. Later, when you create elaborate reports that rival slick magazine layouts, the spreadsheet software can find the fonts on disk and make them available to you.

What's a Font?
A font is a complete collection of letters, numbers, punctuation marks, and mathematical symbols that have been designed to fit together. Good old manual and electric typewriters typically came in one of two fonts: Pica or Elite. Also popular are Helvetica, Courier, and Times-Roman. The text in this box is Helvetica, while the main body of text throughout this book is Century. Selectively mixing the fonts on a page—using one font for headlines, another for body text, and so on—helps you emphasize your message.

The Install program can create a small, medium, or a large set of fonts for you to use when you work in the spreadsheet. Unless you have almost no space on your hard disk, generate at least the medium-size font set. While you'll have little need of so many fonts right away, in a couple of months you may find uses for a wide variety of type styles in your spreadsheets.

Generating fonts can eat up a lot of time. Don't be afraid to leave your computer running and grab lunch while the Install program finishes its work. Eventually, the program finishes. You may have to press a key to clear the final screen, but, once the program is done, a DOS prompt appears on your display. You're ready to run 1-2-3.

Having completed this chapter, you:

- *Should have an in-depth under-standing of 1-2-3's installation procedures*

- *Might be able to generalize your experience to installing other com-puter programs*

- *Are ready to run your 1-2-3 spreadsheet software*

Part II
Spreadsheet Basics

Magic. A computer turns you into a magician. It gives you the power to complete tasks quickly, to produce attractive documents, and to do jobs that you might not even attempt without a computer. The key to the magic is having software that handles all (or most) of your business needs. 1-2-3 is the right software.

As you become proficient in your use of 1-2-3, you'll be able to breeze through tasks that can take hours with paper and pencil. For example, recording and summarizing monthly sales figures, keeping track of billable hours and writing invoices, drawing graphs that show revenues plotted against promotional spending, and even performing regression analyses on experimental data are all simple tasks for 1-2-3.

Here's the caveat: There's a learning curve. Few people can use the computer immediately to project next year's sales without at least some instruction and practice. On the other hand, the learning curve is very steep. In about 20 minutes, the average novice can know enough about 1-2-3 to shift forever from a desktop adding machine or calculator to the spreadsheet software. In another 20 minutes, you can learn to lay out simple spreadsheets that clearly report on the status of your business. In a matter of hours, you can learn to create and modify fairly sophisticated spreadsheets that let you fiddle with numbers to see how, for example, changes in sales volume might affect your department's bottom line.

The 10 chapters in Part II will get you up to speed with your 1-2-3 spreadsheet. The first chapter introduces 1-2-3, explains what appears on the display when you start up the software, and shows how to use the spreadsheet to do some basic math. Subsequent chapters build on your understanding of the spreadsheet until you know enough to create snazzy documents that contain numbers, calculations, and text that explains the numbers—all spruced up with the spreadsheet publishing capabilities of Wysiwyg.

With a commitment of an average of 20 minutes per chapter (some run a little longer and some a little shorter), Part II should take less than three and a half hours of your time. Spread that over a week or two, and you'll be as proficient with the spreadsheet as many users ever become. You'll also be ready to move on to more advanced topics—performing complex math with 1-2-3, managing lists of data, and plotting graphs that represent your numeric data in pictures.

Introducing the Worksheet

You're ready to start 1-2-3. Everything we discussed in Part I was to prepare you for this moment. Starting up is easy, but once you're in 1-2-3 you might wonder what to do next. This chapter leads you through the start-up, and explains the concept of the electronic spreadsheet. It gives you a short tour of Lotus 1-2-3 and even reveals how to use 1-2-3 to do simple mathematical calculations.

Because there's so much to cover before you become productive with the spreadsheet, this chapter is a little longer than most. However, once you're familiar with the spreadsheet environment, further chapters will go by more quickly.

Start Up 1-2-3

How you start 1-2-3 depends entirely on how you installed the software on your computer. We assume, as explained in Part I, that you can get to a DOS prompt and that you'll follow along from there. Here's how to proceed once a DOS prompt appears on your display.

Use the CD command to make the 1-2-3 program directory current. The program directory is the one you specified to the Install program when you transferred the software to your hard disk. To use the CD command, type *cd \dirname*, where *dirname* is the name of the 1-2-3 program directory, and then press Enter.

In this chapter, you'll:

- *Learn what an electronic spread-sheet is*

- *Learn the parts of 1-2-3's spread-sheet "environment"*

- *See how to get around in the spreadsheet*

- *Use 1-2-3 to solve some simple math problems*

Start 1-2-3 by typing *123* and pressing Enter.

A Note to Mouse Enthusiasts
Whether you're using 1-2-3 Release 2.3 or 3.1, it is possible to work with a mouse. For Release 3.1 users, there is a little work involved before you can bring the mouse into action, even if the mouse is already attached to your computer. Release 2.3 users with a mouse attached should find the mouse ready for action when they first start up 1-2-3. However, so that everyone can start with the mouse at once, we've left its introduction until later in this section. Please bear with us and we'll put the mouse to work when we reach Chapter 11.

Welcome to the Spreadsheet

Almost immediately your software displays a copyright screen that tells you what edition of 1-2-3 you're running. After a slightly longer wait, the copyright screen vanishes and the spreadsheet appears. It looks something like what you see in Figure 5.1.

The spreadsheet display has several components. Let's look at the major ones in an order that helps relate each component to the others.

Find the 1-2-3 Program Directory

If you used the directory name that the Install program suggested when you installed 1-2-3, your program files are in a directory called 123R23, or 123R31—it depends on which release of the software you're using. If you're not sure where the program files are, you can find them easily.

At the DOS prompt, enter *dir* and then look for a directory name that sounds as if it holds your 1-2-3 files. If the names 123R23 or 123R31 aren't listed, perhaps the files are in a directory named 123, LOTUS, or LOTUS123. When you find a likely directory name, enter the DOS command *dir \123r23*.exe*. Substitute the directory name of choice for the name *123r23* in the command. This tells DOS to list any files that contain an .EXE extension in the target directory. If one of the listed files is 123.EXE, then you've found the 1-2-3 program directory.

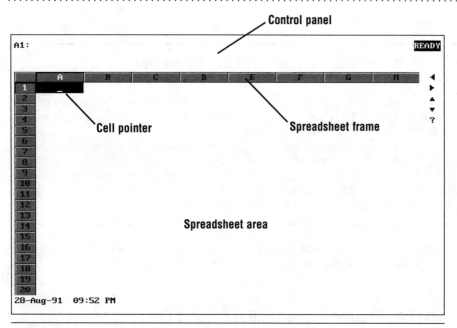

FIGURE 5.1: Lotus 1-2-3 as it appears the first time you run it on your computer.

The Spreadsheet Frame

The spreadsheet frame, or border, is the large inverted L that has letters in it across the display and numbers running down the left of the display. This frame delineates the boundaries of the spreadsheet. Perhaps further discussion of the frame will make sense as we talk about the spreadsheet itself.

The Spreadsheet

The spreadsheet is the area below and to the right of the spreadsheet frame. Actually, the spreadsheet covers a much greater area than what appears on the monitor. You see, the spreadsheet is like a very large bingo card. It has column letters across the top and row numbers down the side, and there's a place at the intersection of each column and row where you can place information.

In bingo, if the number B4 comes up, you can place a marker at cell B4 on your card. You can place something in cell B4 of your spreadsheet any time you want. The intersection of any column and row can hold information—a

Release 3.1's Layered Worksheeet

If you think of the worksheet as a piece of ledger or graph paper, Release 2.3 offers only one sheet to work with at a time. In Release 3.1, you can work with a stack of worksheet pages as many as 256 layers deep. Just as a unique letter or letter pair identifies each spreadsheet column, so does a letter or letter pair identify a spreadsheet layer. The cell address A:A1 that appears in the top left of the display identifies cell A1 in spreadsheet layer A.

This book discusses work in only one layer of the sheet. Throughout our discussions, we'll point out any places where the three-dimensional capabilities of Release 3.1 might cause confusion.

number, words, and even formulas—and the column letter and row number that together describe a cell's location is the "cell address."

The Cell Pointer Identifies the Current Cell

At this moment, you can see the cell address A1 followed by a colon in the top left corner of the display. Those of you using 1-2-3 Release 3.1 actually see the address A:A1, but the initial A: isn't important at this stage of the discussion. The *Release 3.1's Layered Worksheet* box explains a bit more about the expanded cell address.

The Action Is in the Control Panel

The space on your monitor above the worksheet frame is 1-2-3's "control panel." The control panel holds the current cell indicator in its top left corner, the status indicator in its top right corner, and the edit line directly beneath the current cell indicator. Later on you'll see that 1-2-3 also uses the control panel to display menus of commands that you can apply to perform many spreadsheet-related tasks.

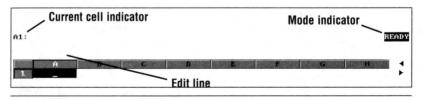

FIGURE 5.2: The top few rows of the display make up 1-2-3's control panel.

The characters in the top left of the display make up the "current cell indicator." They reveal what cell will end up holding information should you type something on the keyboard and press Enter. Another way to tell which cell is the current cell is to find the cell pointer in the spreadsheet area.

This is a no-brainer. The cell pointer is the rectangle whose color matches that of the spreadsheet frame. Centered in the rectangle is a dash that may or may not be flashing—a cursor just like the one that appears after a DOS prompt. At this moment, the cell pointer is in cell A1—at the intersection of column A and row 1. You can change that in a jiffy.

Move the Cell Pointer to Make Another Cell Current

Pressing the cursor control keys moves the cell pointer. Try it. Move the cell pointer one cell to the right by pressing the RightArrow key—that's the key with the arrow pointing to the right. The cell pointer moves, and the current cell indicator changes to reflect the new current cell: B1.

Press the DownArrow key and the pointer moves to cell B2. Now press the RightArrow key several times in succession. Eventually, the pointer comes up against the right edge of the display. Then, when you continue pressing Right-Arrow, the spreadsheet starts moving to the left beneath the cell pointer. You can recognize the spreadsheet's movement by the changing column letters in the frame.

NumLock Must Be off to Move the Cell Pointer
On many keyboards, the cursor controls share keys with numbers on the numeric keypad. When the NumLock light on your keyboard is off, the keypad provides cursor control. When that light is on, the keypad produces numbers rather than cursor movement. If your computer's cursor controls are in the numeric keypad, make sure the NumLock light is off while you work with 1-2-3. Pressing the NumLock key turns the light on if it's off, and off if the light is on.

If you press RightArrow enough, the column letters will go to X, Y, and Z, and then they'll start over with AA, AB, AC, and so on all the way to column IV. Likewise, if you press DownArrow enough, the spreadsheet begins to slide upward on the display, and the row numbers increase to as high as 8,192. With 256 columns and 8,192 rows, you can understand why only a part of the spreadsheet shows at one time.

The Mode Indicator

The indicator in the top right corner of the display reads READY when you first start 1-2-3. This means that the software is awaiting commands—either to move the cell pointer, accept data entry into the current cell, or perform other spreadsheet maintenance tasks.

While you work, the mode indicator's message changes to reflect whatever task is at hand. When you start typing a number, the indicator changes to read VALUE. Later, you'll see that the mode indicator can also read LABEL, MENU, EDIT, and POINT.

Back to A1: The Home Key

Pressing any of the cursor-movement keys moves the cell pointer in the direction the arrow on the key points. When the cell pointer hits the edge of the display, it continues to move to the next cell in the desired direction. However, the spreadsheet moves under the pointer rather than the pointer moving over the spreadsheet.

Much of your work in the spreadsheet will take place near the sheet's top left corner. To let you get there in a hurry when you're galloping among other cells, simply press the Home key. The cell pointer jumps directly to cell A1. Press the Home key now so that the cell pointer returns to its starting position.

Put the Sheet to Use

You have a sense of how to get from cell to cell in the sheet, but you haven't yet seen any reasons to do so. Remember that you can store information in spreadsheet cells. See how that works by typing the number 8. Now look at the line directly beneath the current cell indicator in the top left corner of the display. The number you typed appears there, and the cursor jumps from within the cell pointer to the space immediately following the number. The cursor tells you where any further characters will appear should you continue typing.

The line beneath the current cell indicator is the "edit line." Anything you want to store in a spreadsheet cell appears on the edit line as you type it. Go ahead and type a second 8. It displaces the cursor on the edit line, so that now the number 88 appears there. To store the number 88 in the current cell,

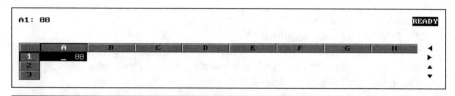

FIGURE 5.3: The current cell indicator reveals that cell A1 contains the number 88. You can see the number in the spreadsheet below the worksheet frame.

press the Enter key—the number (along with the cursor) jumps from the edit line down into cell A1. At the same time, the current cell indicator reveals that cell A1 contains the number 88. Your display should match the one shown in Figure 5.3.

Press the DownArrow key so that the cell pointer moves to cell A2. The current cell indicator reads *A2:* and reveals that there is nothing in that cell. Now press UpArrow and return to cell A1. Once again the current cell indicator reveals the cell's contents.

Some Math in the Spreadsheet

OK, what's the point of seeing a cell's contents in two places on the display? You can see the number 88 in cell A1. Why have it appear in the top left of the display as well?

The answer is, what appears in the spreadsheet isn't always what resides in a cell. A cell can contain values or formulas. Formulas are mathematical expressions of the type you might enter into an adding machine. When a cell contains a formula, the formula's result shows in the worksheet. You can see the formula only by looking at the current cell indicator. Move the cell pointer to cell A2 by pressing the DownArrow key, and let's create a simple formula to see how this works.

Build a Simple Formula

With the cell pointer in cell A2, type the characters *+8+8* and press Enter. You've just created a formula that adds the value 8 to the value 8. You see the formula's result, 16, in cell A2.

The formula itself appears next to the current cell indicator.

Now press the DownArrow key and move the cell pointer to cell A3. You're going to create a formula in this cell similar to the one you created in cell A2.

> **Why Start a Formula with Plus?**
> Throughout this book we begin each formula with a plus sign. This guarantees that 1-2-3 will interpret the entry as a formula. As you'll see later on, starting with a plus sign has other advantages as well.

However, this formula is going to add the value in cell A1 to the value in cell A2 and return the result.

Try it. Type *+A1+A2* and press Enter. The value 104 appears in cell A3, and the new formula appears adjacent to the current cell indicator.

The Power of 1-2-3

Here, then, is the true power of 1-2-3. First, you can use the spreadsheet to store numbers. You can also store formulas that use various numbers to calculate values—much as you would an adding machine. Most importantly, you can write formulas that refer to numbers in different cells.

The formula in cell A3 means, "Add the values from cells A1 and A2." It's an algebraic expression, and cells A1 and A2 are the variables. This means that if you change either of the values in cells A1 and A2, the formula should calculate a new result. Try it.

Move the cell pointer to cell A1. Replace the value in that cell with the number 10. To do this, simply type *10* and press Enter. The value 10 ends up in cell A1, and the formula in cell A3 returns 26! You've reused the formula in

---

What if You Blow It?

One thing that holds many new spreadsheet users back is a nagging concern that they might press the wrong button and commit some catastrophic error. Don't be concerned. As you fiddle about with formulas, your worst mistake is likely to be a typographical error. When you press Enter, 1-2-3 will beep and the word EDIT will appear in the top right corner of your display. This tells you that you've made a mistake.

Don't panic. Press the key marked Esc (for Escape). The Escape key almost invariably lets you back out of any accidents you have with the spreadsheet. There may be other ways to recover from mistakes as well, but for now simply press Escape once or twice and retype the formula that gave you trouble.

When You Finish Practicing
We're not quite ready to explain how to end a session with 1-2-3 gracefully. For now, if you're finished for the day, simply turn off your computer. In Chapter 7, we'll see how to get out of 1-2-3 without shutting down the machine.

cell A3 without recreating it. That formula will continue to read +A1+A2 no matter what values or formulas you store in those cells.

More about Math

1-2-3 can perform calculations other than addition. For example, the symbol for subtraction is a minus sign, as in *+6–3;* the symbol for division is a slash, as in *+21/7;* and the symbol for multiplication is an asterisk, as in *+5*2.* There are other mathematical symbols as well, but we'll leave them for a later discussion.

Create some formulas on your own so you get an idea of how easy it is to do so. Start each formula by moving the cell pointer to a cell that will receive the formula. Then, type a plus sign, a number or a cell address, an arithmetic operator, another number, and so on until you've completed the desired mathematical expression. Press Enter to store your formula in the cell.

Having completed this chapter, you:

- *Know how to start 1-2-3 from a DOS prompt on your own computer*

- *Are familiar with the various elements of the spreadsheet display*

- *Can move the cell pointer around in the sheet*

- *Understand the meaning of the "current cell"*

- *Know how to enter numbers in the spreadsheet*

- *Can write simple formulas that refer to values stored in spreadsheet cells*

Label the Worksheet

When you want to identify the contents of a folder, you label the folder. When you want to identify the contents of a worksheet, you label the sheet. A label is a textual spreadsheet entry. It can consist of words, sentences, combinations of words and numbers, punctuation marks—essentially, any entry that isn't a number or a formula is a label. You use labels to identify the meanings of the numbers in your spreadsheets and to create reports that any reader will understand.

Labels Augment Numbers and Formulas

Even at its simplest, being able to enter numbers and formulas into the sheet gives you a lot of power. Once you've entered a formula that refers to several cells, you can change the values in the referenced cells as often as you want and obtain new results from the formula. One use for such formulas is immediately apparent: calculating totals. You might, for example, wish to record the sales income generated by each person on your team and then calculate the total income for the team. That's what we'll do in this chapter.

Before we proceed, consider what we're about to do. We'll enter some values in a column and then write a formula. Each value will represent a sales person's revenue, and the formula will calculate the total revenue. The finished product, shown in Figure 6.1, will be meaningless to anyone who doesn't know what the numbers mean. That's where the labels come in.

In this chapter, you'll:

- *Learn to use words to label the numeric entries in your spreadsheets*

- *Discover some of the differences between text and values*

- *Point to cells to create some simple formulas*

- *Begin to work with your first spreadsheet model*

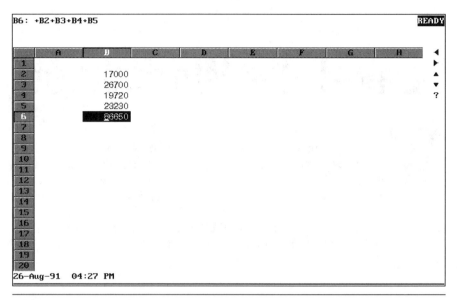

FIGURE 6.1: You know that the numbers in this spreadsheet represent sales revenues. Will anyone else know?

Build the Sales Model

To emphasize the benefits of labeling a worksheet, start up 1-2-3 and then enter the sales values that appear in cells B2, B3, B4, and B5 of Figure 6.1. Remember, to enter a value, move the cell pointer to the desired target cell, type the value, and then press Enter. Make sure your worksheet has entries in cells B2, B3, B4, and B5 that match the ones in the illustration.

Now enter a formula in cell B6 to calculate the total of the other values. The formula that you'll create will be +B2+B3+B4+B5, but rather than type it as you did formulas in Chapter 5, let's apply a feature of 1-2-3 called "POINT mode."

Point to Build Formulas

Make sure that the cell pointer is in cell B6—the cell that will hold the summary total. Type a plus sign (+), but don't type another character. Now press the UpArrow key on the cursor-control keypad. The cell pointer moves up!

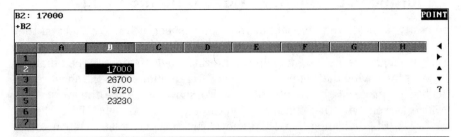

FIGURE 6.2: You're entering a formula into cell B6 using POINT mode, and cell B2 is the first of the cells you're referencing.

More importantly, look in the control panel. The cell address B5 appears following the plus sign on the edit line. Also, the mode indicator changes to POINT. Press UpArrow a second time, and the cell pointer moves to cell B4. Press UpArrow twice more so that the pointer highlights cell B2 and the edit line reads +B2. That's the first expression that you want in the summary formula. Figure 6.2 shows the top of the display as it should look at this moment.

The next thing that goes in the formula is another plus sign, so type one. It appears on the edit line, making the entry there *+B2+*, and the cell pointer jumps back to its starting point in cell B6.

Point to the next cell that the formula should reference. To do this, press the UpArrow key 3 times so the formula in the control panel reads *+B2+B3*. Type a plus sign and point to cell B4 and then type a final plus sign and point to cell B5. The formula +B2+B3+B4+B5 should now appear on the edit line in the control panel.

Press Enter to store the formula in cell B6—that's the cell that was current when you began creating the formula in the first place. Cell B6 in your worksheet should display the value 86,650 to match the worksheet in Figure 6.1.

Point Mode Is Important

You can use POINT mode to build even the most complex formulas. Its great advantage over typing cell addresses is that POINT mode lets you see the cells you're referencing even if those cells aren't on the display when you begin creating the formula. After you type an arithmetic operator such as +, –, *, or /, you can use the arrow keys to highlight any cell that you want to use in a the formula you're creating.

Point mode has many other practical applications. For example, you can use POINT mode to select cells whose contents you wish to erase, copy to other cells, or move to other areas of the worksheet. We'll explore further uses of POINT mode in later chapters.

Label the Worksheet to Reveal Its Meaning

Honestly, what do the numbers in your spreadsheet mean? We told you they were sales figures, but no one casually looking at your display would have a clue. We'll give readers some help by entering labels to identify the numbers.

Start by moving the cell pointer to cell B1. The numbers in the sheet represent sales made in the month of May. To show this, type the word *May*. Notice as you type that the mode indicator in the top right of the display reads LABEL, indicating that 1-2-3 knows you're typing a label. When you've completed the word, press Enter, and 1-2-3 stores your entry in cell B1. Your worksheet should match the one in Figure 6.3.

	A	B	C	D	E	F	G	H	
1		May							►
2		17000							▲
3		26700							▼
4		19720							?
5		23230							
6		86650							
7									

FIGURE 6.3: A label in cell B1 identifies the month in which the values were established.

OK, all of the numbers came from May, but what does each number represent? Move the cell pointer to cell A2 and enter the label *Mike*. The value in cell B2 represents Mike's sales revenue for May. Drop down to cell A3 and enter *Herb*, then enter *Bobbie* in cell A4, and enter *Dana* in cell A5. Finally, enter the label *Total* into cell A6. Your worksheet should match the one in Figure 6.4.

A6: 'Total									READY
	A	B	C	D	E	F	G	H	
1		May							►
2	Mike	17000							▲
3	Herb	26700							▼
4	Bobbie	19720							?
5	Dana	23230							
6	Total_	86650							

FIGURE 6.4: Entering each sales person's name in column A helps to clarify the entries in column B.

Align Labels for a Tidy Look

The worksheet is looking pretty clear, but we can do even better. You've probably noticed that while the numbers in your spreadsheet fall near the right end of each cell, the labels fall at the left ends of the cells. What you might not have noticed is that 1-2-3 inserted a "label prefix" at the beginning of each of the labels you entered.

With the cell pointer on the word *Total* in cell A6, look at the entry following the current cell indicator in the control panel (shown in Figure 6.4). It reads *'Total.* The apostrophe is a label prefix. It tells 1-2-3 that the entry in the cell isn't a number or a formula. Because you started the entry by typing a letter, 1-2-3 assumed you wanted to enter a label and automatically inserted the label prefix. While the prefix doesn't appear in the spreadsheet, it is nonetheless a part of the cell's contents.

Don't Like an Entry? Delete It

If you're using 1-2-3 Release 2.3, and you don't like a cell entry that you've just committed to the spreadsheet, don't panic. You can erase the entry in a flash. Move the cell pointer to the cell whose entry you wish to erase and then press the Delete key. The procedure for erasing cells in 1-2-3 Release 3.1 is a bit more complex. We'll examine it in the next chapter.

There are several types of label prefixes, and the prefix that you use determines where in the cell the label appears. The apostrophe label prefix causes a label to align with the left end of a cell. A quotation mark (") label prefix makes a label align with the right end of a cell, and a caret (^) prefix centers a label.

By default, 1-2-3 inserts an apostrophe label prefix when you enter a label without first typing a label prefix. You can override the default simply by starting a label entry with a prefix. Let's give it a try.

Practice Aligning Labels   The label *Total* in cell A6 doesn't stand apart from the other labels in column A. If it were aligned with the right end of the column, perhaps you'd notice it more easily. With the cell pointer in A6, type a quotation mark (") and then type the word *Total.* When you press Enter, a right-aligned label replaces the earlier version.

The term "by default" means, "That which the software does if you don't tell it to do otherwise."

Typing the Prefix Is Arbitrary

When you begin a cell entry by typing a letter, 1-2-3 automatically assumes that you're entering a label and inserts an apostrophe label prefix. If you begin an entry by typing an apostrophe, 1-2-3 interprets the apostrophe as a prefix, and the apostrophe doesn't appear in the worksheet even though it's part of the cell's contents.

If you want a label entry to begin with an apostrophe, a quotation mark, or a caret, you must start with a label prefix, and then type the desired punctuation mark. For example, if you want the label *"Hello."* to appear in cell C3, you must enter the characters *'"Hello."* into the cell.

The label *May* in cell B1 almost seems to be in a column of its own. Often a label that heads a column looks best when centered in the column. Move the cell pointer to cell B1, type *^May* and press Enter. Your spreadsheet should match the one shown in Figure 6.5.

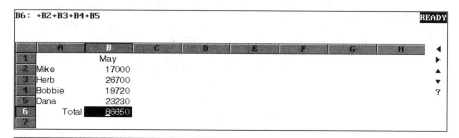

FIGURE 6.5: The label in cell B1 starts with a caret prefix and so is centered in the cell. The label in cell A6 begins with a quotation mark and aligns with the right of the column.

Labels Can Be Long

So far you've entered only very short labels in the sheet. Each of your entries fits with room to spare inside the width of a column. Let's see what happens if you enter a label too long to fit in a column.

Move the cell pointer to cell A9 and type this sentence. As you type, notice that the letters appear on the edit line in the control panel. Press Enter to complete the entry, and the label appears in the spreadsheet—extended out across columns B, C, D, E, and F. Don't let the appearance fool you.

How Long?
Labels in 1-2-3 can be longer than your monitor can display. In 1-2-3 Release 2.3, a label can be as many as 240 characters long. In Release 3.1 a label can be up to 512 characters. Actually, these length limits apply to any cell entries, including formulas.

The long label resides entirely in cell A9. Because there's nothing to the right of the label, 1-2-3 displays all of it. However, if there were an entry in cell B9, you'd see only nine characters of the label in cell A9. Enter the number 7 into cell B9, and then move the cell pointer back to cell A9 to see how this works.

```
A9: 'Move the cell pointer to cell A9 and type this sentence.        READY

        A          B          C       D       E       F       G       H     ◄
  1                May                                                       ►
  2   Mike         17000                                                     ▲
  3   Herb         26700                                                     ▼
  4   Bobbie       19720                                                     ?
  5   Dana         23230
  6          Total 86650
  7
  8
  9   Move the ce       7
 10
```

FIGURE 6.6: Making an entry in cell B9 results in an occultation of the long label stored in cell A9—but the label is there, as the control panel reveals.

Figure 6.6 shows the worksheet. As you can see in the control panel, the label *Move the cell pointer to cell A9 and type this sentence.* still resides in cell A9, but most of it is buried behind the entry in cell B9. In a later chapter we'll see how you can adjust the widths of columns to accommodate longer or shorter labels.

There's little more to learn about labels at this point. We've used only a few to illustrate their usefulness in clarifying the numeric contents of a spreadsheet. It would be good exercise for you to fiddle around in the spreadsheet a bit more until you're comfortable combining labels, values, and formulas to describe simple business situations. Later chapters will assume that you've mastered the basics of working with numbers and labels.

Having completed this chapter, you:

- *Can create formulas by pointing at cells*

- *Are ready to generalize POINT mode to upcoming spreadsheet tasks*

- *Know the difference between values and formulas and labels*

- *Understand that 1-2-3 automatically inserts a prefix when you enter a label*

- *Can override 1-2-3's default label prefix to affect a label's alignment and tidy up a worksheet*

- *Shouldn't wonder what happens to a long label when part of it seems to disappear*

- *Are ready to look at 1-2-3's menus and see what they let you do*

An Introduction
to Menus

In only two chapters you know how to build simple spreadsheets. With numbers, formulas, and labels you can record activity in your business, sum up periodic data, and write simple reports to explain your numeric entries. All of this becomes far more useful when you apply 1-2-3's menu commands to manipulate the spreadsheet.

1-2-3 has an impressive—perhaps even intimidating—complement of commands that you use to copy and move data in the sheet, alter the appearance of numeric entries, change the widths of columns, perform statistical analyses, manage databases, graph data, save and retrieve files, and so much more. Don't worry, we're not going to cover all of that in this chapter. Rather, we're going to get started with 1-2-3's menu commands and apply them to some simple spreadsheet chores.

The Menu, Please

Let's take a look at 1-2-3's main menu for the moment with no other task in mind. To activate the menu, start in READY mode. No matter where the cell pointer is, press the slash key (/). A menu appears in the control panel. Figure 7.1 shows 1-2-3's main menu, the top line of words above the spreadsheet frame.

In this chapter, you'll:

- *Learn how to use 1-2-3's menus*

- *Discover multicell "range" references*

- *Copy the contents of one cell to other cells*

- *Erase the contents of cells*

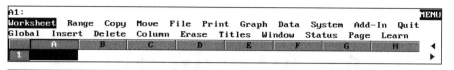

FIGURE 7.1: 1-2-3's main menu appears in the control panel when you press the slash key.

How Does a Menu Work?

The key to working with 1-2-3's menus is to read what appears in the control panel. Right now, the menu offers 11 choices for Release 2.3 users and 10 choices for users of Release 3.1. Whichever release of the software you're using, there's a menu pointer on the first menu item—that's the Worksheet option.

The menu pointer works a lot like the cell pointer. You can move it about by pressing cursor-movement keys. Move the pointer to the right by pressing the RightArrow key, and back to the left by pressing LeftArrow. When you try to move the pointer beyond the edge of the display, it jumps back to the item at the opposite end of the screen.

At the moment, the menu pointer is on the Worksheet option. A second row of options appears beneath the first row. That second row reveals what you'll encounter should you select the currently highlighted item. Press Right-Arrow once so that the menu pointer falls on the Range selection. Notice that the list of options that the Range selection leads to is different from the list that the Worksheet option offers. Press RightArrow again, and you'll see that the Copy command on the main menu lets you "Copy a cell or range of cells." Use the RightArrow and LeftArrow keys to cruise about the main menu until you've examined all of the available choices.

Go Deeper: Choose a Menu Item

Press either the RightArrow or LeftArrow key until the menu pointer is on the Worksheet option and then press Enter. This is one way to select a command from a 1-2-3 menu—highlight the item and press Enter. A new menu appears, and you can see that the first item, Global, on that menu in turn leads to further menu options. Explore this menu a bit by navigating with the RightArrow and LeftArrow keys—read the information that appears beneath

Dialog Boxes in Release 2.3

1-2-3 Release 2.3 lets you use a mouse to get around in the spreadsheet, build formulas, and make selections from menus. Dialog boxes are for mouse users. With or without a mouse, you can access all of 1-2-3's commands via menus alone. However, dialog boxes offer a host of options from which a mouse user can make many selections rapidly and then lock in those selections without selecting each of the items from menus. We'll look more at dialog boxes in Chapter 10.

the menu as you highlight each of the choices. When you've examined the options, highlight the word Global and press Enter.

What appears at this juncture depends on whether you're using 1-2-3 Release 2.3 or Release 3.1. In either case, a new menu appears on the display, but Release 2.3 users will also find their spreadsheets buried beneath something called a "dialog box." Read the *Dialog Boxes in Release 2.3* box for a brief explanation of this phenomenon.

OK, you've worked your way several layers deep into 1-2-3's menu system and now have a sense of how many options there are. Don't panic. You can get a lot done using only a few of the choices. What's important at this point is that you learn to work with the menus. If there's something you want to do, and you don't know the appropriate commands, highlight each menu item in turn and read the "long prompts" that appear beneath the menu.

Escape Backs Away from Trouble

Even if you select a menu item that leads someplace you don't want to be, you're not really in trouble. Pressing Escape "backs up" one level through the menu tree. Try it now. We're deeper into the menu than we need to be, and there's some work we need to do in the worksheet before we actually apply any of the menu commands.

Press Escape once, and you'll return to the Worksheet menu. Press Escape a second time to reach the main menu and press it a third time so the worksheet returns to READY mode. We'll enter a few numbers and labels in the sheet so that we can apply 1-2-3's Range Erase and Copy commands.

Don't do anything tricky. Enter the value *3* into cell A1 and *7* into cell A2. Then enter the label *Test* into cell A4. Your worksheet should match Figure 7.2. Now let's take the menus for a spin.

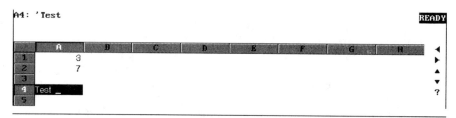

FIGURE 7.2: You'll use these simple entries to apply some of 1-2-3's menu commands.

Use the Menus to Copy a Cell

Any rectangular group of cells— even a single cell —is a range.

One task that you'll perform often is copying information from one location in the sheet to another. Sometimes you want to reuse a label that you've already entered and it's faster to copy the label than to retype it. Other times you'll copy a rectangular group of cells—called a range—for use in several areas of the sheet. Most often, you'll copy a formula from one cell to many other cells—we'll explore the latter two uses of the Copy command in Part III.

For now, let's copy the label from cell A4 to cell B4. To do that, place the cell pointer in cell A4 and press the slash key. Move the menu pointer to the item Copy and press Enter. Read the control panel.

The Corners Identify a Range
1-2-3 uses special notation to identify ranges. The address of a single cell is the cell's column letter followed by the cell's row number. The address of a range is the cell address of the range's top left corner, followed by two periods, and then by the address of the range's bottom right corner. For example, the expression A1..B3 identifies the rectangle of cells that includes A1, B1, A2, B2, A3, and B3. In 1-2-3 Release 3.1, a range reference might also include the worksheet layer letter. So, the expression A:A1..A:B3 identifies range A1..B3 in worksheet layer A.

1-2-3 prompts you to identify the range to copy from and offers a default range. In Release 2.3 the range is A4..A4, and in Release 3.1 the offered range is A:A4..A:A4. In any case, that's the range you want to copy, so press Enter to accept it.

Now 1-2-3 prompts you to identify the range to copy to. You can either type the target address or point to it. Press the RightArrow key to highlight cell B4 and press Enter. The label *Test* appears in cell B4.

Practice with the Copy Command

There's a lot more to learn about copying cells in the worksheet. We devote an entire chapter to the topic in Part III. The point of using it here was to get you using 1-2-3's menus.

Practice further with the command by copying the value from cell A1 to cell B1 and then copy from cell A2 to cell B2. Remember to begin each copying procedure by placing the cell pointer in the cell to copy from. Then, press slash to bring up the menu, select Copy, and press Enter. Finally, press the RightArrow key and press Enter. For further practice, copy from cell A1, A2, or A4 to cells farther away in the sheet than column B.

A Graceful Exit from 1-2-3

At the end of Chapter 5, we promised to show you a graceful way to end a session with 1-2-3. Sometimes you'll want to stop using 1-2-3, but then go on to work in DOS or to use some other software. To do this, select Quit from 1-2-3's main menu.

Erasing Cells for Release 3.1 (and 2.3) Users
A box in Chapter 6 explains how to erase cells in 1-2-3 Release 2.3 by pressing the Delete key. While that method doesn't work in Release 3.1, there is a way to erase cells that works in every release of 1-2-3: Apply the Range Erase command. To erase the contents of the current cell, press slash and select Range from the main menu. Then, select Erase from the resulting menu. Finally, press Enter to tell 1-2-3 that you want to erase the current cell. The Range Erase command can remove the contents from all the cells in a range of any size.

When you've finished practicing with the Copy command and you want to quit for the time being, press the slash key. Select Quit from the main menu, and 1-2-3 displays a two-item menu that asks whether you really want to quit. Select Yes to confirm your desire.

At this moment, 1-2-3 beeps at you and displays yet another menu. This menu points out that you haven't saved your work and asks if you really want to quit. There's no need to save this simple practice worksheet, so choose Yes once more to end the session (we explore how to save your work in the next chapter). 1-2-3 vanishes from the display, and a DOS prompt appears.

Having completed this chapter, you:

- *Understand how 1-2-3's moving cursor menus work*

- *Have a good sense of the enormousness of 1-2-3's menu tree*

- *Know how 1-2-3 identifies a spreadsheet range*

- *Can apply the Copy command to replicate cell entries*

- *Know how to erase cells in all releases of 1-2-3*

- *Can gracefully end a session with 1-2-3*

- *Should be able to apply your experiences with menus to more complicated spreadsheet tasks*

- *Are ready to apply your understanding of ranges to broader applications*

8

Save Your Work for Later

So far the spreadsheets we've created haven't been very challenging. You could build any of them in minutes, so losing them at the end of a work session hasn't been costly. If you always lost your work at the end of the day, there would be no point at all in working. That's why 1-2-3 lets you save your spreadsheets on disk.

To explore how 1-2-3 saves files, we'll begin by creating a slightly more ambitious worksheet than the ones in preceding chapters. This gives you a chance to review the concepts and techniques you've already learned. Then we'll save the sheet on disk and get a good idea of how to work with 1-2-3's file saving and retrieving commands.

Review the Basics

It never hurts to practice. And besides, you'll apply the few things you've already learned about 1-2-3 in almost every spreadsheet you create. Building the model shown in Figure 8.1 will help you to reinforce your basic skills. After you build the model, we'll use 1-2-3's file saving commands to store it on disk.

In this chapter, you'll:

- *Learn how to save a spreadsheet on disk so you can return to it again and again*

- *Create a small practice worksheet to review basic spreadsheet tasks*

- *Make a new directory on your hard disk to hold spreadsheet files*

- *Learn how to change the data directory during the current work session*

- *Save your practice worksheet in the new data directory*

- *Erase the entire worksheet without quitting from 1-2-3*

- *Retrieve your practice worksheet from disk*

	A	B	C	D	E	F	G	H
1	3rd Quarter Sales							
2								
3		Jul	Aug	Sep				
4	Patti	35900	33800	31700				
5	Jim	24000	27300	32700				
6	Kelly	28900	28700	26500				
7	Shannon	31800	32700	31900				
8	Stacy	35600	38200	39100				
9	Totals	156200	160700	161900				
10								

FIGURE 8.1: Instructions in the text explain how to create this simple model, so you can practice your spreadsheet skills.

Apply Your Knowledge

Here's how to proceed: Start 1-2-3 from DOS so that you're facing a blank worksheet, and make sure the cell pointer is in cell A1. The label in cell A1 begins with a number—you'll have to start with a label prefix when you type this entry (see the *Numbers as Labels* box for an explanation of why). Enter *'3rd Quarter Sales*.

Numbers as Labels
In Chapter 6 we explored how the label prefix you type affects the alignment of a label in a cell. We also saw that you can begin an entry by typing a prefix, or let 1-2-3 insert a prefix automatically. It's important to understand that 1-2-3 doesn't add a label prefix if the first character that you type while making an entry is a number or a plus sign. When you type a number first, 1-2-3 assumes that you're entering a value. If you then type some letters, as you do when you enter *3rd Quarter Sales*, 1-2-3 doesn't recognize the entry as a value—and it's too late to add the label prefix automatically. To prevent any confusion, when you want to enter a label that begins with a number, start by typing a label prefix character.

Enter each of the labels shown in range A4..A8—no tricks for any of these. When you type the entry for cell A9, begin with a right-alignment prefix. That is, enter the characters *"Totals* into cell A9. Similarly, enter each of the labels in range B3..D3 beginning with a caret label prefix to center them in the columns. The entry in cell B3 should be *^Jul,* cell C3 should contain *^Aug,* and cell D3 should contain *^Sep.*

Enter each of the values in range B4..D8, and then enter the summary formulas in range B9..D9. The formula in cell B9 is +B4+B5+B6+B7+B8. Likewise, the formulas in cell C9 and D9 are +C4+C5+C6+C7+C8 and +D4+D5+D6+D7+D8, respectively. Enter the formulas either by typing them out as they appear on this page or by using POINT mode the way you learned in Chapter 6.

By the time you've entered the last formula, your worksheet should match ours.

Save Your Work

It's time to save your masterpiece—or is it? Actually, you could save the spreadsheet right now, but a little advanced preparation will save you some headaches later on. You see, you haven't yet established a directory on your hard disk to receive the files you create with 1-2-3.

If you save right now, 1-2-3 will try to put your spreadsheet in the directory that contains the 1-2-3 program files. Rather than jumble so many files together, let's create a new disk directory to hold your spreadsheets. Then, we'll see how to place a copy of the sheet on disk.

Create a Data Directory

Actually, you can't create directories from within 1-2-3. This is a task that you must perform in DOS. Fortunately, you don't need to end your 1-2-3 session to be able to work in DOS—there's a command on the 1-2-3 menu that activates DOS without removing the spreadsheet from RAM.

Get to DOS by pressing the slash key and selecting System. The spreadsheet vanishes, and a DOS prompt appears. But never fear, the spreadsheet that you just created is still in RAM. Let's create a data directory.

Start by switching to the root directory. To do this, enter the DOS command *cd *. Now issue the MD (Make Directory) command. You can assign any directory name you wish, but the remainder of this book will assume that you're working with a directory called 123DATA, so use that name.

Type *md 123data* and press Enter. DOS creates the new directory in the root directory of your hard disk. Return to 1-2-3 by typing *exit* and pressing Enter. Almost immediately the spreadsheet that you created earlier reappears on the display. You're not quite ready to save the file.

The System command on 1-2-3's main menu lets you use DOS without quitting from 1-2-3.

Make the Data Directory Current

Back in Chapter 3 we explored how to make a directory current when you're working in DOS. You can do the same thing within 1-2-3; however, in the spreadsheet you use menus. When you make a directory current, 1-2-3 uses that directory automatically when you save a file for the first time. Also, 1-2-3 looks in the current directory when you ask the software to retrieve a file.

To make your new data directory current, press slash and select File. The resulting menu offers many options, but the Save, Retrieve, and Directory (Dir) selections will serve most of your needs early in your spreadsheet career. Move the menu pointer to Directory (Dir, if you're using Release 3.1) and press Enter.

1-2-3 prompts you to identify the desired directory to make current. Following the prompt is a path name to the directory that is already current— C:\123R23 for Release 2.3 users, and C:\123R31 if you're using Release 3.1. Whatever appears there, it will vanish when you start typing a new directory path.

Type *C:\123DATA*—or the path name to whatever directory you want to use for data storage—and press Enter. 1-2-3 returns to READY mode. Now you're ready to save the spreadsheet.

Save the Spreadsheet

You rely on menu commands to save the work that you do in 1-2-3. Start by pressing slash. Then select File from the main menu and Save from the next one. 1-2-3 prompts you to enter a name under which to save the file, and as you can see by the directory path following the prompt, the current directory is C:\123DATA.

Type a file name. Use the name PRACTICE. Notice as you type that the filename replaces the characters at the end of the path in the control panel. When you finish typing the name, your control panel should read *Enter name of file to save: C:\123DATA\PRACTICE*. Press Enter to save the worksheet. The drive light on your CPU flickers briefly, and 1-2-3 returns to READY mode.

What's That Asterisk Do?

When you select /File Save, 1-2-3 displays a prompt, *Enter name of file to save:*, followed by a directory path, such as *C:\123DATA*.WK1* or *C:\123DATA*.WK**. The directory path has two purposes. First, it identifies where 1-2-3 wants to save the file—that would be the directory named 123DATA on the C drive. Second, the path produces a listing of spreadsheet files already stored in the target directory.

The characters *.WK1, used by Release 2.3, tell 1-2-3 to list any files that have a .WK1 extension. The characters *.WK*, used by Release 3.1, tell 1-2-3 to list files that have any Lotus worksheet extension—.WK1, .WK3, and .WKS. There are no files in the 123DATA directory because we haven't saved any yet. Consequently, no files appear in the listing. You'll see a listing later, after you create and save one or more spreadsheet files. We'll explore the usefulness of the listing at that juncture.

Retrieve the File to Prove That You Saved

Assuming that you've followed along successfully, there's a copy on disk of the worksheet that now appears on your monitor. Take a chance and wipe out the spreadsheet in RAM. To do this without leaving 1-2-3, you apply the Worksheet Erase command.

Press slash and select Worksheet. Then select Erase. 1-2-3 asks if you really want to erase the sheet. Select Yes. The spreadsheet should go blank. If the sheet doesn't go blank, there's a beep, 1-2-3 warns you that you haven't saved, and another Yes/No menu appears, then something's not right— choose No and work through this chapter again starting at the *Create a Data Directory* heading.

You Didn't Type an Extension. . . .
Notice when you select /File Retrieve that the file you saved as PRACTICE now has a file extension. 1-2-3 Release 2.3 automatically adds a .WK1 extension when it saves a file, and Release 3.1 adds a .WK3 extension. This helps you to identify worksheet files whether you're working in 1-2-3 or in DOS.

Now retrieve the spreadsheet file that you saved just a moment ago. Press slash and select File. Then select Retrieve. 1-2-3 prompts you to enter the name of the file to retrieve and offers in the control panel a listing of files from which to choose. You can either type the file name PRACTICE or use the arrow keys to highlight that file name with the menu pointer and then press Enter. If PRACTICE is the only file listed in the control panel, it's already highlighted, so you merely need to press Enter to retrieve it.

Having completed this chapter, you:

- *Are a little more practiced with the basics of working in the spreadsheet*

- *Know how to get into DOS without unloading 1-2-3*

- *Have seen how the DOS MD command creates directories on your disks*

- *Are able to select a directory in which 1-2-3 will save worksheet files*

- *Know how to save a spreadsheet in the current data directory*

- *Can erase a worksheet without quitting from 1-2-3*

- *Know how to retrieve a spreadsheet from disk into 1-2-3*

9

Clarify Your Worksheets

Y ou're becoming proficient with 1-2-3. By now you can create simple models that add up data collected from various parts of your business. To top it off, you can save your models on disk and retrieve them later so that the work you do in one spreadsheet will survive even when you need to work on a different model.

You're working too hard. Knowing just a few more techniques will let you simplify your formulas and make it even easier to clarify the meanings of the values in the sheet. You can handle the barest basics. This chapter helps you push the envelope by revealing an alternative way to work with menus, a faster way to write formulas, and a way to doctor up numeric entries so they look like dollars rather than simply numbers.

Find a File You've Saved

If you worked through Chapter 8, you've saved a worksheet named PRACTICE on your hard disk. Save a little energy by re-trieving that file or return to the *Apply Your Knowledge* section in Chapter 8 and follow the instructions there to recreate the model. To retrieve the file, start up 1-2-3 as usual. Select /File Retrieve, and 1-2-3 prompts for the name of the file to retrieve.

What you do next depends on your set-up. There may be a listing of file names

In this chapter, you'll:

- *Discover how to simplify summary formulas with @functions*

- *Make your numbers look like dollar amounts by applying numeric display formats*

- *Learn a new way to select commands from menus*

- *Change the widths of columns to accommodate wide cell entries*

beneath the prompt in the control panel. Is the name PRACTICE in that list? If the list stretches across the entire screen, press the RightArrow key repeatedly and move the menu pointer across the display. When the pointer reaches the rightmost file name, more names may "scroll" into the control panel as you continue pressing RightArrow. The file names are in alphabetical order, and eventually you should come to the name PRACTICE.

If you don't find PRACTICE in the listing, then perhaps the file is in a different directory. In Chapter 8, we explained how to create a data directory to hold the spreadsheets you create in 1-2-3. Perhaps you've quit from 1-2-3 since then, and you haven't used the /File Directory command to reestablish 123DATA as the current directory. No matter. You can tell 1-2-3 to look for files in different directories even as you issue the File Retrieve command.

Redirect, Please

Redirect any of 1-2-3's File commands to an alternative directory by pressing Escape to clear the existing path and then entering a new path.

To have 1-2-3 look for files in a directory other than the current one, press Escape twice to clear the path listed after the prompt in the control panel. Then, type the path to the directory that contains the desired file, finishing with a backslash (\). For example, press Escape twice to clear the current path and then type *C:\123DATA*. When you press Enter, 1-2-3 lists the worksheet files that reside in the directory named 123DATA. If there is no such directory, 1-2-3 displays an error message to that effect. Clear the message by pressing Escape repeatedly until the spreadsheet is in READY mode. Then, reissue the File Retrieve command and try again.

Use the menu pointer to highlight the file name PRACTICE and press Enter to retrieve the worksheet into RAM. The worksheet appears in Figure 9.1. You're ready to explore more of 1-2-3's features.

	A	B	C	D	E	F	G	H	
1	3rd Quarter Sales								◄
2									►
3		Jul	Aug	Sep					▲
4	Patti	35900	33800	31700					▼
5	Jim	24000	27300	32700					?
6	Kelly	28900	28700	26500					
7	Shannon	31800	32700	31900					
8	Stacy	35600	38200	39100					
9	Totals	156200	160700	161900					
10									

FIGURE 9.1: Either retrieve or recreate this practice worksheet and use it to explore some more of 1-2-3's features.

Shorthand Summary Formulas

So far, we've been working pretty hard to write formulas that add up sequences of numeric cell entries. The summary formula in cell B9 is +B4+B5+B6+B7+B8. Creating such a formula requires a lot of keystroking. There is a shortcut. When you want to add up the values stored in a range— a rectangular grouping of cells—simply apply the @SUM function.

Change the Data Directory for Good

In Chapter 8, you established a directory on your hard disk to hold data files that you create in 1-2-3. If you followed our directions to the letter, the name of your data directory is C:\123DATA. While the main text of this chapter explains how to retrieve files from any directory no matter which directory is the current one, you might prefer to set 1-2-3 so that it always looks for and saves files in the directory named 123DATA.

Here's how to change the default data directory so that C:\123DATA is current whenever you run 1-2-3: Select /Worksheet Global Default Directory. 1-2-3 displays the prompt *Default directory:*, followed by the path to the current data directory. Press Escape to clear the existing path and then type the path to the desired directory — in this case, *C:\123DATA*. Press Enter and then select Update from the resulting menu. Finally, select Quit to return the spreadsheet to READY mode.

The @SUM Function?

The @SUM function is one of a collection of prewritten formulas—called @functions—built into 1-2-3. Most @functions consist of an @ sign (pronounced "at sign"), followed by a function name, followed by one or more items enclosed in parentheses. For example, a typical @SUM function might read @SUM(B4..B8). Its meaning is, "Sum the values stored in range B4..B8."

The items within a function's parentheses are "arguments." Some functions accept only one argument, others accept two or three arguments, and still others accept as many arguments as you can cram into a cell. A few @functions accept no arguments (obstinate little guys).

The @SUM function is one of those that can accept as many arguments as will fit in a cell. The arguments can be range references, single cell references, or numbers. You use commas or semicolons to separate one argument from the next. For example, the formula @SUM(B4..B8,C9,22) returns the sum of the values in range B4..B8, added to the value in cell C9 and to the value 22. Let's put the @SUM function to work in your spreadsheet.

@SUM Applied

Move the cell pointer to cell B9 and enter *@SUM(B4..B8)*. The formula is somewhat shorter than the original addition formula, but it returns the same result. Now let's create a second @SUM formula using POINT mode.

Move the cell pointer to cell C9 and type the characters *@SUM(*. Press the UpArrow key five times until the cell pointer highlights cell C4. You're going to establish a range reference, so it seems that you need a way to highlight all of the cells in range C4..C8 at once. You can.

Pressing the period key in POINT mode to anchor the cell pointer is an important technique to learn.

Notice that the edit line in the control panel reads *@SUM(C4*. This means that the cell pointer is "unanchored" and free to move anywhere in the spreadsheet. Now press the period key. The edit line suddenly changes to read *@SUM(C4..C4*. You've just anchored the pointer in cell C4. Now press the DownArrow key. The cell pointer stretches!

Each time you press DownArrow, the highlight stretches down one cell. Also, the edit line in the control panel changes to represent a new range reference. Press DownArrow enough times so that the highlight covers range C4..C8—that's the range you want to sum. Now finish the @SUM formula by typing a closing parenthesis and pressing Enter.

We'll look more closely at @functions in Part III. For now, practice a bit more with the @SUM function by using POINT mode to enter the formula *@SUM(D4..D8)* into cell D9.

Cell Formats Make Dollars and Sense

The numbers in your practice worksheet apparently represent something to do with sales in the third quarter. What the numbers don't tell is whether they represent sales volume—for example, that Patti sold 35,900 items in July—or they represent sales revenue in dollars. You can apply a numeric display format to make sense out of the numbers.

Display Formats Defined

A numeric display format changes the appearance of a number. The number itself doesn't change, only its appearance in the worksheet does. A display format can make a number appear with standard punctuation (commas to delineate thousands), with a currency symbol, in scientific notation, and so on. All of this will make the most sense when you apply a display format to the values in your spreadsheet.

Start by placing the cell pointer in cell B4. Then select /Range Format. The resulting menu offers quite a selection of formats. The one that interests us is the Currency option, so select Currency. 1-2-3 asks how many decimal places you'd like to show in each cell and suggests two as a likely choice. Type *0* to replace the proffered 2 and then press Enter—there is no decimal component to any of the cell entries.

Use Menus Efficiently
Until now we've encouraged you to move the menu pointer from item to item as you make selections from 1-2-3's menus. When you do this, the long prompts that appear in the control panel clue you in to what each menu command will do should you apply it. There is a shortcut to making menu selections that can significantly speed your work. Rather than move the menu pointer to an item and press Enter, simply type the first letter of the item's name. For example, to select Range from the main menu, type *r*. To select Worksheet, type *w*. At first, pointing and picking helps you to learn about 1-2-3 and the options available on the menus. Later, as you become more familiar with the menu items, you'll be able to issue commands quickly when you type letters rather than point to pick.

	A	B	C	D	E	F	G	H
1	3rd Quarter Sales							
2								
3		Jul	Aug	Sep				
4	Patti	$35,900	33800	31700				
5	Jim	$24,000	27300	32700				
6	Kelly	$28,900	28700	26500				
7	Shannon	$31,800	32700	31900				
8	Stacy	$35,600	38200	39100				
9	Totals	156200	160700	161900				
10								

FIGURE 9.2: Each of the cells in range B4..B8 has a currency format with no decimal places.

1-2-3 prompts you to indicate a range of cells to format and offers range B4..B4 as the default range. Either type B4..B8 or press DownArrow four times to expand the highlight over range B4..B8. Whichever approach you use to indicate the range, press Enter to complete the command. The values in column B appear with dollar signs and punctuation as shown in Figure 9.2.

Further Practice with Formats

Actually, it would be nice to see dollar signs on each of the entries in range B4..D8—you've formatted only the first column. Move the cell pointer to cell C4 and format the remaining cells: Select /Range Format Currency and enter *0*. Then either type *C4..D8* or use the arrow keys to highlight the range. Finally, press Enter to lock in the new format.

Let's also assign a format to the entries in row 9. Just for the experience, we'll use a currency format with two decimal places for these entries.

When asterisks fill a cell, it probably means the cell's contents are wider than the column holding them.

Start with the cell pointer in cell B9. Select /Range Format Currency and enter *2*. Finally, indicate range B9..D9. Whoops! What appears in each cell isn't a currency format—it's just a bunch of asterisks. This is 1-2-3's way of telling you that a formatted entry is too wide to fit in the cell. The underlying numbers or formulas are still there, as are the display formats, but the column just isn't wide enough to show the number, the dollar signs, and the decimal places. You'll have to make a change.

Adjust the Width of a Column

1-2-3's columns start out being nine characters wide. You can change the width of any column to accommodate the entries that you make in it.

	A	B	C	D	E	F	G	
1	3rd Quarter Sales							◄
2								►
3		Jul	Aug	Sep				▲
4	Patti	$35,900	33800	31700				▼
5	Jim	$24,000	27300	32700				?
6	Kelly	$28,900	28700	26500				
7	Shannon	$31,800	32700	31900				
8	Stacy	$35,600	36200	39100				
9	Totals	$156,200.00	$160,700.00	$161,900.00				
10								

FIGURE 9.3: The practice worksheet with cells formatted and column widths adjusted to accommodate wide entries.

Because the entries in cells B9, C9, and D9 of your practice worksheet are too wide to appear in a nine-character column, it would be appropriate to make those columns wider.

Make a Column Wide

Start with the cell pointer in any cell of column B—that's the column whose width you'll adjust first. Select /Worksheet Column Set-Width. From the resulting prompt, you can see that a column can be anywhere from 1 to 240 characters wide, and that currently the width is 9 characters. Type *12* and press Enter. 1-2-3 widens the column to show up to 12 characters and then returns to READY mode. The summary total appears formatted in cell B9.

1-2-3 lets you set the widths of several columns in a single operation. We'll use that approach to adjust the widths of columns C and D. Start by moving the cell pointer to column C. Then select /Worksheet Column Column-Range Set-Width. 1-2-3 prompts you to identify a range of columns whose widths you want to change. Press the RightArrow key to highlight cells in both columns C and D—any range that spans both columns will do—and then press Enter.

Don't enter a number. Once you've issued a width-setting command, you can adjust column widths by pressing the LeftArrow and RightArrow keys. Try it. Press RightArrow once, and columns C and D expand. Press RightArrow two more times. When the width reaches 12 characters, the formatted contents of cells C9 and D9 appear.

Before you lock in the column width, press the LeftArrow and RightArrow keys a few times to see how 1-2-3 adjusts the widths. Finally, adjust the width to 12 characters and press Enter. Your worksheet should match the one in Figure 9.3. Don't bother to save the modified worksheet—you won't need it in future chapters.

Having completed this chapter, you:

- *Are prepared to explore @functions in much greater detail*

- *Have a sense of how to apply numeric display formats*

- *Know how to choose menu items without pointing and picking*

- *Can adjust column widths to fit your spreadsheet entries*

Customize 1-2-3 with Global Worksheet Commands

A spreadsheet should convey a message. 1-2-3 offers a huge complement of tools to help you make the message clear. As you use these tools, you might discover that you're making the same types of alterations to the spreadsheet again and again. Learning and applying some of the "global" commands can reduce your efforts to customize a sheet.

The global commands let you alter 1-2-3's default settings for a given worksheet. For example, you can change the widths of all the columns or you can change the numeric display format that 1-2-3 uses automatically for numeric entries. The key is to understand the difference between commands that act locally in the spreadsheet and commands that affect the sheet globally.

Should You Go Global?

So far when you've applied display formats or altered column widths, you've worked locally—that is, you've set formats only within selected ranges of cells and you've altered the widths of selected columns. Quite often you end up setting almost every column you use to the same width or you apply the same display format to

---

In this chapter, you'll:

- *Learn to use several 1-2-3 menu commands*

- *Change the way that 1-2-3 automatically formats numbers in the sheet*

- *Learn the difference between "local" and "global" commands*

- *Alter the alignments of labels you've already entered in the sheet*

almost every numeric entry. If this is the case, you might be better off changing the global setting.

The Difference between Global and Local

A local command, such as /Worksheet Column Set-Width or /Range Format, overrides the global setting for a selected part of the sheet.

A global setting is one that affects 1-2-3's defaults. For example, if you set the global column width to 12, then all of the spreadsheet's columns will have a width of 12 instead of the original 9 characters. All of the columns, that is, but the ones whose widths you've set locally. Likewise, if you set the global display format to currency with zero decimal places, all cells display values using that format, except for cells whose formats you've changed using the /Range Format command. Let's change some global and local settings so you have an idea of how this works.

Change the Default Column Width

Start in a blank worksheet and select /Worksheet Global. From the options available, select Column-Width (Col-Width in Release 3.1). As you might expect, 1-2-3 prompts you to enter a column width and reveals that the current width is nine characters. Either press the RightArrow key twice, or type *11* and, in either case, press Enter. Now each spreadsheet column is 11 characters wide.

Experiment with Widths

To compare the effects of the global command with those of a local command, place the cell pointer anywhere in column A and select /Worksheet Column Set-Width. Press the LeftArrow key four times or type *7* and, in either case, press Enter. Use the /Worksheet Column Set-Width command again to set the width of column C to 15.

You've set the widths of columns A and C locally, overriding the global width setting for those columns. That override will remain in effect in this particular worksheet—even if you change the global width—unless you specifically reset the width to conform to the default. Fiddle a little more to see how this works.

Select /Worksheet Global Column-Width and change the default to 7. Now all the columns but C are seven characters wide. On the other hand, while column A is seven characters wide, it isn't set to conform to the new default, it simply happens to coincide. Set the default width once more to see that column A marches to its own drummer: Select /Worksheet Global Column-Width and change the default to 9—column A retains its seven-character width.

Reset to Make a Column's Width Conform

Sometimes you set a column's width and later decide that you should have left it alone—the column would be better off at the default width. If that's the case, don't use the /Worksheet Column Set-Width command. That command fixes a column at the selected width. If you later decide to change the default again, that column's width won't change.

To reset a column to the default, place the cell pointer in the column and select /Worksheet Column Reset-Width. You can reset the widths of several adjacent columns at once by selecting /Worksheet Column Column-Range Reset-Width and selecting the columns by highlighting them or typing a range reference that spans the columns.

Try it. Move the cell pointer to column A, select /Worksheet Column Reset-Width, and press Enter. Column A returns to a width of 9—matching the other columns in the sheet. If you were now to reissue the /Worksheet Global Column-Width command and change 1-2-3's default width, column A's width would conform to the new default. Column C would remain at a width of 15.

Change the Default Display Format

You can alter column widths on both a local and a global level. The same applies to numeric display formats. Give it a try. Select /Worksheet Global Format and choose Fixed. The fixed display format forces 1-2-3 to show a specific number of decimal places in a number, no matter how many decimals the number actually contains. For this exercise, enter *3*.

While the worksheet appears unchanged, you can see the effects of the new global format by making an entry in cell A1. Get there by pressing the Home key and then entering *12*. The entry displays as 12.000. Drop down to cell A2 and enter *14.55555;* it appears in the cell as 14.556.

Formatting Is "Visual Rounding"

Many of the numeric display formats require that you specify a maximum number of decimal places to show for any numeric entry. Suppose that you specify a format with two decimal places. Any number with that format will show those two places. The number 8 will appear as 8.00, the number 3.1415 will appear as 3.14, and so on.

When a number has more decimal places than the selected display format will allow,

1-2-3 rounds the number off visually. So, the number 14.5555 displayed with two decimal places appears as 14.56. It's important to understand that the underlying value is still 14.5555—the display format doesn't round off mathematically. Any rounding that results from an assigned numeric display format is for your viewing pleasure only. Formulas that refer to the formatted cells will use the unrounded values in their calculations.

Override the Default Format

1-2-3's standard display format is General. Reset the global format to General by selecting /Worksheet Global Format General.

The /Range Format command lets you override the global format. To see it work, select /Range Format Currency and enter *0*. Then, press Enter to change the format of cell A2. The entry there displays as $15 and will stay that way no matter how you set the global format.

Just as you can reset column widths to the global default, so can you reset the display formats you've assigned with the /Range Format command. To do this, select /Range Format Reset and indicate the cell or range of cells whose formats you wish to remove.

Change the Default Label Prefix

Remember how we discovered in Chapter 6 that 1-2-3 automatically inserts an apostrophe label prefix when you make a label entry? An apostrophe causes the label to align with the left end of a cell. You can, if you wish, tell 1-2-3 to use an alternative prefix.

Select /Worksheet Global Label-Prefix (in Release 3.1, the commands are /Worksheet Global Label). You can choose to have 1-2-3 align labels to the left or to the right in a cell or to center labels automatically. Changing the global label alignment doesn't change the alignment of labels already entered in the sheet. It changes only the alignment of labels that you enter after issuing the command.

Speed Label-Entry

It's a bit time-consuming to type a label prefix each time you enter a label. When you need to enter several centered labels across a row, or perhaps a bunch of right-aligned labels down a column, typing the requisite prefixes slows you down. Don't do it. When you must enter a series of centered or right-aligned labels in adjoining cells, forgo the caret or quotation mark prefixes. Simply type the characters and press Enter, and let 1-2-3 apply the default label prefix—usually an apostrophe for left alignment. After you've entered all of the adjoining labels, use the /Range Label Center or the /Range Label Right command to realign the newly entered labels.

Chances are you won't want to change the global label prefix. Left-aligned labels are the most common in spreadsheet models. When you need centered and right-aligned labels, it makes the most sense to work on a local scale. We're not going to change the global label alignment, so press Escape several times until 1-2-3 is in READY mode. Let's work a bit locally.

Change Established Label Alignments

While you can affect a label's alignment by starting with the desired label prefix when you first type the entry, that's not the only way to adjust its position in the cell. It's possible to change the alignment of all of the labels in a range even after you've entered the labels.

Enter and Realign Some Labels

See how easy it is to realign labels by entering a few in your worksheet. Enter the label *Jul* into cell D1 and *Aug* into cell E1. The labels end up aligned left in their cells. Now change the alignment.

Start with the cell pointer in cell D1. Select /Range Label Center and indicate range D1..E1. 1-2-3 changes the label prefixes of the selected cells, and the labels end up centered. For practice, select /Range Label Right and indicate the same range. The labels shift to the right in their cells.

The phrase, "indicate range D1..E1" means "either type the characters D1..E1 at the prompt or highlight the range and then press Enter."

Spend some time fiddling with label alignments, cell formats, and column widths until you're comfortable with the various commands that apply to these features. Change the options both globally and locally until you're confident that you understand the difference between them.

Having completed this chapter, you:

- *Have a better idea of how to customize your spreadsheets*

- *Understand the difference between global and local settings*

- *Know how to set column widths, cell formats, and label alignment both globally and locally*

- *Are familiar with the concept of "visual rounding"*

Snazzy Spreadsheets with Wysiwyg

By now you may have created several spreadsheets related to your business. And, in spite of your ability to align labels, format numbers, and change column widths, printouts of your worksheets probably wouldn't attract a lot of attention from the casual observer. If you want to get someone's attention, you've got to add emphasis.

Emphasis is what Wysiwyg is about. Wysiwyg, a program that comes in the box with 1-2-3 Releases 2.3 and 3.1, is a collection of "spreadsheet publishing" tools. With these tools you can apply special shading to selected cells, put boxes around cells, change the fonts and font styles (bold, italic, and under-lined) of your worksheet entries, and more.

Learning about Wysiwyg early in your computing career will help you to produce slick memos, letters, and reports that rival the quality of many brochures, newsletters, and magazines. Also, by introducing Wysiwyg at this point, we make it possible for everyone who has one to use a mouse with the spreadsheet. Release 2.3 users can use a mouse without Wysiwyg, but Release 3.1 us-ers must have the add-in attached before their mice will work in the sheet.

You pronounce the name Wysiwyg as "wizzy-wig."
. . . .
. . . .
. . . .

In this chapter, you'll:

- *Learn how to make your work-sheets sparkle through spread-sheet publishing*

- *Learn what an add-in is*

- *Add spreadsheet publishing tools to 1-2-3 by attaching the Wysiwyg add-in*

- *Apply some Wysiwyg commands and add emphasis to spreadsheet entries*

- *Learn more about working in POINT mode*

Wysiwyg Isn't Part of 1-2-3

Wysiwyg isn't built into 1-2-3. Rather, Wysi-wyg is an add-in. Before you have access to

What's an Add-in?

1-2-3's designers realized that their spreadsheet software couldn't be all things to all people. To overcome that limitation, the spreadsheet's design lets programmers develop software that "attaches" in such a way that it seems to be built right into 1-2-3. Such a software package is an add-in.

1-2-3 comes with three add-ins in the package. The first is called the Viewer, the second is the Auditor, and the third is Wysiwyg. There are commercially available add-in word processors, database managers, printing utilities, graph-drawing packages, and file protection programs. If you prefer to work only with 1-2-3, you might look for some of these add-ins to round out your spreadsheet's features.

its spreadsheet publishing capabilities, you must "attach" Wysiwyg to 1-2-3. Once attached, the spreadsheet publisher acts as if it were part of 1-2-3— you issue Wysiwyg commands by selecting them from menus just as you normally issue commands. At the same time, 1-2-3's menus remain available. Essentially, Wysiwyg adds a host of powerful features to those already available in the spreadsheet.

Attach the Add-in

Chances are that you copied Wysiwyg's files to your hard disk when you first installed 1-2-3. That being the case, you can easily attach it to the spreadsheet. The procedure differs a bit in Release 3.1 from that of Release 2.3, so follow the instructions appropriate to your needs. You needn't be working in a blank spreadsheet, but it's OK if you are.

1-2-3 Release 2.3 Press slash and select Add-In Attach. 1-2-3 displays a list of add-in file names and prompts you to identify the add-in that you want to attach. Press the RightArrow key repeatedly until you've highlighted the file name WYSIWYG.ADN and press Enter. Now 1-2-3 displays a menu that asks what function key you'd like to be able to use to activate the add-in after it's attached. Select No-Key. A title screen appears and then drops away to reveal the spreadsheet—it's slightly altered, but it's still the spreadsheet. Select Quit from the resulting menu and return to READY mode.

1-2-3 Release 3.1 Press and hold down the key marked Alt. While holding down Alt, press the function key marked F10 and then release both keys. This

Attach Wysiwyg Forever

The remaining text in this book assumes that you always work with the Wysiwyg add-in attached to 1-2-3. Working with Wysiwyg makes a lot of sense as long as you're not creating giant spreadsheet models that eat up your computer's RAM. You'll always have spreadsheet publishing capabilities available and you will be able to lay out your models accordingly. Release 3.1 users get the added bonus of being able to work with a mouse— the mouse isn't available in Release 3.1 without Wysiwyg attached.

You can set up 1-2-3 so that every time you start up the spreadsheet software it attaches Wysiwyg automatically. To do this in 1-2-3

Release 2.3, select /Worksheet Global Default Other Add-in Set 1. 1-2-3 offers a menu listing of add-in file names. Highlight WYSIWYG.ADN and press Enter. Select No-Key from the resulting menu and then select No from the menu that follows. Finally, select Quit Update Quit.

To make Wysiwyg available in every 1-2-3 Release 3.1 work session, hold down the Alt key and press function key F10. Select Settings System Set and then select the file name WYSIWYG.PLC from the resulting listing of names. Choose No from the resulting menu and No-Key from the menu that follows. Finally, select Update Quit Quit to return to READY mode.

produces a menu in the control panel. Select Load from the menu, and 1-2-3 displays a list of add-in file names along with a prompt that asks you to select an add-in to "read into memory." Highlight the file name WYSIWYG.PLC and press Enter. Select No-Key from the resulting menu—you don't need to be able to activate Wysiwyg by pressing one of the function keys. A title screen appears to tell you that Wysiwyg is loading and then drops away to reveal the spreadsheet. Select Quit from the resulting menu and return to READY mode.

Retrieve Some Data to Doctor

Before you put Wysiwyg to work, it will be useful to have some data in the spreadsheet. People who have worked through earlier chapters created a simple model and stored it on disk in a file named PRACTICE. If you're one of those people, retrieve the spreadsheet into RAM. If you haven't yet created the practice sheet, skip back to Chapter 8 and work through it until you've built the model and saved a copy of it on disk. The practice worksheet appears in Figure 11.1.

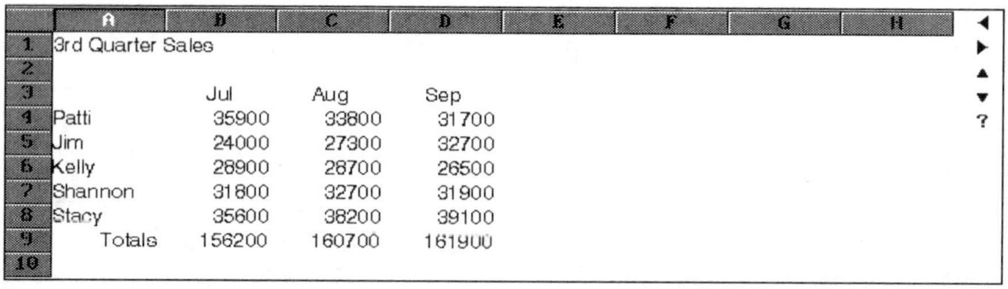

FIGURE 11.1: You might have created this practice worksheet when you read Chapter 8. You'll use it in this chapter to apply some of Wysiwyg's commands.

Add Some Pizzaz with Wysiwyg

The best introduction to Wysiwyg is one that quickly shows you what it can do to a simple spreadsheet model. The exercise you're about to do whips through several Wysiwyg commands that significantly alter the appearance of the sheet. Be aware that nothing you'll do with Wysiwyg changes the contents of the spreadsheet cells. You can think of Wysiwyg formatting as equivalent to assigning numeric display formats—the appearance of cells might change, but the underlying contents remain unscathed.

Beef Up the Title

The title of a document should grab a reader's attention. The title in our practice worksheet accomplishes this only in as much as it's at the top of the page. Let's make it stand out by enlarging it and putting it in boldface.

Move the cell pointer to cell A1 because that's the cell that contains the title. Then, to access Wysiwyg's menu, type a colon (:) rather than press the slash key. Do it, and Wysiwyg's main menu appears in the control panel.

Take a few moments to scan the menu. Move the menu pointer from one item to the next and read the long prompts associated with each item. Most of the items on Wysiwyg's main menu lead to further menus, but you can see from the long prompt that the commands that interest us at the moment are probably under the Format option. Select Format from the menu.

	A	B	C	D	E	F	G	H	
1	3rd Quarter Sales								◄ ►
2									▲ ▼
3		Jul	Aug	Sep					?
4	Patti	35900	33800	31700					
5	Jim	24000	27300	32700					
6	Kelly	28900	28700	26500					
7	Shannon	31800	32700	31900					
8	Stacy	35600	38200	39100					
9	Totals	156200	160700	161900					
10									

FIGURE 11.2: When you set the title in a 24-point font, it definitely stands out from the rest of the worksheet.

Change the Title's Font

First let's make the title larger than the other text in the spreadsheet. You do this by changing the font in which 1-2-3 renders the title. Select Font. Wysiwyg offers eight fonts from which to choose. Of the eight choices, be aware that the default font is font 1. That is, 1-2-3 with Wysiwyg automatically renders all cell entries in Font 1 until you specifically issue commands to the contrary.

Font 1 is probably 12-point Swiss. To remain consistent, stick with the Swiss font, but go with the 24-point size. Select 3 from the menu. Wysiwyg prompts you to identify a target range; press Enter to indicate cell A1. Now the title most definitely stands out—the font is much larger, and the column's height has increased to accommodate it. Your worksheet should match the one in Figure 11.2.

A "point" is a unit of measurement common in typesetting. One point is equal to one seventy-second of an inch (1/72").

Set the Title in Boldface. . . . And, Hey, Add an Underline

Big is good, but bold is better. Give the title added emphasis by making it boldface as follows: Press colon and select Format Bold Set. Press Enter to indicate cell A1 as the target range. Set the title apart even more by underlining it. You know the drill: Press colon and select Format Underline. But wait a minute.

You can apply one of three styles of underlines. A standard single underline would look pretty thin next to the large, boldfaced title. Even a double underline would look out of place. So, go ahead and choose Thick from the menu and then press Enter to indicate A1 as the target cell. The worksheet is starting to look interesting.

"Unanchor" the Cell Pointer

When 1-2-3 is in point mode, there can be either a cell reference or a range reference representing whatever it is you're highlighting. When there's a cell reference only, the cell pointer is free to move in the spreadsheet. When there's a range reference, the cell pointer is anchored—and when the range reference is to more than one cell, the range highlight's anchored corner is the one opposite the cursor. The cursor identifies the "free" corner of a point mode range highlight. Figure 11.3 illustrates this concept.

Notice the range reference adjacent to the "range" prompt in the control panel. In most cases, 1-2-3 offers a range highlight when it prompts you to select a range on which to act (when you're assigning a numeric display format, for example). You can unanchor the highlight, if you wish, by pressing the Escape or the Backspace key. This lets you move the pointer to some other cell where you can reanchor it by pressing period.

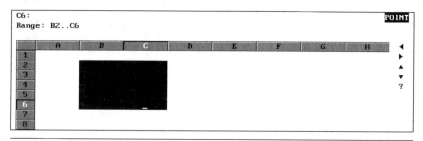

FIGURE 11.3: The "free" corner of a range highlight is the corner that contains the cursor.

Dolly Up the Data

The spreadsheet entries as they already appear aren't very eye-catching. It might be nice to set the month names apart a bit from the data and add some shading and boxes to emphasize the values and separate them from the summary totals. Start by emphasizing the month name column headers.

Boldface and Boxes

Move the cell pointer to cell B3. Then press the colon and select Format Bold Set. Indicate range B3..D3 as the range to format.

	A	B	C	D	E	F	G	H
1	**3rd Quarter Sales**							
2								
3		Jul	Aug	Sep				
4	Patti	35900	33800	31700				
5	Jim	24000	27300	32700				
6	Kelly	28900	28700	26500				
7	Shannon	31800	32700	31900				
8	Stacy	35600	38200	39100				
9	Totals	156200	160700	161900				
10								

FIGURE 11.4: Doctoring up the title, the column headers, and the data cells has transformed the spreadsheet.

Now put some boxes around the data. Press the colon and select Format Lines. Take a moment to explore the resulting menu. Highlight each selection in turn and read the associated long prompt. You'll see that you can draw lines around ranges or around each of the cells in a range. You can also draw lines on just one side of each cell in a selected range. There are options for drawing double lines and for drawing heavy lines. We're going to put lines around each of the cells in a selected range, so select All from the menu.

Wysiwyg prompts you to indicate a range. The default range offered is B3..B3, so you know that the cell pointer is anchored in cell B3. Actually, you're not going to include cell B3 in the range—you're putting boxes only around the cells in range B4..D8. Fortunately, you can clear the default range reference by pressing either the Escape or the Backspace key.

Try it. Press Escape once, and the default reference changes to read B3. Now move the cell pointer down to cell B4 and press the period key to reanchor the cell pointer. Use the cursor keys to highlight across and down to cell D8. Finally, press Enter to complete the command sequence. Lines appear around each of the cells in range B4..D8. Your worksheet should match the one in Figure 11.4

Separation Lines and Shading

Remember how you used to write out mathematical equations in school? You'd write one number under the next until all of the numbers you were going to add up appeared with the decimal places properly aligned and then you'd draw a line under the numbers. As you performed the addition, you'd write your answer under the line. Such a calculation might appear as follows:

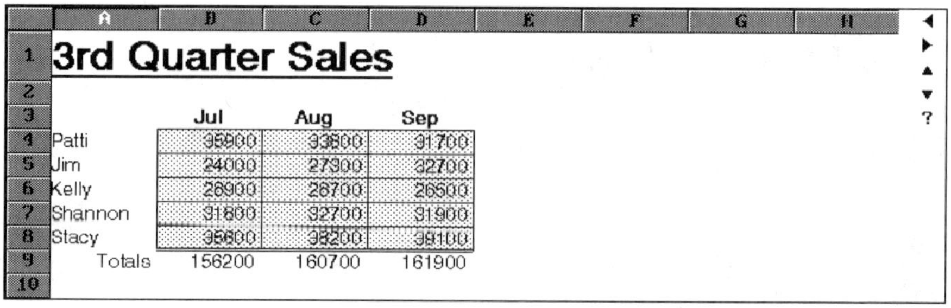

FIGURE 11.5: This is how the practice worksheet should look before you save it at the end of this chapter.

$$
\begin{array}{r}
75.2 \\
108 \\
+\ \ \underline{16.5} \\
199.7
\end{array}
$$

To emphasize this line in your spreadsheet, move the cell pointer to cell B9, and proceed as follows: Press colon and select Format Lines Double. Choose Top and then indicate range B9..D9.

The totals in row 9 will stand out a bit more if you shade the data in range B4..D8. To do this, select :Format Shade. You can select light shading, dark shading, or even opaque shading to completely black out the contents of a range. Choose Light and then indicate range B4..D8. Remember, to indicate the range using POINT mode, press Escape to unanchor the cell pointer, move the pointer to cell B4, press period, and then highlight the range. The finished worksheet should match the one in Figure 11.5.

Slash or Colon

Through the remainder of this book, we'll use a simple convention to describe the menu sequences you need to accomplish the tasks at hand. As in previous chapters, if you need to press slash to access 1-2-3's menus, we show the sequence beginning with a slash. For example, the commands to erase the current cell might read, "select /Range Erase and press Enter."

If you need to press the colon key to begin a Wysiwyg menu sequence, we'll begin our instruction with the colon rather than a slash. Our instructions to apply light shading to a range of cells might read, "select :Format Shade Light and indicate range B4..D8."

Save This File for Later

You have a pretty good idea of what Wysiwyg can do for your spreadsheets. Actually, we've discussed only a fraction of the add-in's features. Please continue to fiddle on your own with the selections on Wysiwyg's menus. For now, focus especially on the options that you find when you select :Format. But before you make more changes to the practice worksheet, save a copy of it on disk. We'll come back to it in a later chapter.

To save, select /File Save. Notice that 1-2-3 offers to save the worksheet under its original file name. That's acceptable, so press Enter. 1-2-3 displays a new menu asking whether you wish to save this new file in place of the earlier version on the disk. Choose Replace—you won't need the original rendition of the model now that you've souped it up with Wysiwyg.

Having completed this chapter, you:

- *Have a good sense of what add-ins are*

- *Have set Wysiwyg to attach every time you start up 1-2-3*

- *Are familiar with the types of capabilities that Wysiwyg adds to 1-2-3*

- *Know how to access Wysiwyg's spreadsheet publishing features*

- *Can unanchor and reanchor the cell pointer while 1-2-3 is in POINT mode*

- *Are prepared to create attractive documents that will grab a reader's attention*

Mousing around the Sheet

Mouse users: Forgive us for taking so long to get around to this. Especially if you're using 1-2-3 Release 2.3, you may already have mastered the mouse—Release 2.3 lets you use a mouse whether or not Wysiwyg is attached. Release 3.1 allows a mouse only when Wysiwyg is active, so it made the most sense to leave a discussion of mice until you all were working with the add-in.

Working with a mouse is quite simple, particularly when you know the basics of working in a spreadsheet without a mouse. You might find the mouse easier to use than the keyboard. A mouse can replace cursor-movement keys for navigating in the sheet, making menu selections, and highlighting ranges. What's more, a mouse lets you select options from dialog boxes, perhaps even more quickly than you can select them via menus.

If you already have a mouse attached to your computer, this chapter will get you up to speed so you can use the mouse in every session with 1-2-3. Even if you don't have a mouse, you might want to read along. Once you see how a mouse works with the spreadsheet, you may decide to get one for your desk.

How Does That Rodent Run?

If 1-2-3 is running, you have a mouse properly installed on your computer, and you followed all the instructions for

---

In this chapter, you'll:

- *Learn the basics of working with a mouse*

- *Use the mouse to navigate among spreadsheet cells*

- *Apply the mouse to issue menu commands*

- *Select cells and ranges in POINT mode using the mouse*

- *Work with dialog boxes if you're using a mouse with Release 2.3*

Clicking Is Key
Your work with the mouse relies heavily on "clicking" objects on the display. To click something—a cell or a menu item, for example—you move the mouse pointer to the item and then rapidly press and release the left mouse button. Double-clicking an item means moving the mouse pointer to the item and pressing and releasing the left mouse button twice in rapid succession.

permanently attaching Wysiwyg in Chapter 11, then there's a little arrowhead somewhere on your display. That arrowhead is tied directly to the mouse on your desk. To see how the mouse and the arrowhead, or "mouse pointer," are connected, hold the mouse down gently on your desk and move the mouse around in small circles. The mouse pointer moves in synchrony with the mouse.

Move with the Mouse

The simplest use of the mouse is to use it to position the cell pointer in the sheet. Do this by moving the mouse around on the desk until the mouse pointer falls on the cell where you want the cell pointer. Then, quickly press and release the left mouse button. The cell pointer jumps directly to the mouse pointer. You can make an entry in the current cell as always. Use the mouse to click several cells on the display and see the effect on the cell pointer's location.

Pictures that you click to accomplish tasks with a mouse are called icons. The triangles to the right of the worksheet are 1-2-3's navigation icons.

There's a second way to move the cell pointer with a mouse. It involves clicking those little triangles on the right edge of your display under the mode indicator. Try it. Click the triangle that points to the right and the cell pointer moves right. Click the triangle that points down, and the cell pointer moves down. Try clicking the triangle that points right repeatedly until the cell pointer reaches the right edge of the display and the spreadsheet moves left under the pointer.

Once you've moved the cell pointer well off to one side, you might want to get it home in a hurry. Clicking the top left corner of the worksheet frame is equivalent to pressing the Home key on the cursor control keypad.

The Mouse and Menus

If you like the mouse to navigate, then you might be pleased that the mouse can also issue menu commands. Before you use the mouse to issue a command, enter a value into cell B2. Then we'll use the mouse to assign a numeric display format.

Get to B2 by clicking the cell and then enter 7. Now slide the mouse away from you until the mouse pointer moves above the worksheet frame on the display. This activates 1-2-3's main menu. Click Range on the menu, click Format on the next menu, and click Currency on the next one. Click anywhere to indicate that you want to use two decimal places and then double-click cell B2 to complete the Range Format command. The first click on B2 selects that cell as the range to format. The second click finishes the command sequence.

Let's apply the mouse to access the menus once more. Start by clicking cell B3 and then enter the value 8. Now use the Range Erase command to clear the entries from cells B2 and B3—slide the mouse away from you to activate the menu. Click Range and then click Erase. While 1-2-3 prompts you to indicate a range to erase, use the mouse to highlight range B2..B3. Here's how to do it.

Move the mouse pointer to cell B2. Press and hold the left mouse button and then slide the mouse toward you until the cell pointer expands to highlight range B2..B3. Once you've highlighted the range, release the mouse button and click anywhere on the display to complete the command sequence.

Holding down the mouse button while moving the mouse is called "dragging."

The Right Mouse Button Provides Escape
Remember how you can press Escape to "back up" out of the menu tree? That is, if you've chosen an incorrect menu command, pressing Escape backs out to the menu from which you selected the command. Pressing the right-hand mouse button has the same effect—unless you've already backed out to either 1-2-3 or Wysiwyg's main menu—and then pressing the right-hand button simply swaps menus. On the other hand, if the mouse pointer isn't in the control panel when you click the right-hand button, you can even escape out of the main menus and back to READY mode. The right-hand mouse button doubles for the Escape key in almost all spreadsheet situations.

Access Wysiwyg with the Mouse

It's a snap to use Wysiwyg's menus with a mouse—there's little difference from using 1-2-3's menus. Move the mouse pointer into the control panel to activate the menu. Then click once with the right mouse button. This switches 1-2-3's menu out of the control panel, and Wysiwyg's menu appears in its place. While the Wysiwyg menu is up, the mode indicator in the top right of the screen reads WYSIWYG. Click the right mouse button again to switch back to 1-2-3's menus.

For Release 2.3 Users—Dialog Boxes

The mouse is much more powerful in 1-2-3 Release 2.3 than it is in Release 3.1. This is in part because of Release 2.3's dialog boxes or dialog settings sheets. With a mouse, you can quickly select several options from a dialog box. Without a mouse you might have to issue several sequences of menu commands to select the same options. You can get some idea of this quite quickly by activating a dialog box to see how it works with a mouse.

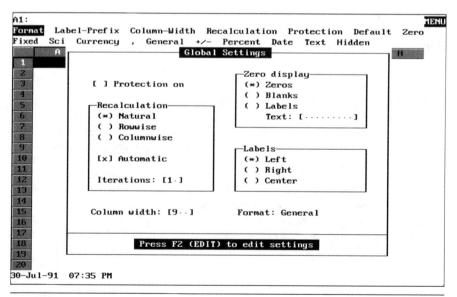

FIGURE 12.1: A dialog box reveals at a glance what settings you've already established in 1-2-3.

Move the mouse pointer up to activate the menu. Make sure you're using 1-2-3's menu, and not Wysiwyg's. Click Worksheet and then click Global. A dialog box appears superimposed on the spreadsheet as shown in Figure 12.1. You can discern from the dialog box several things about the worksheet. Most of those things aren't familiar just yet, but you should recognize the column width setting (in the bottom left of the dialog box) and the label alignment options (the lower right box within the dialog box.)

Right now the global column width is nine, and the default label alignment is Left. Change the label alignment setting by clicking Right in the box labeled *Labels.* The menu disappears from above the dialog box, and an asterisk appears next to the option you clicked. You could select from among other options in this dialog box as well, but we haven't explored those features of 1-2-3 just yet, so leave them alone.

The point is, once you've clicked the desired settings in the dialog box, you can either lock in those settings by clicking the OK button in the bottom right of the dialog box or you can discard the changes by clicking Cancel. In either case, the menu reappears, and you can return 1-2-3 to READY mode by moving the mouse pointer out of the control panel and clicking the right-hand mouse button several times in succession.

The Mouse Is in Your Hands

There's more we could say about working with a mouse in 1-2-3. However, the little we've covered should be enough to get you through most of the spreadsheet tasks you're likely to encounter. We can't assume that all readers are using a mouse, so further text will discuss matters in terms of menu command sequences. If you're using a mouse, you'll have to decide when it's appropriate to work with dialog boxes rather than work through the menus with us. We'll try to point out special situations where working with a mouse might be more appropriate than working with the keyboard.

Having completed this chapter, you:

- *Understand how the mouse controls the mouse pointer*
- *Know how to navigate by clicking cells and navigation icons*
- *Can use the mouse to access menus and highlight ranges*
- *Should be able to generalize your experience with the mouse to other software that uses mice*

13

Hard Copy: Print a 1-2-3 Spreadsheet

A spreadsheet on the computer is great for you and for anyone who's willing to look over your shoulder to see your latest model. However, your spreadsheets aren't going to reach a wide audience until you start printing them on paper. Once you've doctored up the data with Wysiwyg, you can print a model so that it looks on paper almost exactly as it looks on the display.

Retrieve the Practice Model

It's easiest to see the effects of printing when there is data in the spreadsheet—printing a blank worksheet simply ejects blank paper from your printer. You've already created an attractive model and saved it in a file named PRACTICE, so retrieve that worksheet from disk. Also, make sure that the Wysiwyg add-in is attached to 1-2-3.

If you haven't created the practice worksheet and you don't have Wysiwyg set to attach automatically when you start up 1-2-3, then please hop back to Chapter 11 and follow the instructions there for working with Wysiwyg. Those instructions, in turn, will send you back to Chapter 8 for instruction on building the practice model. Before you're ready to print, your spreadsheet should match the one in Figure 13.1.

In this chapter, you'll:

- *Learn how to make printed copies of your spreadsheets*
- *Follow five easy steps to printing*
- *Learn a few tricks to troubleshoot your printer*

101

	A	B	C	D	E	F	G	H
1	**3rd Quarter Sales**							
2								
3		Jul	Aug	Sep				
4	Patti	35900	33800	31700				
5	Jim	24000	27900	32700				
6	Kelly	28900	28700	26500				
7	Shannon	31800	32700	31900				
8	Stacy	35600	38200	39100				
9	Totals	156200	160700	161900				
10								

FIGURE 13.1: You should recognize this practice worksheet from earlier chapters. Retrieve it now so that you can apply the five steps to printing a spreadsheet model.

Follow the Five Steps to Printing

Printing from 1-2-3 can seem so easy that it doesn't deserve a chapter in a book. Actually, only the basics of printing are easy. If you want no more than to print exactly what appears on the display, then there are five steps to that end. Once you've mastered the five steps, you may go on to explore some of 1-2-3's more advanced printing options. This chapter will stick with the easy stuff.

1. Make Sure Your Printer Is On and Ready

Most printers have a light that comes on when the power is on. A second light comes on when the printer is ready to accept information from the computer. This second light might be labeled Ready, or On Line, or simply Line. If your printer lacks such indicators, then you just have to trust that turning on the power makes it ready to print.

If your printer's power is on, and the On Line indicator never lights, look for a button on the printer labeled Off Line or Line. Pressing that button allows the printer to connect to the computer—or disconnects the printer from the computer—depending on the status of the On Line light. In any case, make whatever settings are necessary on the printer so that you know it's connected to your computer.

2. Align the Paper in the Printer

If you're using a dot-matrix printer or some other machine that has a tractor feeder, then you need to make sure that the top of a page of paper aligns with the top of the printer's print head. This isn't a concern if you're using a laser printer or other printers that can feed single sheets of typing paper.

A tractor feeder is a collection of sprocketed wheels that engage the edges of perforated computer paper and feed the paper into a printer.

3. Tell 1-2-3 What Range to Print

Actually, you'll be printing with commands from Wysiwyg's menu, so select :Print. Mouse users, remember that you can activate Wysiwyg's menus by pointing at the control panel and clicking the right-hand mouse button. Now select Range and then Set from Wysiwyg's menus.

Wysiwyg prompts you to identify a range to print. Indicate range A1..E10. Any range that's smaller than an 8.5 × 11-inch sheet of paper and that contains the data you wish to print will do, though the positioning of the data in the print range will affect the data's position on the finished page. A dotted line appears around the print range so that you'll know which data are in the print range and which are outside of it should you return to the spreadsheet to make further modifications.

4. Preview the Printout

This step is optional. Still, you can save paper by previewing a printout to make sure you like its appearance before committing it to paper. If you don't like what you see in the preview, drop out of the print menus and doctor up the spreadsheet a bit more before printing.

Select Preview from the print menu, and a graphical representation of your document appears on the display. When you're satisfied that you know what it will look like on paper, press any key to clear the display.

> **Don't Confuse the Print Menus**
> There are two print menus in 1-2-3 once Wysiwyg is attached. It's easy to use the wrong menu. Make sure the word WYSIWYG appears in the mode indicator before you select Print, or you won't find the options we describe in the text. We could argue that there are reasons to use the 1-2-3 Print menu, but nothing we'll cover in this book requires it. Chances are you'll find all the printing power you need on Wysiwyg's print menus.

5. Select Go

Selecting Go from the print menu tells Wysiwyg to print whatever falls within the print range in the spreadsheet. It usually takes a while for Wysiwyg to send the necessary information to the printer, but eventually your printed document should emerge. 1-2-3 returns to READY mode after printing.

And If It Doesn't Print?

There are a host of reasons why your spreadsheet won't print on your printer. We can't possibly anticipate all the problems you might encounter, but this short list suggests a few things you can try before asking someone else for help.

Check the Cable

One thing to check right away is whether the cable that connects the printer to your computer is loose. Press the plug onto the socket on your computer and tighten the screws that hold it there. Seat the other plug firmly on the printer.

Use the Right Port

"Port" means "place where you plug in a device." The two most common types of ports are serial and parallel.

Is 1-2-3 trying to print on the proper printer port? Explaining the types of ports and how printers work with them is beyond the scope of this book. However, we can suggest a way that you might get 1-2-3 to use the right port if it isn't already.

From READY mode, select :Print Configuration Interface. You can see from the settings/dialog box that appears on the display that the selected interface is Parallel 1. That's selection 1 on the current menu. Select 2 from the menu and then again walk through the five steps to print. If you don't get a printout, select :Print Configuration Interface and then select 3. Then try again to print. Work through the choices on the :Print Configuration Interface menu until you've tried them all or until 1-2-3 prints the selected range.

Check the Printer Driver

Are you using the correct driver for the printer? The printer's name appears on the display when you select :Print Configuration. It's in the settings dialog box under the heading Configuration: Printer. If the wrong printer name appears there, you might be able to replace it by selecting Printer from the menu (from READY mode, the menu sequence would be :Print Configuration Printer) and then selecting the name of the appropriate printer.

If Your Printer Isn't Listed
If your printer's name doesn't appear on the list when you select :Print Configuration Printer, you'll need to exit from 1-2-3 and run the installation program. Now that 1-2-3 is on your hard disk, you can run install by switching to the directory that holds the 1-2-3 program files and then entering *install*. Follow the Install program's instructions for installing printers to run with 1-2-3.

Save Your Changes

If you do end up changing configuration settings to get 1-2-3 to print, you should update the configuration file so that your modifications will be in effect the next time you run the spreadsheet software. The configuration file is a disk file than contains a record of your custom settings. 1-2-3 consults that file at start-up so that it knows what features you want active in the worksheet.

To update the configuration file, escape back to READY mode. Then, select :Display Default Update. Choose Quit to return to READY mode.

Having completed this chapter, you:

- *Are familiar with the five easy steps to printing with 1-2-3*

- *Can set a print range in your worksheet*

- *Know how to preview a document before committing it to paper*

- *Are aware of some of the trouble spots that can interfere with printing*

- *Should be able to print other spreadsheets you create in 1-2-3*

Use Names Instead of Addresses

In small worksheets, it's easy to keep track of the cells and ranges that you want 1-2-3 to use when you write formulas and issue menu commands. However, as your worksheets become larger, you might find it difficult to remember just where you entered that sales commission percentage or what is the range reference for the table of monthly production numbers. There's nothing about the address A6..C12 that tells you the range contains test scores. If, on the other hand, range A6..C12 also had the name *testscores,* at least you'd remember the name.

This chapter reveals 1-2-3's range naming capabilities. It explains how to create range names and how to use them as you write formulas and issue menu commands. By the end of the chapter, you'll have a good sense of how range names can simplify your work with 1-2-3.

Uses for Range Names

You can assign names to any range—even to individual cells. Once you've named a cell, you can type the name in place of the cell's address when you create a formula. You can also type the name when you want to indicate the cell as you issue menu commands. All of this applies as well to working with ranges that you've named—if you would normally specify a range as you issue a menu command, you can just as well type a range name to identify the range.

In this chapter, you'll:

- *Learn to use range names in place of cell addresses*

- *Learn some reasons to use range names rather than cell addresses*

- *Assign names to cells and ranges*

- *Use range names in formulas*

- *Use range names when you issue menu commands*

- *Learn about 1-2-3's Help facility*

A Range Naming Scenario

Suppose that you're calculating bonuses for your retail sales people. It was an unusually grueling shopping weekend during the holiday rush, and you've decided to award discretionary bonuses in the area of 2.75% of revenue generated by each person. As you work in the spreadsheet, you find that you're entering the value .0275 repeatedly to calculate the bonuses. A range name might simplify the task.

You could enter the value .0275 once, and assign a range name to the cell holding it. Then you'd type the range name each time you created a formula to calculate the bonus. What's more, once you'd entered the formulas, you'd be able to change your mind about the bonus percentage simply by changing the value entered in the named cell. Give it a try.

Prepare the Bonus Percentage Cell

The idea in naming a cell is to use a name that you'll remember several hours later when you need to refer to the cell. Keep the names short and simple, but make them descriptive. For example, you might name the cell for this exercise *percentage,* but that's rather long. The name *pcnt* might be just as memorable, so assign it to cell B1.

You can enter a percentage by following a number with a percent sign. 1-2-3 converts the entry 23% into the value .23.

To assign a range name, select /Range Name Create. 1-2-3 prompts you to enter the name. Type *pcnt* and press Enter. Then 1-2-3 asks you to identify the range to name. Indicate cell B1.

OK, cell B1's name is *pcnt,* but you can't tell by looking. You can clarify the issue by entering a label in cell A1 that reveals the name of cell B1. Move the pointer to cell A1 and enter the label *pcnt.* Finally, before you enter any percentage calculations, enter the value *.0275* into cell B1.

Write a Percentage Formula

Move the cell pointer to A4 and enter the name *Pat.* Move to cell B4 and enter *3290*—that's how much Pat brought in during the stellar shopping weekend. Now move the pointer to C4 and type the first percentage calculation: *+B4*pcnt.* Press Enter to complete the formula. The value 90.475 appears in cell C4.

Enter the value *5858* into cell B7 to represent the revenue of a second sales person. Then enter a percentage calculation in cell C7. To do that, move the pointer to C7 and type *+B7*pcnt.* The formula returns 161.095.

Help Can Guide You through Your Work

1-2-3 has an extensive built-in Help facility. At any time in a work session that you have questions about what you're doing, simply press the HELP key—that's the function key labeled F1 either at the left end of your keyboard or just above the number keys across the top of the keyboard.

When you press the HELP key (alternatively, mouse users can click the question mark to the right of the worksheet), a window of information appears superimposed on the spreadsheet. The information in the window is about whatever task you're performing when you activate Help—for example, if you've selected /Print when you press HELP, the Help window teaches you about printing.

Using arrow keys, you can make selections in the Help window to find further information about any spreadsheet-related topic. Select the Index option from any Help display to produce a listing of all of the topics available. When you're finished with help, press the Escape key. The Help window vanishes, and you're left exactly where you were in the sheet before you accessed Help.

Notice in the control panel that the formula reads +B7*PCNT. 1-2-3 displays cell and range names in formulas to help you understand the formulas' meanings.

Use a Range Name in a Command Sequence

Wherever you indicate a range while issuing a menu command sequence, you can enter a range name rather than typing a range reference or highlighting cells. The demonstration of this might be more interesting with a multicelled range, so let's create another name in the sheet.

Enter the values in your worksheet as indicated in the following list:

Cell	Entry
B10	8
B11	9
C10	7
C11	12

Now, assign a name to the range that contains the entries: Select /Range Name Create and enter the name *test*. Then indicate range B10..C11. Use the name to assign a numeric display format to each of the cells in the range.

Select /Range Format Fixed and enter *2*. Then type the name *test* and press Enter. The new entries assume the fixed format and show two decimal places of zeros.

Name Ranges On Your Own

The benefits of range names may not be entirely clear at this point in your spreadsheet career. We've worked very little with ranges of cells and certainly haven't created any large spreadsheets.

You may have created some large models by now, and you might see the advantage of naming key cells and ranges in those sheets. As you become more sophisticated in your spreadsheet designing, you'll discover more and more situations in which range names can simplify your work.

Having completed this chapter, you:

- *Understand some of the advantages of working with range names*

- *Know how to name spreadsheet cells and ranges*

- *Can use range names as references when you write formulas*

- *Know how to use range names as you issue menu command sequences*

- *Have a sense of how to use the Help facility*

- *Are better prepared to work with large spreadsheet models*

Part III
Formulas and
Functions

You've learned an enormous amount about 1-2-3, and we haven't hidden the fact that there's a lot more to learn. The menu trees contain several hundred commands, and we've applied no more than a couple dozen of them.

All the same, you can harness much of 1-2-3's power without resorting to menu commands. Part III shows you how. It digs deeper into the business of expressing your problems mathematically. We've already explored how to do basic math in the sheet, we've learned to write formulas, and we've even touched on @functions—the most powerful of 1-2-3's math tools.

Still, on the level that we've applied formulas, we've barely taken advantage of the spreadsheet software. For example, once you've created a formula, as we did to calculate totals back in Chapter 8, you can copy the formula about in the spreadsheet so that it will calculate the totals of other ranges of cells.

There are more than 90 functions that help with your calculations. There are functions to do trigonometry and exponentiation, functions to help you work with calendar dates, and even functions that let you do a type of "arithmetic" with labels rather than with numbers.

This section won't turn you into a spreadsheet formula master, but it will lay the groundwork. Once you've finished with the chapters in Part III, you'll have a solid understanding of how to write formulas, of how to copy formulas about in the sheet, and of how to apply various categories of @functions to solve your complex calculations.

Copy Formulas

The Copy command is one of the workhorses of the spreadsheet environment. With it you can enter a label or a value and then copy the entry as needed throughout the sheet. As we've applied the command so far, you've copied only from one cell to another cell. However, you can copy from one range of cells to another range and from a single cell to a range of cells.

But where the Copy command really shines is with formulas. When you enter a formula that performs calculations on the entries in one column, copies of the formula can perform calculations on the entries in other columns. This is, perhaps, one of the greatest time-savers of 1-2-3.

Some Simple Copy Jobs

We can paint a thousand scenarios in which you'd copy cells. Perhaps the quickest path to enlightenment is to ignore the underlying reasons and simply apply the command to some hypothetical spreadsheet data. Following are two quick demonstrations of the Copy command.

From One Range to Another

Just as the Copy command can copy entries from one cell to another, so can it copy from one range to another. Start in a blank worksheet and enter labels as shown in Figure 15.1 to see how this works.

In this chapter, you'll:

- *Use the Copy command to use a single formula again and again*

- *Discover how 1-2-3 thinks about formulas*

- *Learn how the Copy command deals with cell contents and cell formats*

- *Explore the differences between 1-2-3's Copy command and the Copy command in Wysiwyg*

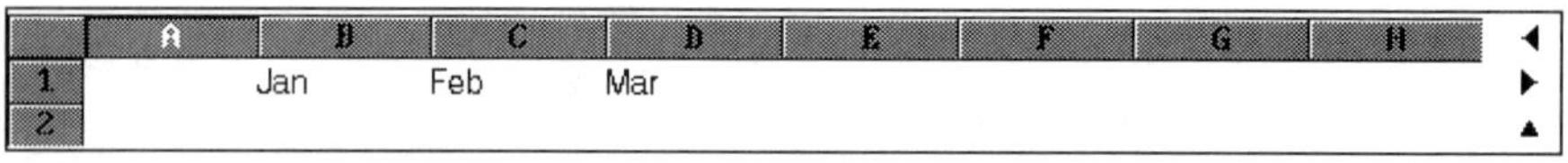

FIGURE 15.1: Enter the labels shown in row 1 to see how 1-2-3 can copy from one range to another.

To copy the labels to row 10, select /Copy and indicate range B1..D1 as the range from which to copy. When 1-2-3 prompts you to indicate a target range, indicate cell B10—you need only identify the top left corner cell of the destination range. This technique works for ranges of any reasonable size.

From One Cell to Many

Suppose that for some reason you want to copy a label or a value into each cell of a three column by five row range—range A15..C19, for example. Let's try it with the label *Jan* that currently appears in cell B10.

Move the cell pointer to cell B10 to make the job easier and then select /Copy. Press Enter to identify B10 as the cell from which to copy and then indicate range A15..C19 as the target range. 1-2-3 fills the range.

Reuse a Formula

Now that you have a sense of the power of the Copy command, put it to work at a really big job. Let's copy a formula from one cell to several other cells. Start by erasing the current worksheet—select /Worksheet Erase Yes and then Yes a second time. Now enter the values shown in Figure 15.2.

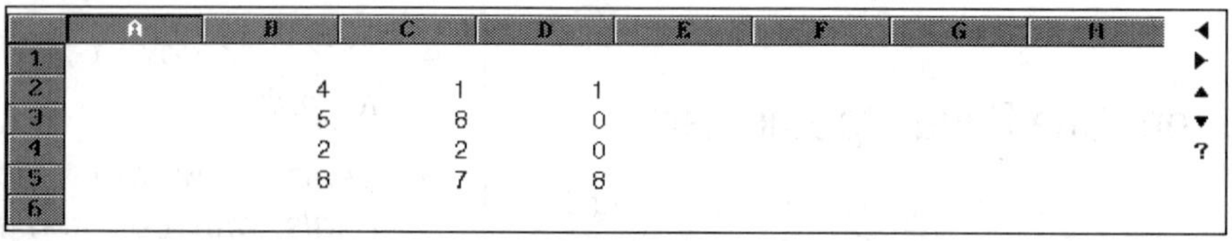

FIGURE 15.2: Enter the values shown to learn how to copy a formula.

Formula Power

We'll use an @SUM formula to exercise the Copy command. Enter the formula *@SUM(B2..B5)* into cell B6. Remember that this formula sums the values in range B2..B5. Now copy the formula across the row.

With the cell pointer in B6, select /Copy and press Enter to indicate cell B6 as the cell from which to copy. Indicate range C6..D6 as the target range. Now examine the formula in cell C6. It isn't the formula that you entered in cell B6! It's better than that. The formula in cell C6 is the one that you probably would have typed there to sum the entries in range C2..C5.

Hello, Relative Cell References

The formula in cell C6 reads @SUM(C2..C5). Likewise, the formula in cell D6 reads @SUM(D2..D5). This phenomenon is a product of 1-2-3's "relative cell references." You see, by default, a formula in 1-2-3 calculates its result relative to the formula's position in the spreadsheet. Cell references in the copies of formulas also calculate relative to their new locations in the sheet. Let's look at it another way.

Relative References Explained

Imagine the formula +A1+A2 entered in cell A3. To 1-2-3 this means, "add the value that is two cells up to the value that is one cell up from the cell holding this formula." 1-2-3 displays cell addresses in formulas for our benefit, but all it keeps track of is where the referenced cells are relative to the cell holding the formula.

When you copy the formula +A1+A2 from cell A3 to cell B3, the copy still means, "add the value that is two cells up to the value that is one cell up from the cell holding this formula." Two cells up is cell B1, and one cell up is B2, so the formula adds up the values from cells B1 and B2.

That's what happened when you copied the @SUM formulas. The formula in cell C6 is summing the values directly above it in the sheet—just as the formula we copied from sums the values directly above it. You see, for many applications, you can write a single formula and copy it as needed throughout a spreadsheet.

Copy Twice with Wysiwyg

1-2-3's Copy command copies more than just a cell's contents—it also copies a cell's numeric display format. The Copy command will copy certain of the formatting options that you apply with Wysiwyg, but there's a hitch. Because the Copy command was designed first to work only with 1-2-3, there are certain Wysiwyg formatting options that the Copy command can't replicate. Confusing as it may be, there's a separate Copy command in Wysiwyg to copy such formatting options as range shading and lines.

A Quick Exercise Illuminates the Problem

To see how 1-2-3 and Wysiwyg distribute their responsibilities for copying cells, first apply some formatting options to the entries in range B2..D6. Select /Range Format Fixed and enter *2*. Then indicate range B2..D6 as the range to format.

Select :Format Lines All and indicate range B2..D6 to place boxes around each of the cells in the range. Select :Format Bold Set and indicate range B2..D5 to set the entries in those cells in boldface. Finally, select :Format Lines Double Top and indicate range B6..D6 to place double lines between the data and the formulas. Your worksheet should match the one in Figure 15.3.

A	B	C	D	E	F	G	H
1							
2	4.00	1.00	1.00				
3	5.00	8.00	0.00				
4	2.00	2.00	0.00				
5	8.00	7.00	8.00				
6	19.00	18.00	9.00				
7							

FIGURE 15.3: This simple worksheet showcases several of 1-2-3 and Wysiwyg's formatting options.

You've applied quite an array of formatting options. Let's see how they copy.

Use /Copy to Copy the Range

Select /Copy and indicate range B2..D6 as the source range. Indicate cell B9 as the target range. What copied and what didn't copy? As you can see in Figure 15.4, the numeric display formats and the boldfacing appear in the target range.

	A	B	C	D	E	F	G	H	
1									◀ ▶
2		4.00	1.00	1.00					▲
3		5.00	8.00	0.00					▼
4		2.00	2.00	0.00					?
5		8.00	7.00	8.00					
6		19.00	18.00	9.00					
7									
8									
9		4.00	1.00	1.00					
10		5.00	8.00	0.00					
11		2.00	2.00	0.00					
12		8.00	7.00	8.00					
13		19.00	18.00	9.00					
14									

FIGURE 15.4: The /Copy command copies cell contents, numeric display formats, fonts, and font attributes to the target cells.

To copy the lines, select :Special Copy. Indicate range B2..D6 as the range to copy from and indicate cell B9 as the target range. There's a rule of thumb in all of this.

The /Copy command copies a cell's contents along with any cell formatting that affects the appearance of the cell's contents. That is, /Copy gets numeric display formats, special fonts, and font styles. The :Special Copy command copies only the cell formatting options that you apply via the :Format menu. That would be fonts, font styles, lines, and shading.

It may be a pain to keep this all straight, but remember a simple guideline: If you copy a range or cell, and the copy doesn't match the original very closely, remember which Copy command you applied (/Copy or :Special Copy) and copy once more using the other command.

/Copy copies a cell's contents and formatting that alters the appearance of the contents. :Copy copies Wysiwyg formatting options only.

Having completed this chapter, you:

- *Have a grip on one of 1-2-3's most powerful menu commands*

- *Know several variations on the use of the Copy command*

- *Understand the behavior of relative references when you copy formulas*

- *Are aware of the differences between the /Copy command and the :Special Copy command*

- *Should be able to save time by issuing the Copy commands to reuse spreadsheet entries*

References Aren't Absolutely Relative

I n Chapter 15, we saw the advantage provided by the relative nature of formulaic references. You can reuse a formula with relative references by copying it wherever you want in the spreadsheet. As you saw, you can copy a formula that sums the entries in a column so that the copies will sum entries in adjacent columns. This is particularly useful when your worksheet contains consecutive columns of daily, monthly, or quarterly data.

Sometimes it's inappropriate for your formulas' references to be relative. For example, you'll see later in this chapter that relative references can make it hard to calculate percentages. In the meantime, you might need to create formulas whose copies always refer to the same cells. More likely, you'll want certain of a formula's references to be relative and other of its references to stick with selected cells even when you copy the formula. A formulaic reference that doesn't adjust to its location in the spreadsheet when you copy it from one cell to another is an "absolute" reference.

Absolutes Immediately

A standard formulaic reference to a cell is simply the cell's address embedded in the formula. To make such a reference absolute, you precede each portion of its address with a dollar sign. Let's see how this works.

In this chapter, you'll:

- *Learn about "absolute" formula references that aren't relative*

- *See how absolute references differ from relative ones*

- *Apply the ABS key to create absolute references in POINT mode*

- *Stumble upon a spreadsheet error message*

- *Discover the EDIT key and use it to alter a cell's contents*

- *Use the Copy command and absolute references to calculate percentages*

Type an Absolute Formula

Start by entering the formula *+A1+8* into cell A3 of an otherwise blank worksheet. The formula returns 8 because cell A1 is blank—a blank cell has the numeric value of 0. For the sake of comparison, move the cell pointer to cell A4 and type *+$A$1+8*. Press Enter to store the formula in the cell. This formula also returns 8.

Hop up to cell A1 and enter *4*. Then enter *7* into cell B1. The formulas in cells A3 and A4 return 12—they each add 8 to the value in cell A1. Let's see what happens when you copy the formulas into adjacent cells of column B. Select /Copy and indicate range A3..A4 as the source range. Then indicate cell B3 as the target range. The copied formulas return different values.

To see why, put the cell pointer in cell B3 and check out the cell's contents in the control panel. The formula in B3 reads +B1+8. The formula in cell B4, however, still reads +$A$1+8. No matter where in the worksheet you copy a formula with an absolute reference, the reference remains fixed on its original cell.

Create Absolute References While Pointing

We had you type a cell address when you created the absolute reference a moment ago. 1-2-3 offers a special tool for you to create absolute references if you prefer to build formulas using POINT mode. Try one.

Move the cell pointer to cell A5 and type a plus sign. Now press UpArrow four times until the cell pointer highlights cell A1. Here's where the trick comes into it. Before you type the next arithmetic operator, press the ABS function key—that is, press the key labeled F4 among the function keys at the left or along the very top of your keyboard. Dollar signs appear on the edit line in the reference to cell A1.

Type a plus sign and then type *10*. Finally, press Enter to complete the formula.

Mixed Absolute and Relative References

It's possible to create formulas that contain both relative and absolute cell references. You might use such formulas to calculate percentages when each entry in a sequence represents a part of a total. Set up a small model to see how this works.

A Percentage Calculation Scenario

The model that you'll create calculates the percentage of sales generated by each sales person in a small office. Start by erasing the current worksheet— select /Worksheet Erase Yes Yes. Then enter labels and values as shown in Figure 16.1.

	A	B	C	D	E	F	G	H
1		Sold	Percent					
2	Mun	108						
3	Joe	77						
4	Sherman	39						
5	Mark	44						
6								

FIGURE 16.1: Enter the labels and values shown so you can use absolute references to calculate percentages.

The worksheet shows the sales volumes of four telephone sales people during one day of business. Calculate the total volume for the office by entering the formula @SUM(B2..B5) into cell B6. Then tidy up the worksheet by inserting a line between rows 5 and 6: select :Format Lines Double Top and indicate range B6..C6. You're ready to calculate the percentage of sales that each salesperson carried for the day.

An Experiment with References

Given the simple worksheet you've just created, how might you calculate the percentage of sales that Mun generated? To calculate a percentage, you divide an individual total by the grand total. So, you might move the cell pointer to C2 and enter the formula +B2/B6. Go ahead and do that. You'll discover that Mun generated about 40% of the sales.

The formula you've created is rather limited. To see why, copy it down column C: Select /Copy, indicate cell C2 as the range to copy from, and indicate C3..C5 as the target range. The resulting formulas return ERR.

The Meaning of ERR

1-2-3 displays ERR as the result of a formula that doesn't make sense. Sometimes an ERR results when you use inappropriate arguments within an @function's parentheses. Other times, you'll see an ERR when a formula tries to calculate something that's mathematically impossible. For example, the formula +A1/0 returns ERR because it's mathematically incorrect to divide by zero.

Examine the formula in cell C3. You'll see that it reads +B3/B7—in other words, it divides the value in cell B3 by zero. You can't divide by zero, so 1-2-3 displays the ERR to alert you that something is wrong. Were you to examine the formulas in cells C4 and C5, you'd see that they also divide by zero. The percentage formula would do a better job if its reference to cell B6 hadn't changed when you copied it down the column.

Make B6 Absolute

Pressing the EDIT key (function key F2) brings a cell's contents onto the edit line of the control panel.
....
....
....

Move the cell pointer to cell C2. We'll fix the formula there. But rather than retype it as we might have done in the past, we'll "edit" the formula and change only the parts of it that are causing trouble. Press the EDIT key—the function key labeled F2.

Immediately, 1-2-3 displays the percentage formula on the edit line of the control panel. A cursor appears after the entry, and you can move that cursor to the left or right by pressing appropriate arrow keys. Press LeftArrow twice so that the cursor is under the second B in the formula. Then type a dollar sign ($)—it appears on the edit line to the left of the cursor. Move the cursor so that it falls under the 6 in the formula and type a second dollar sign. The formula should read +B2/$B$6. Press Enter to store the modified formula in the current cell.

Select /Copy and press Enter to accept cell C2 as the range from which to copy. Then indicate range C3..C5 as the target range. 1-2-3 copies the modified formula down the column, and appropriate decimal values appear in column C. Examine the new formula in cell C3, and you'll see that the formula's first reference adjusted in the copy, while the second reference is stuck to cell B6—the formula calculates Joe's sales percentage.

Edit Cell Entries

You can edit any entry that you've already made in the sheet. Start by highlighting the cell that contains the entry and then press the EDIT key (function key F2). 1-2-3 brings the cell's contents onto the edit line of the control panel.

In EDIT mode, the LeftArrow and Right-Arrow keys move the edit cursor. The Delete key erases the character over the cursor, and the Backspace key erases the character to the left of the cursor. 1-2-3 inserts the characters that you type to the left of the edit cursor. If you decide that you don't like the changes you've made as you edit, press Escape to quit from EDIT mode and leave the cell contents intact. Otherwise, finish editing by pressing Enter. 1-2-3 doesn't record the changes you make in EDIT mode until you press Enter.

	A	B	C	D	E	F	G	H	
1		Sold	Percent						▶
2	Mun	108	40%						▲
3	Joe	77	29%						▼
4	Sherman	39	15%						?
5	Mark	44	16%						
6		268							

FIGURE 16.2: Assigning a percent format makes the decimal values in column C reveal the percentages that they represent.

You can further clarify the spreadsheet by applying an appropriate numeric display format. To do this, select /Range Format Percent, enter *0* to display no decimal places, and then indicate range C2..C5 as the range to format. The completed worksheet should match the one in Figure 16.2.

Having completed this chapter, you:

- *Have a good sense of the difference between relative and absolute formulaic references*

- *Know how to create absolute references both while typing formulas and while using POINT mode*

- *Understand the meaning of ERR in the spreadsheet*

- *Can modify the contents of a cell without retyping the cell's entry*

- *Know how to apply absolute references to calculate percentages*

17

More about @Functions

Applying spreadsheet @functions is like have a math whiz in your office. If there's some arcane calculation that you have to do—for example, calculating the standard deviation of a collection of test scores—but you can't remember how, or worse, you never learned how in the first place, you can probably apply an @function to the task. In almost all cases, to apply an @function, you need know nothing beyond the function's purpose and its syntax. Heck, if you want, you can apply an @function without even knowing its purpose.

This chapter explains the general rules that apply to @functions and then provides an overview of the types of calculations that @functions can perform. For simplicity, we divide the functions into several categories depending on the types of problems they help you solve. When you finish the chapter, you should be well prepared to experiment on your own with the wealth of functions available in 1-2-3.

In this chapter, you'll:

- *Learn more about 1-2-3's built-in @functions*

- *Get an overview of the types of calculations that @functions perform*

- *Look at @functions that perform calculations in the following categories:*

  - *Math and trigonometry*

  - *Conditional math (explored indepth in Chapter 18)*

  - *"Special" spreadsheet-related calculations*

  - *Unusual "math" with labels*

  - *Calendar- and time-related arithmetic*

  - *Statistics*

  - *Business math*

@Functions Defined. . . with Emphasis on Advantage

An @function is a prepackaged collection of calculations that you might perform often in a spreadsheet. In essence, an @function is 1-2-3's shorthand for formulas that you could write using arithmetic operators, but that would be so complex as to become prohibitive. Let's consider a typical calculation.

The Average of a Range of Values

Here's a calculation that can eat up a lot of formula-writing time. The average of a collection of numbers is the sum of the numbers divided by the number of numbers. The average tells you what to expect of a typical participant in an experiment or a survey.

	A	B	C	D	E	F	G	H	
1	Name	Score							◀
2	Bobbie	78							▶
3	Stacy	89							▲
4	Pat	76							▼
5	Shannon	86							?
6	Carrie	65							
7	Cindie	68							
8	Carol	72							
9	Charlotte	88							
10	Kirstin	77							
11	Alyson	84							
12									

FIGURE 17.1: A formula to calculate the average of these test scores would be quite hefty without @functions.

For example, suppose that you have a column of test scores as shown in Figure 17.1 and you want to know the average of those scores. You could enter the following formula into cell B12:

+(B2+B3+B4+B5+B6+B7+B8+B9+B10+B11)/10

That's a lot of work. It's much easier to enter the function *@AVG(B2..B11)*. Either formula reveals that the average score on the test was 78.3.

Order of Precedence

Some mathematical calculations have precedence over others, so 1-2-3 performs those calculations first when it evaluates a formula. For example, 1-2-3 performs calculations of exponentiation before it performs multiplication and division. Multiplication and division happen before addition and subtraction. In evaluating the formula +8+2*3^2, 1-2-3 first squares the value 3 (the caret means, "raise to the power of"), returning 9, and then multiplies 2*9, returning 18. Finally, 1-2-3 adds 8 and 18, returning 26.

When the precedence of several calculations in a cell is equal, 1-2-3 works through the calculations from left to right. To override this algebraic standard, enclose in parentheses the calculations that you want performed first. The formula +B2+B3+B4+B5/4 divides the value in cell B5 by 4 and then adds the result to the sum of the entries in B2, B3, and B4. Modified with parentheses, the formula +(B2+B3+B4+B5)/4 sums the entries in range B2..B4 and divides the total by 4.

A Reminder about Syntax

Remember that @functions have a standard syntax. Almost all @functions consist of an @ sign (pronounced "at-sign"), followed by a function name, and then by a list of arguments enclosed in parentheses. Some functions accept long lists of arguments, others accept only one argument, and a few accept no arguments at all (obstina little guys).

The Realm of @Functions

There are more than 90 @functions in 1-2-3. Few users remember all of the functions and how to apply them. Fewer still use even a fifth of the functions available. It's not so important to memorize everything there is to know about these gems. Rather, try to develop a sense of how to apply @functions. Then be aware of the categories of problems that the functions can solve. When you face a challenging calculation, dig a little in your spreadsheet's documentation and you'll probably find a function or two to help out with the problem.

The following material introduces the @functions by category, so you'll have a good idea of the tools available to perform calculations in your spreadsheets. Each subsection contains a short list of functions representative of the functions in the category. Listing and describing all of 1-2-3's @functions is beyond the scope of this book.

Mathematical Functions

The functions in this group handle calculations that you would find on a standard scientific calculator. These would include trigonometric functions, logarithmic functions, rounding functions, and even a function to calculate the square root of a number. Here is a short list of functions found in the category:

Absolute Values   The function @ABS(*value*) returns the absolute value of *value,* where *value* is a number, a numeric formula, or a reference to a cell that contains a formula. Hence @ABS(10) is 10, and @ABS(–30) is 30.

Sines, Cosines, and Tangents   The functions @SIN(*value*), @COS(*value*), and @TAN(*value*) calculate the sine, cosine, and tangent of *value,* respectively. *Value* can be a number, a numeric formula, or a reference to a cell that contains a number.

Integers Only   The function @INT(*value*) returns the integer portion of *value.* The expression @INT(578.32) returns 578. The @INT function doesn't round off, it simply truncates the decimal portion of a number.

Round off Mathematically   The function @ROUND(*value,places*) rounds off numbers mathematically. It returns the value of *value* rounded to the number of decimal places determined by the *places* argument. Hence, the expression @ROUND(123.456,1) returns 123.5. Round to ones, tens, hundreds, and so on by using a negative *places* argument. @ROUND(123.456,–1) returns 120.

The Mystical Value of PI   While no computer has returned the true value of PI, 1-2-3's @PI function provides a useful approximation of the value. The @PI function has no arguments—simply enter @PI as needed.

Quick Square Roots   The function @SQRT(*value*) returns the square root of *value,* assuming that *value* is a number, a cell reference to a number, or a formula that resolves to a number. The @SQRT function can't calculate imaginary numbers, so don't bother using it to calculate the roots of negative numbers.

Logical Functions

This category of functions may seem a bit odd. It will make more sense after you read Chapter 18. Except for the @IF, the @TRUE, and the @FALSE functions, each of the logical functions can return only 1 or 0. The result 1 means that a certain condition is met, and the result 0 means that the condition isn't met. These functions let your formulas test the status of the worksheet.

Conditional Math with @IF   The @IF function is rather complex and so forms the basis of its own chapter, Chapter 18. In a nutshell, the function examines the truthfulness of a mathematical statement such as +A1=B1. If the statement is true, then the function returns a specific result. If the statement is false, then the @IF function returns a different result.

Is the Add-in There?   The function @ISAPP("*name*") returns 1 if an add-in named *name* is attached to 1-2-3 and 0 if such an add-in isn't attached. The function works in 1-2-3 Release 2.3, but not in Release 3.1.

Does the Cell Contain ERR?   The function @ISERR(*value*) returns 1 when *value* is an ERR and 0 when *value* isn't ERR. Typically, *value* might be a reference to a cell that contains a formula that might sometimes return ERR.

Special Functions

This group of functions is "special" because no one has thought of a better way to classify it. The functions in the category perform calculations that probably wouldn't make sense anywhere outside a spreadsheet. Special functions return information about spreadsheet entries and ranges. They also help to locate information stored in tables. Here's a sampler.

What's Under the Cell Pointer?   The @CELLPOINTER function tells your formulas what's going on in the current cell. For example, the formula @CELLPOINTER("*address*") returns the absolute address of the cell holding the cell pointer. The formula @CELLPOINTER("*width*") returns a number that reveals the width of the column holding the pointer.

The Number of Columns in a Range   The function @COLS(*range*) returns the number of columns that *range* spans. *Range* must be a reference to a cell or a range in the sheet. The @ROWS function determines how many rows there are in a range.

Find Items in Tables   The @VLOOKUP and @HLOOKUP functions find information stored in tables. These functions are tricky enough that we devote an entire chapter to discussing them later in Part III.

String Functions

The string functions are a bit difficult to summarize. These functions help you when you perform string manipulations—when you do "math" with labels. The string functions perform such tasks as chopping characters from the ends or beginnings of labels finding specific character strings within labels, and replacing selected characters in labels with other characters. You might use string functions when you create large collections of textual data such as employee records or customer mailing addresses. We examine the topic of string manipulation more closely in Chapter 20. Here's a tickler.

The word "string" refers to a sequence of characters that have no numeric value. In 1-2-3 it is virtually synonymous with "label."

Compare Two Strings   Do two labels contain the identical characters? The @EXACT function can tell. The expression @EXACT(*"string1"*,*"string2"*) returns 1 if the strings match, and 0 if they don't match. Hmm . . . maybe this should be in the Logical category?

Is the String Embedded?   The @FIND function returns a number that identifies a string's location if it occurs inside of a longer string. For example, the expression @FIND("ted","fretted",0) returns 4—the string *ted* begins with the fourth character from the leftmost character in *fretted*. The function's third argument, 0, tells 1-2-3 to begin its search for *ted* at the character that is zero characters from the leftmost character in *fretted*.

Learn a Label's Length   The function @LENGTH(*string*) returns a number that reveals how many characters there are in *string*. For example, @LENGTH("commission") returns 10. Blank spaces count as characters, so the expression @LENGTH("percent sold") returns 12.

Calendar-related Functions

This category might as well be Date and Time Functions. As with string functions, date and time functions are hard to explain without spending a little time at it. Chapter 19 covers the topic more carefully. Here we'll tell you that the date and time functions provide a means for 1-2-3 to keep track of time in the spreadsheet. Functions in this category calculate the current date, day, month, or year, and the current hour, minute, or second.

What Day of the Month Is It?   The function @DAY(*datenum*) tells you what day of the month *datenum* represents. Likewise, @MONTH(*datenum*) tells you what month of the year *datenum* identifies; @YEAR(*datenum*) identifies *datenum*'s year. *Datenum* must be a date serial number—something that we'll discuss in Chapter 19.

The Time Now Is. . .   The functions @SECOND(*timenum*), @MINUTE (*timenum*), and @HOUR(*timenum*) return values that identify the second within a minute, the minute within the hour, and the hour within the day, respectively, that *timenum* represents. *Timenum* must be a time serial number—we'll talk about time serial numbers in Chapter 19.

Statistical and Database Functions

Statistical functions let you calculate statistics of the data in your spreadsheets. Database functions help you to manipulate information stored in databases. Some of the calculations you'll do with databases involve statistics, so there's some overlap in these two categories. We've combined them here. We don't discuss database functions, however, until late in Part IV.

Find the Middle Ground   The @AVG function, as you know, calculates the average of a range of values. Actually, the function calculates averages for lists of values. For example, the expression @AVG(A1..B2,C1,25) calculates the average of the values in range A1..B2, the value in cell C1, and the value 25.

Standard Deviation and Variance   The @STD and @VAR functions work just as the @AVG function does. @STD calculates the population standard deviation (the square root of the variance) of the values in the argument list, and @VAR calculates the population variance.

High and Low   The @MAX function also works the same way the @AVG function does. It accepts a list of arguments and returns the greatest value from the list. @MIN returns the lowest value from the list.

Financial Functions

Financial @functions are the power tools of business computing. With them you can rapidly calculate future values of investments, periodic payments on loans, the present values of future amounts, and several types of depreciation. Following is a short list.

The Value of an Investment   Want to know how much money you'll have in ten years if you put $100 in the bank each month until then? The @FV function will tell you. The function's syntax is @FV(*payment,interest,term*), where *payment* is the amount of each period payment, *interest* is the periodic interest rate, and *term* is the total number of payments. Suppose the bank pays 5.25% annual interest. The appropriate @FV function would be @FV(100,.0525/12,120). Your bank account will hold $15,738 in ten years.

Your Monthly Payment on a Loan   You need to borrow $6,500 and the best you can find is a three-year loan at 17.5%. What will you pay each month? To find out, use the @PMT function. The function's syntax is @PMT(*principal, interest,term*). Your loan principal is $6,500. The interest rate per term is 17.5%/12, and the total number of terms is 12*3, or 36. To calculate your loan payments, enter *@PMT(6500,.175/12,12*3)*. The function reveals that you'll pay $233 a month on your loan.

@Function Overkill

That's enough. There are plenty more @functions. But, by now, you understand how to work with these powerful tools. Your software's Help facility has a complete listing of the functions and can help you to learn their proper syntax and application. Also, the @function guide that came in the box with your spreadsheet software explains the functions quite clearly.

Having completed this chapter, you:

- *Understand the basics of using @functions*

- *Have a good idea of the range of calculations that @functions can perform*

- *Should recognize opportunities to apply @functions in your models*

If It's So, Then . . .

You make decisions all the time based on the things going on around you. If it's cold, wear a coat. If the room is dark, turn on the light. Quite often, you'll want spreadsheet formulas to make similar decisions: If the stock price is above $35 a share, sell; if a customer's purchase exceeds $350, calculate a 10% discount.

1-2-3 offers several tools to help you express these conditional statements mathematically. The calculations rely on a type of math called Boolean algebra—the concept is much easier to understand than to pronounce. This chapter introduces the basics of conditional math and gets you started applying these very powerful concepts.

The Key to Conditionals

At the heart of conditional math is Boolean algebra. Boolean algebra is a system of calculations in which an expression can result in one of two values: zero or one. When you understand how Boolean expressions work, you'll pretty much understand everything you need to know about conditional math.

Boolean Expressions Explained

A Boolean expression is a statement that can be either true or false. When the statement is true, the expression has the value 1. When the statement is false, the expression's value is 0. Consider the expression +A1=B1 entered in cell A3 of the spreadsheet in Figure 18.1. In fact, don't consider it—set up a worksheet to match it.

In this chapter, you'll:

- Gain an understanding of the concept of conditional math
- Learn how the @IF function can make decisions on its own
- Build a small retail discount model to see the @IF function at work

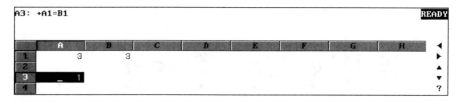

FIGURE 18.1: The Boolean formula in cell A3 of this worksheet returns 1 because the entries in cells A1 and B1 are equal in value.

The statement is true at this point because the values in A1 and B1 are equal. Now try changing the value in cell A1—enter 7. When the number hits the cell, the formula in cell A3 returns 0. The statement +A1=B1 is no longer true.

Twists on Boolean Equations

There are many types of Boolean expressions. +A1=B1 is an expression of equality. Equally valid are statements of inequality. For example, the formula +A1>B1 is true when the value in cell B1 is less than the value in A1. Other valid statements include +A1<B1, +A1>=B1, and +A1<=B1. The question is, how do you work this into spreadsheet calculations?

The @IF Function at Work

The @IF function will handle most of your conditional math problems. It's quite easy to apply. The function's syntax is @IF(*condition,true-result, false-result*). The *condition* argument should be a Boolean expression that returns either 1 or 0. The *true-result* argument determines what the function returns if the expression is true. The *false-result* argument determines the function's result if the expression is false.

Try a simple @IF statement in the worksheet you've just created. Move to cell A5 and enter *@IF(A1=B1,100,−100)*. The formula means, "If the value in cell A1 equals the value in B1, return 100, otherwise return −100." At the moment, the formula returns −100 because cell A1 doesn't equal cell B1.

A Practical Application

The expression @IF(A1=B1,100,–100) isn't all that useful. You'll have to consider your own problems to figure out when and how to apply the @IF function. One scenario that we suggested earlier might provide some inspiration. Let's use the @IF function to calculate a discount for purchases of more than $350.

The Discount Calculation

Select /Worksheet Erase Yes Yes to erase the stuff you've done so far. Then enter values as shown in Figure 18.2. The values represent purchases made by a customer in a retail store. We've omitted such details as labels to identify the items bought and fancy formatting so that we can get right to the formulas.

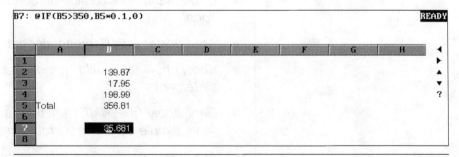

FIGURE 18.2: These values are the amounts that a customer spent to buy several items in a retail store.

Enter the formula *@SUM(B2..B4)* into cell B5—that calculates the total spent by the customer. Label that cell *Total* by entering the word into cell A5. Then drop down to cell B7 and enter the discount calculation. It should read @IF(B5>350,B5*.1,0). The formula returns 38.68 as shown in Figure 18.3. The customer gets the discount because the total spent exceeds $350.

```
B7: @IF(B5>350,B5*0.1,0)                                    READY
```

FIGURE 18.3: The @IF formula in cell B7 calculates a 10% discount because the customer's total purchases exceed $350.

Now change one of the values in range B2..B4 so that the total spent is less than $350. Move the cell pointer to cell B2 and enter *125*. The discount calculation returns 0; there is no discount because the customer hasn't spent enough money.

Tidy Up the Calculation

Actually, in this type of calculation, you're probably more interested in how much the customer owes you than in the amount of the discount. You can change the formula to reflect this need.

The total the customer should pay equals the total price for all items bought, minus the result of the discount formula. Edit the formula in cell B7 appropriately. Place the cell pointer in B7 and press the EDIT key (function key F2.) Press LeftArrow until the edit cursor is under the @ sign and then type *+B5–* so that the formula reads *+B5–@IF(B5>350,B5*0.1,0)*. Finish editing by pressing Enter.

Test your work by entering the value *139.87* back into cell B2. The formula in cell B7 returns the amount that the customer should pay.

Having completed this chapter, you:

- *Understand the basics of conditional math*

- *Are familiar with Boolean algebra*

- *Know how to build conditional statements*

- *Can apply the @IF function to solve simple conditional problems*

- *Are prepared to deal with other complex spreadsheet mathematics*

Work with Dates and Time

Much of what you do in the worksheet is date or time related. You record the dates of business transactions, the projected completion dates of projects, the target dates for meeting business plans, and on and on. Chances are that you've already recorded dates in some of your spreadsheets—perhaps you've entered them as labels such as '12/17/91 or 'January 7, 1992. That's Ok for a lot of what you do, but it's just not right.

1-2-3 has its own scheme for working with dates. If you were to ask the software, it would tell you that time began on January 1, 1900. Each day since then has its own serial number. January 1, 1900 is day 1, January 2, 1990 is day 2, and so on through the end of the next century. By enumerating days in this way, 1-2-3 gains the ability to handle dates mathematically. Knowing one date, your spreadsheet can tell you what day falls seven days, thirty-one days, or even several hundred days later. Also, 1-2-3 can use date serial numbers in conditional statements to identify date values that fall before or after known dates. Especially when you work with databases, as we'll do in Part IV, understanding and applying date serial numbers is crucial.

In this chapter, you'll:

- *Learn how 1-2-3 handles dates in the spreadsheet*

- *Discover how date serial numbers let you do math with dates*

- *Apply a few @functions that help you manipulate dates mathematically*

- *Use a numeric display format to make a number appear as a date*

- *Learn how to remove formulas from cells, leaving behind their results*

- *Get a quick overview of time in the spreadsheet environment*

@Functions Simplify Serial Numbers

You may be relieved that you don't have to learn 1-2-3's system of date serial numbers. While it's important to work with these serial numbers, 1-2-3 offers a complement of @functions that convert familiar date entries into the necessary date serial numbers and back. These @functions are easy to apply with only a little practice. Let's look at a few of them at work.

Convert a Date to a Serial Number

Year numbers in this century run from 0 to 99. Year numbers in the next century run from 100 to 199. Hence, @DATE(101,1,1) is January 1, 2001.

We think of dates in terms of the month, the day, and the year. For example, unless you're European, the expression 6/3/92 clearly represents the third day of June, 1992. Knowing this, you can use the @DATE function to calculate the serial number for that date.

The function's syntax would be @DATE(92,6,3). Try it. Start in a blank worksheet, and enter *@DATE(92,6,3)* into cell A1. The function returns 33758. To 1-2-3, that's June 3, 1992.

Numeric Display Formats for Dates

Date serial numbers might be perfect for 1-2-3, but the number 33758 doesn't tell the average human much at all. By applying one of the date-related numeric display formats, you can make date serial numbers meaningful to your biological audiences.

Select /Range Format Date. There are several formatting options. Start by applying the first of them. Select 1 and then indicate cell A1 as the range to format. Oops. There's that asterisk thing again. Remember that 1-2-3 displays asterisks when a formatted cell entry is too wide for the cell containing it. Select /Worksheet Column Set-Width and increase the width of column A by one character. The date displays as 03-Jun-92. Figure 19.1 shows the @DATE function entered in five cells, each with its own date format.

A Little Date Arithmetic

As you might guess, there's no trick to doing math with date serial numbers. For example, in cell A2 calculate the date that falls one week after the date

	A	B	C	D	E	F	G	H	
1	Date 1	03–Jun–92							►
2	Date 2	03–Jun							▲
3	Date 3	Jun–92							▼
4	Date 4	06/03/92							?
5	Date 5	06/03							
6									

FIGURE 19.1: Each of the cells in column B contains the function @DATE(92,6,3). Labels in column A identify the corresponding formats in column B.

in cell A1. To do this, move the cell pointer to A2 and enter the formula +A1+7—there are seven days in a week. The result is 33765. Select /Range Format Date 1 and press Enter to display the serial number as 10-Jun-92.

	A	B	C	D	E	F	G	H	
1	03–Jun–92								►
2	10–Jun–92								▲

FIGURE 19.2: This is how your practice worksheet looks after you enter and format an @DATE function in cell A1 and an addition formula in cell A2.

Sometimes it's important for your formulas to know when a particular date falls within a month. For example, if the date is after the fifteenth of the month, then the formula should calculate a late payment. The @DAY function can help with this problem.

@DAY and the Late Payment Calculation

If your formulas could look at the formatted date functions, they'd see as you do that the entry in cell A1 falls before June 15. The @DAY function can be the eyes of your formulas.

If you were to enter the expression *@DAY(A1)* in your practice worksheet (that's the worksheet shown in Figure 19.2), it would return 3—that is the day of the month represented by the date serial number in cell A1. Suppose that cell A1 holds the date on which a customer makes a monthly payment of $256. The payment is due on the first, and you add a 1.5% late fee to the customer's debt if you don't receive payment by the fifteenth.

One way to calculate the late fee would be to create an @IF formula that incorporates the @DAY function. Try it in your worksheet. Move the cell pointer to cell C1 and enter *@IF(@DAY(A1)>=15,256*.015,0)*. The function returns 0 because the payment came in on the sixth. However, what happens when the date in cell A1 falls after the fifteenth? Move the pointer to A1 and

> **Date and Time Serial Numbers?**
> The @NOW function returns a serial number that has both a date and a time component. For example, at noon on January 1, 1992, the @NOW function returns 33604.5. The date-related @functions ignore the decimal component of a serial number, and the time-related functions ignore the integer component. The date and time numeric display formats also differentiate a serial number's components appropriately.

enter *@DATE(92,6,17)*. Now the formula in cell C1 returns 3.84—that's the damage for paying late.

1-2-3 also has an @MONTH function that returns the month of the current year and an @YEAR function that returns the year as a serial number from 0 to 199. The serial number 0 represents 1900, and the serial number 199 represents 2099.

@NOW for the Moment

Quite often you want nothing more than to record the current date in your spreadsheet. Use the @NOW function. The @NOW function accepts no arguments—you simply enter *@NOW* into any cell. 1-2-3 reads your computer's built-in clock and returns the current date as a date serial number.

Because the @NOW function relies on your system's clock, it changes in value each time you update the spreadsheet. That is, whenever you make an entry, 1-2-3 reevaluates the @NOW function and changes it to reflect the current time of your system clock. Tomorrow an @NOW function in your sheet will return a value different from the one it returns today.

Preserve the Present

Sometimes you want to record the day's date in the sheet so that it will appear there when you next work in that particular file. If you enter *@NOW*, 1-2-3 updates the function's result when you retrieve the worksheet; the function won't reveal the date of the spreadsheet's last use.

If you wish to lock in the function's current value, apply 1-2-3's /Range Value command. To do this, enter *@NOW* in a cell. Then, without moving the cell pointer, select /Range Value and press Enter twice. The /Range Value command will replace any formula with the formula's current value.

A Brief Overview of Time

This topic sounds rather metaphysical. Actually, it's quite simple. You see, 1-2-3 thinks of time as a percentage of a day. For example, at 6:00 AM, 25% of a day has passed. At noon, 50% has passed. If you want to record the time of day in your spreadsheet, use the @TIME function.

A	B	C	D	E	F	G
1 Time 1	08:30:10 AM					
2 Time 2	08:30 AM					
3 Time 3	08:30:10					
4 Time 4	08:30					
5						

FIGURE 19.3: Each cell in column B contains the function @TIME(8,30,10). The labels in column A identify the display formats of corresponding cells in column B.

1-2-3 speaks standard military time—to 1-2-3, 1:00 PM is 13:00.

Hours Are Like Days

The function @TIME(8,30,10) represents 10 seconds after 8:30 AM. It returns .3542824074. Look familiar? It makes just as much sense as a date serial number. Once you've entered an @TIME function, you can assign a numeric display format to reveal the meaning of the resulting time serial number. To assign a numeric display format to a time serial number, select /Range Format Date Time and then find the desired time format on the resulting menu. Figure 19.3 shows the function @TIME(8,30,10) entered into several cells having different time display formats.

1-2-3 contains @SECOND, @MINUTE, and @HOUR functions that do for times what @DAY, @MONTH, and @YEAR do for dates. Be aware as you explore the time-related functions on your own that 1-2-3 understands standard military time. For example, to enter the time 3:00 PM, you would type *@TIME(15,0,0)*.

Having completed this chapter, you:

- *Understand 1-2-3's odd convention for keeping track of time*
- *Know how to create dates and times in the spreadsheet*
- *Are able to make serial numbers appear in the sheet as the dates and times they represent*
- *Can apply the /Range Value command to convert formulas into their current values*
- *Have a sense of how to do math with dates and times*
- *Are prepared to deal with issues of time as you learn about database applications*

20

Label Arithmetic

Suppose that your worksheet contains a column of first names and a column of last names, and what you really want is a column of first and last names together? Or, what if it's the other way around? The first and last names are in a single column, and you want to separate them into two columns. What if you want to devise sequential invoice numbers and append the first letter of each customer's name? All of these tasks are possible with label, or string, arithmetic. Perhaps of equal importance, many applications of string arithmetic arise as you learn to work with databases.

The idea of doing math with labels may seem a bit odd—labels have a numeric value of 0, so what's the point of using them to do math? Actually, the math we're talking about applies to the structure of the labels themselves. Using the string-handling @functions, you can attach one label to another, chop pieces out of a label, replace characters in a label with other characters, and so on.

"Add" Two Labels

The most basic of tasks in label arithmetic is that of adding two labels together. Computerists once decided that the term for this should be "concatenation," and the name stuck. Let's play a bit in an otherwise blank worksheet and learn how to concatenate two labels.

Concatenate Your Names

Enter your first name into cell A1 and your last name into cell A2. Then, drop the cell

In this chapter, you'll:

- Learn about the mathematical differences between labels (strings) and numbers

- Discover how 1-2-3 can add labels together and perform other label calculations

- Consider some uses for label arithmetic

- Examine a few of 1-2-3's label-handling @functions

143

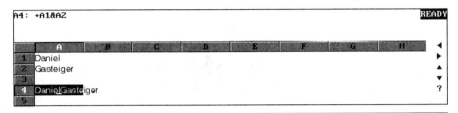

FIGURE 20.1: Enter your first and last names in a blank worksheet in preparation to concatenate them.

The ampersand is 1-2-3's string concatenation operator.

pointer to cell A4 and enter the formula *+A1&A2*. Your names appear concatenated in the cell. If you were the author of this book, your worksheet would match the one in Figure 20.1.

A Label Is a String
The term "label" is a convention from spreadsheet computing that describes a specific class of cell entries. A label entry can be any character string that has no numeric value. The term "string" applies to such character strings whether or not the strings are cell entries. A number, entered into the spreadsheet is still a number, but a string entered into the sheet is a label.

Literal Strings

There's something wrong. How often do you need to arrange your names into a single word? Typically, there's a space between your first name and your last. The concatenation formula doesn't insert a space, but it would if it included a literal string.

Literal Is Just What It Says

A literal string is the label arithmetic equivalent of a number. For example, a numeric spreadsheet formula might read +A1+5—it adds the literal number 5 to whatever value resides in cell A1. Suppose that you want to concatenate a specific sequence of characters with a label in the sheet. It's almost as simple as entering *+A1&here's the string,* but there's a catch. You must enclose a literal string in quotation marks. Let's see how this works.

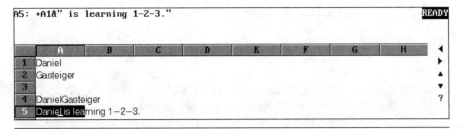

FIGURE 20.2: The formula in cell A5 concatenates a literal string with the label stored in cell A1.

Move the cell pointer to cell A5 and enter the formula *+A1&" is learning 1-2-3."* The expression " is learning 1-2-3." is the literal string in this formula. Notice that the first character in the expression is a space. You must account for spaces this way in your string formulas—to a computer, a space is no less a character than a letter or a number. The author's practice worksheet appears in Figure 20.2.

How can you correct the first concatenation formula? By concatenating a space character between the two cell references. Here's how.

Return the cell pointer to cell A4 and press the EDIT key (function key F2). Press the LeftArrow key twice so that the edit cursor is under the second letter A in the formula. Type quotes ("), a space character, quotes, and an ampersand (&). The new entry should be +A1&" "&A2. Press Enter when your formula matches ours.

It's quite common to speak of a string as a "string value." For example, it's acceptable to say, "The formula returns a string value."

A Few String @Functions

Concatenation is the tip of the label arithmetic iceberg. There are 19 @functions that in some way manipulate strings. A few of those functions are quite simple. They perform such tasks as changing all the letters in a string to uppercase or to lowercase. Other string @functions are a bit more complicated. Some locate strings within other strings or replace pieces of strings with other strings. We can't explore all of the string @functions, but let's try out a few of them to get a feel for their potential.

Cut off a Few Characters

One string-related task that we suggested earlier is that of finding a person's first initial when you have the person's name entered in a cell. The @LEFT function should do the job nicely—it returns a string taken from the left end of another string. The function's syntax is @LEFT(*string,length*), where *string* is the string from which you want to return characters, and *length* is the number of characters you want to return. For example, the expression @LEFT("Restaurant",4) returns the string *Rest*.

Try it out in the worksheet you've already started. Move the cell pointer to cell A6 and enter *@LEFT(A1,1)*. The formula returns your first initial. The @RIGHT function works just as the @LEFT function does, but it returns characters from the right end of a string.

Uppercase, Lowercase, or Proper

Do you prefer your label entries in uppercase? Enter the formula *@UPPER(A1)* into cell A7. How about lowercase? Enter *@LOWER(A1)* into cell A8. Perhaps your entries are entirely uppercase, and you'd prefer that each word have only its initial letter capitalized. Enter the formula *@UPPER(A1)&" "&@UPPER(A2)* into cell A9—it returns your name in uppercase characters. Now enter the formula *@PROPER(A9)* into cell A10—it capitalizes the first letter of every word and converts any other letters to lowercase. Your worksheet should look something like the one in Figure 20.3.

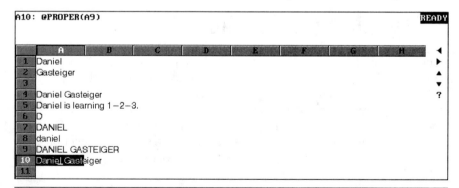

FIGURE 20.3: Cells A6, A7, A8, A9, and A10 of this worksheet contain the formulas @LEFT(A1,1), @UPPER(A1), @LOWER(A1), @UPPER(A1)&" "&@UPPER(A2), and @PROPER(A9), respectively.

Transform Your Label Entries

Sometimes you face an entire column of labels that simply aren't pleasing. For example, all 300 names listed in column A of a worksheet are in uppercase, and you'd rather have them lowercase with initial capitals. The @PROPER function, the /Copy command, and the /Range Value command can quickly convert the labels.

Try this in columns E and F of your practice sheet: Enter a sequence of 10 labels in uppercase characters down column E. In cell F1, enter the formula @PROPER(E1). Select /Copy,

indicate cell F1 as the cell to copy, and indicate range F2..F10 as the target range. The formulas convert the labels as desired.

Select /Range Value and indicate range F1..F10 as the range from which to copy. Indicate cell E1 as the target range. The /Range Value command replaces the uppercase labels in column E with the current "values" of the formulas in column F. Finally, select /Range Erase and indicate range F1..F10 to remove the unneeded formulas from the worksheet.

On Your Own

At first string arithmetic may seem a bit arcane. With any luck, our examples suggest a few tasks to which you can put your knowledge of string @functions. Eventually, you'll discover that you can apply these concepts to your work with databases. In the meantime, fiddle a bit on your own with the techniques we've explored and with some of the other string-related @functions.

Having completed this chapter, you:

- *Are aware of the difference between a string and a number*

- *Know how to concatenate strings and can combine first and last names or cities, states, and zip codes from several cells into a single cell*

- *Understand the concept of literal strings*

- *Can use the @LEFT, @UPPER, @LOWER, and @PROPER string functions to find first initials of names or change the case of entries in your spreadsheets*

- *Are prepared to deal with other topics that might involve string arithmetic*

Find Information in Tables

Tables belong in spreadsheets. In a world laid out in columns and rows, information often comes packaged that way. For example, why not store tax tables in the sheet? Or tables of interest rates? Of course, once you put the data into tables, you need a convenient way to get needed information out of the tables.

1-2-3 has a small complement of @functions whose purpose is to pull information out of tables for use in your spreadsheet calculations. These @functions are fairly easy to apply, and you'll find uses for them in many of your spreadsheet applications.

A Simple Table Scenario

Suppose that you volunteer at a local animal shelter. One of your responsibilities is to log in each new dog and establish a feeding schedule. The animal shelter's veterinarian has supplied a table that lists dog weights and dog activity levels as you see in Figure 21.1. The numbers within the table are ounces of food appropriate for a particular dog weight and activity level.

Unfortunately, the veterinarian doesn't use a computer, and has provided you with the table on paper. You'll need to recreate it in the worksheet before you'll be able to apply the techniques we're about to discuss. There are no tricks. Simply enter the labels and values exactly as shown—remember to start each of the labels in range C4..E4 with a caret (^) prefix to center it in its cell.

In this chapter, you'll:

- *Discover how to look up information stored in tables*

- *Learn about @functions that work with tables of data*

	A	B	C	D	E
1					
2			Activity level		
3					
4	Weight in		Low	Med	High
5	pounds	10	5	6	7
6		20	7	9	12
7		30	12	14	16
8		40	16	17	18
9		60	18	21	24
10		80	24	26	29
11		100	29	32	35
12					

FIGURE 21.1: This table lists dog weights down its left column and activity levels across its top row.

Look Up a Feed Quantity

A dog named Spooner comes into the shelter. She weighs in at 60 pounds and seems a bit hyperactive. Of course with a table as small as the one in Figure 21.1, you can scan the numbers visually and see right away that she should get 24 ounces of food a day. But if this were a very large table, the task might be prohibitive. Besides, in many applications, such as models that involve tax and commission tables, you need to use the looked up value in further calculations.

The @VLOOKUP function can return the proper value for your spreadsheet calculations. It has the syntax @VLOOKUP(*val,table,offset*). The *val* argument is a number or a string that you want to locate in the left column of the table; the *table* argument identifies the table range; and the *offset* argument identifies which column of the table holds the information for which you're looking.

What's Your Offset?

The *offset* argument in an @VLOOKUP function identifies its target column a bit differently from the way you might expect. The @VLOOKUP function thinks of the columns in a table in terms of how far each one is "offset" from the table's leftmost column. An offset of 1 means, "the column that is one column to the right of the leftmost column." An offset of 2 means, "the column that is two columns from the leftmost column." An offset of 0 identifies the leftmost column itself.

Move the cell pointer to cell A14 and enter *Spooner.* Then enter the formula *@VLOOKUP(60,B5..E11,3)* into cell B14. It should return 24.

Lookup Functions Fudge

1-2-3 found Spooner's weight in the table without a hitch, and so was able to return a recommended feed amount. What happens when you try to look up a value that isn't actually in the table?

A second dog, named Olive, comes into the clinic. Olive is a bit sluggish and weighs 77 pounds. Olive's weight isn't in the table, so 1-2-3 uses a different strategy to return a value. When the @VLOOKUP function can't find the lookup value, it locates the first value in the lookup column that exceeds the lookup value and then drops back a row to find its result. This will make more sense when you log Olive into the clinic.

To log Olive in, first enter her name into cell A15 and then enter the formula @*VLOOKUP(77,B5..E11,1)*. It returns 18. Because the function can't find Olive's weight, 77 pounds, in the lookup column, it stops looking when it finds 80 pounds. Then it drops back one row and returns 18 from the offset column.

Lookup Labels

The @VLOOKUP function can find labels in the lookup column as well as numbers. You might rely on this capability to find information about a particular person from a table of employee names and other vital statistics. Or, you might have an inventory database in which to look up quantities or prices of products. Let's use the dog food table and a variant of the @VLOOKUP function to see how this works.

Horizontal Lookups

The "V" in @VLOOKUP stands for vertical. There is a sister function to @VLOOKUP called @HLOOKUP. The function's syntax is identical to that of the @VLOOKUP function, but it looks across the table's top row for the lookup value and uses the offset argument to locate a specific table row.

Suppose that you want to know how much food to give to a dog of medium energy if you know that the dog weighs 40 pounds. Drop down to cell B17 and enter the formula @*HLOOKUP("Med",B4..E11,4)*. It returns 17 from the row that is four rows down from the top row of the table. Note that the table range in this example includes row 4—the row that contains labels identifying activity levels. The @HLOOKUP function finds the label *Med* in that row and then scans down four rows to return a result.

Having completed this chapter, you:

- *Have a handle on dealing with information stored in tables*

- *Understand the basics of working with the @VLOOKUP and @HLOOKUP functions*

- *Might recognize opportunities to create tables for use in your spreadsheet models.*

Part IV
Manage Large Lists
of Information

Who doesn't deal with lists of information—whether or not you work with computers? Certainly everyone uses a phone book from time to time. If not, perhaps you have your own address books. No? Then maybe you've eaten in a restaurant—even at a fast-food place—where you've read a list of the foods that the restaurant serves. Still not convinced? Do you peruse the stock listings in the newspaper? Television schedules? Movie listings? The ingredients lists on cereal boxes?

The point is, you already know what a database is. It's simply a list of information. In 1-2-3, there are certain rules about how you lay out a list to make it a database, but the rules follow naturally from what you already know about the spreadsheet.

There are advantages to storing information in a 1-2-3 database. For example, once you've created a database, you can use 1-2-3's commands to re-arrange list entries into alphabetical or numerical order. You can also use menu commands to locate specific information very rapidly. Finally, there are some powerful @functions that perform statistical analyses with information stored in a database.

This section explains what constitutes a database in 1-2-3. It shows you how to create a database and how to manipulate information in the database. Along the way, you'll apply some of the knowledge that you've acquired from reading earlier chapters in the book. You'll also recognize many opportunities to apply database management techniques in your own spreadsheets.

22

1-2-3: Database

A database is a list of information. Perhaps the most omnipresent example of a database is the telephone directory. In it you find listings of people's first and last names, their street addresses, and their phone numbers. Arranged in alphabetical order, entries in the phone directory provide rapid access to specific entries from among tens of thousands.

When you create a database in a spreadsheet, you make large collections of information at least as accessible as entries in a phone book. In fact, there are things you can do with a spreadsheet-based database that most people would never try to do with the white pages. For example, suppose you want to list database entries in reverse alphabetical order? Or, suppose that your database contains the production data for several of the products that your plant produces and you want to arrange the products in order of highest production to lowest? These are just a few of the things that 1-2-3's database management commands let you do with lists of information.

The Structure of a Database

1-2-3 has a fairly rigid definition of what constitutes a database. All of the information about any one list item must reside in a single worksheet row. For example, in an address database, each row might contain one person's first and last name, street address, city, state, and zip code. In a production database, each row might contain a production date, a product name, a production site, and a quantity produced. Figure 22.1 shows a small production database.

In this chapter, you'll:

- *Review the meaning of "database"*

- *Learn what constitutes a database in 1-2-3*

- *Become familiar with some of the terms associated with databases*

- *Create a database model to use throughout Part IV of the book*

- *Arrange database entries in alphabetical and numerical order*

	A	B	C	D	E	F	G
1							
2							
3							
4							
5	Date	Product	Site	Quantity			
6	03-Feb-92	Rubber flange	West St.	4200			
7	03-Feb-92	Black Inflation	N. Plant	4100			
8	03-Feb-92	02 Ring Gasket	West St.	12000			
9	04-Feb-92	Rubber flange	West St.	1200			
10	04-Feb-92	Black Inflation	N. Plant	4300			
11	04-Feb-92	02 Ring Gasket	West St.	12000			
12	05-Feb-92	Black Inflation	N. Plant	4300			
13	05-Feb-92	02 Ring Gasket	West St.	12000			
14	05-Feb-92	Rubber flange	West St.	3000			
15							

FIGURE 22.1: Each row of a database contains a *record,* and each column identifies a *field.*

A Practice Database

The bad news is that we're asking you to create the database in your spreadsheet so you can use it to learn about 1-2-3's database commands. It shouldn't take too long—just be cautious about a few things.

First, remember to use the @DATE function to enter each of the dates in column A. For example, enter the formula *@DATE(92,2,3)* into cell A6. Set the width of column A to 10 characters and apply the Date 1 numeric display format to its entries. Also, remember to start each of the entries in cell B8, B11, and B13 with apostrophe label prefixes. Set the width of column B to 18 so that it accommodates the product names.

Some Useful Database Terms
Each row of a database in 1-2-3 is a *record,* and each column is a *field.* To help you keep the information straight, each database field must have a *field header* at the top of the column. The database in Figure 22.1 has four fields, and their headers appear in row 5.

You're ready to manage a database. But first, save the spreadsheet on disk so you'll have it when you work through Chapters 23–26. Save the spreadsheet under the name PDBASE so there won't be any confusion when you need to retrieve it later on. Now let's manipulate some data.

For Mouse Users It's a Drag to Set Widths

If you're using a mouse, and Wysiwyg is active (as we're assuming it is), then you don't need to issue the /Worksheet Column Set-Width command to alter the widths of columns. Instead, move the mouse pointer to the line in the spreadsheet frame that marks the right edge of a column whose width you want to change. Drag (that is, press down the mouse button and move the mouse while you're holding down the button) to the left or right depending on how you want to alter the column's width.

The dotted line that appears reveals whether you've changed the width enough to fit your label entries. The column's right edge shifts to where the dotted line is at the moment you release the mouse button.

Sort the Database

One of the simplest and most useful database tasks is rearranging the records to highlight certain aspects of the data they contain. For example, it might be useful to arrange the records in this database in order from highest to lowest production or to arrange them so that all the West Street plant production is in one group and the Northern plant production is in another group. Rearranging a database alphabetically or numerically is called *sorting* the database. There are three steps.

1. Set the Data Range

Before 1-2-3 can sort records, you must identify the records to sort. To do this, select /Data Sort. If you're a 1-2-3 Release 2.3 user with a mouse, and you want to practice a bit with dialog boxes, check out the box titled Dialog with Data Sort. The box explains steps 1 and 2 of sorting a database. Rejoin us at the step 3. If you don't have a mouse, or you're using Release 3.1, select Data-Range from the menu and indicate range A6..D14 as the range of data to sort.

Don't include the database field headers in the Data range of the Data Sort command.

2. Select a Sort Key and a Sort Order

You must select a sort "key." That is, you must identify to 1-2-3 the database field on which to base, or key, the order of the sorted records. Are you

Dialog with Data Sort

If you're a mouse user, there's a bit more to learn about dialog boxes. The one that appears on the display when you select /Data Sort gives you access to several settings needed to sort a database. To identify the Data range, click the dotted line that follows the prompt *Data range* in the dialog box. A flashing cursor appears in the box to show that 1-2-3 is ready for you to indicate a range. Rather than type the range, activate point mode. Press the ABS key. That's the function key numbered F4. The dialog box vanishes, and 1-2-3 goes into POINT mode. Now, drag with the mouse to highlight range A6..D14 and

then click anywhere in the sheet. The dialog box returns, and the range setting appears in the Data Range Setting box.

Set the Primary key to identify which database field should determine how 1-2-3 sorts the records. You're putting the records in order by production totals, so click *Primary-Key*, press the ABS key, and then double-click any cell in column D. When the dialog box reappears, there is an asterisk next to the *Descending* setting. This means that 1-2-3 will sort the records from largest to smallest— that's what you want to do, so click *OK* at the bottom of the dialog box.

alphabetizing by product name, or listing in descending numerical order by production totals?

We're sorting by production totals, so select Primary-Key and indicate any cell in column D. After you indicate the sort key, 1-2-3 asks whether you want to arrange the records in descending or ascending order. Type *D* for descending and press Enter. You're ready for step 3.

3. Tell 1-2-3 to Do It

1-2-3 knows what to sort and how to sort it. Get the job done by selecting Go. In a flash, records line up in descending numerical order. You can see quite easily that there were more 02 Ring Gaskets produced than any other item.

Resorting Is Simple

Should you prefer to sort the records into a new order, part of your work is already done. Once you've set the Data range, you don't need to do it again unless you add or delete database records. 1-2-3 remembers the Data range.

To see how this works, select /Data Sort Primary-Key and indicate a cell in column A as the primary sort key. This time, enter *A* for ascending sort order and then select Go. 1-2-3 reorders the records chronologically.

Having completed this chapter, you:

- *Know what structure data must have to be considered a 1-2-3 database*

- *Have learned the terms associated with databases*

- *Understand how to set a Data range to sort a database*

- *Know the reason for setting a sort key*

- *Have greater understanding of the mouse if you're a Release 2.3 mouse user*

23

Ask Questions about Your Data

A rranging database records alphabetically or numerically can help you to locate selected information in a hurry. Knowing a person's last name, for example, you can use an address database's last name field as the primary sort key and then visually scan to find the name in the database.

For small databases like the one you prepared in Chapter 22, you can find records quickly even without first sorting the data. However, in very large databases, sorting the data may not make the records significantly more accessible. Even when alphabetized, a database of several thousand records prohibits visual searching. The /Data Query commands let you find records easily in large databases.

A Command That Locates Records: /Data Query Find

The /Data Query Find command locates all the records in a database that meet specified criteria. For example, you might want to find all records of people whose last names begin with the letter "P." Or, you might want to find the records of people whose sales exceeded $35,000. Retrieve the practice database that you created in Chapter 22, and we'll see how to apply the /Data Query Find command.

In this chapter, you'll:

- *Learn how to make 1-2-3 search a database for specific information*
- *Create a Criteria range*
- *Perform several database queries*

Retrieve the Practice Database

If you created and saved the database as instructed in Chapter 22, retrieve it now. Our instructions were to save the worksheet under the file name PDBASE. If you haven't yet created that worksheet, please go back to Chapter 22 and follow the instructions for building the worksheet and storing it on disk. The practice database appears in Figure 23.1.

	A	B	C	D	E	F	G
1							
2							
3							
4							
5	Date	Product		Site	Quantity		
6	03−Feb−92	Rubber flange		West St.	4200		
7	03−Feb−92	Black Inflation		N. Plant	4100		
8	03−Feb−92	02 Ring Gasket		West St.	12000		
9	04−Feb−92	Rubber flange		West St.	1200		
10	04−Feb−92	Black Inflation		N. Plant	4300		
11	04−Feb−92	02 Ring Gasket		West St.	12000		
12	05−Feb−92	Black Inflation		N. Plant	4300		
13	05−Feb−92	02 Ring Gasket		West St.	12000		
14	05−Feb−92	Rubber flange		West St.	3000		
15							

FIGURE 23.1: Retrieve the practice database that you created in Chapter 22.

The Steps to Query Find

There are four steps to performing a /Data Query Find operation. The steps are:

1. Establish a Criteria range in the spreadsheet.

2. Enter a selection criterion.

3. Establish the database range settings.

4. Issue the Find command.

Let's take the steps one at a time.

1. Establish a Criteria Range

The Criteria range is an area of the spreadsheet that you prepare to tell 1-2-3 what records you want to find in the database. A Criteria range looks like a small database: It has field headers that match the headers of the corresponding database. There must also be one or more rows beneath the field headers to hold any criteria that you'll enter in step 2.

The easiest way to create a Criteria range is to copy the field headers from the database into a row that won't interfere with other things in the spreadsheet. The design of the practice database left some rows at the top of the spreadsheet that you can use for a Criteria range. So, copy the database field headers to row 1 by selecting /Copy and indicating range A5..D5 as the source range and cell A1 as the target.

2. Enter a Selection Criterion

The selection criterion tells 1-2-3 what information to find in the database. You enter selection criteria in the second row of the Criteria range. The selection criterion is a representation of the information that you'd like to find in the database. For example, if you're looking for records that contain the words "Rubber flange" in the Product field, you'd enter the words *Rubber flange* in the Product field of the Criteria range.

Let's try it. We're interested in examining the production data for rubber flanges, so enter the label *Rubber flange* into cell B2. Your worksheet should match the one in Figure 23.2.

	A	B	C	D	E	F	G
1	Date	Product	Site	Quantity			
2		Rubber flange					
3							
4							
5	Date	Product	Site	Quantity			
6	03–Feb–92	Rubber flange	West St.	4200			
7	03–Feb–92	Black Inflation	N. Plant	4100			
8	03–Feb–92	02 Ring Gasket	West St.	12000			
9	04–Feb–92	Rubber flange	West St.	1200			
10	04–Feb–92	Black Inflation	N. Plant	4300			
11	04–Feb–92	02 Ring Gasket	West St.	12000			
12	05–Feb–92	Black Inflation	N. Plant	4300			
13	05–Feb–92	02 Ring Gasket	West St.	12000			
14	05–Feb–92	Rubber flange	West St.	3000			
15							

FIGURE 23.2: The Criteria range in this worksheet is in range A1..D2 and contains the label *Rubber flange* to identify records that you wish to find.

3. Establish the Database Range Settings

You don't have to take this step every time you search for database records. After you establish the database range settings, you don't have to do it again

The database Query Input range, unlike the Data Sort Data range, must include the database field headers.

. . . .
. . . .
. . . .

unless you change the dimensions of the database by adding or deleting records. 1-2-3 remembers the settings until you deliberately change them, so this step in the /Data Query Find process simply goes away.

This time through the procedure you do need to establish the settings, so select /Data Query. You must tell 1-2-3 what range is the database Input range and what range is the Criteria range. Select Input and indicate range A5..D14. The Input range identifies the database and must include the field headers as well as the database records. Next select Criteria and indicate range A1..D2. The Criteria range can include more than two rows, but for the querying operations we will do in this book, these two rows will be enough.

You're ready to find the rubber flanges, but before you do, save the practice database worksheet, again under the name PDBASE. We'll come back to it in later chapters, and there's no sense in recreating the Criteria range and reestablishing the database range settings as you work through each chapter.

4. Issue the Find Command

No trick here. Select Find from the Data Query menu. The cell pointer jumps to row 6 and expands to highlight the entire record. As you can see in Figure 23.3, row 6 contains the first of the rubber flange records.

	A	B	C	D	E	F	G
1	Date	Product	Site	Quantity			
2		Rubber flange					
3							
4							
5	Date	Product	Site	Quantity			
6	03–Feb–92	Rubber flange	West St.	4200			
7	03–Feb–92	Black Inflation	N. Plant	4100			
8	03–Feb–92	02 Ring Gasket	West St.	12000			
9	04–Feb–92	Rubber flange	West St.	1200			
10	04–Feb–92	Black Inflation	N. Plant	4300			
11	04–Feb–92	02 Ring Gasket	West St.	12000			
12	05–Feb–92	Black Inflation	N. Plant	4300			
13	05–Feb–92	02 Ring Gasket	West St.	12000			
14	05–Feb–92	Rubber flange	West St.	3000			

FIGURE 23.3: Given the criterion *Rubber flange* in the Criteria range, the /Data Query Find command highlights the first of the Rubber flange records in the database Input range.

But wait. There are more Rubber flange records. In find mode (note the mode indicator in the top-right corner of the display), 1-2-3 can highlight only one record at a time. To view the next Rubber flange record in the database, press DownArrow. Then press DownArrow again to view the final Rubber

When You Select Find
When you issue the /Data Query Find command, 1-2-3 scans the database record by record. It compares the cells in the Criteria range with the corresponding cells of each record. When the cells exactly match, 1-2-3 marks the record as a match, and lets you move the highlight to the record. The trick here is that a blank cell in the Criteria range will match any entry in the database. You don't need to make entries in each cell of a Criteria range because a blank cell matches all entries—only cells that contain entries affect the record selection.

flange record. When you've finished perusing the found records, press Enter or Escape. Then select Quit and return to READY mode.

Criteria Wildcards

It's often not necessary to type out entire field entries to identify the records that you want to find. Rather, you can use wildcard characters to shorten your database-matching criteria.

The asterisk (*) wildcard matches any and all sequences of characters in a label. Use it in combination with a known character or character string to select groups of labels. For example, you might be searching an address database for everyone whose last name starts with "P." The criterion P* in the appropriate name field will do the trick.

The tilde (~) is another interesting wildcard. You use it to identify records that you don't want to find. For example, you could use the criterion ~R* in the Product field of our practice Criteria range to select all the records but the ones whose product name begins with "R." Try it. Enter the label in place of the one already stored in cell B2. Then select /Data Query Find. You won't

You Can Also Match Numbers
The examples In this chapter, show how to find database records that contain specific label entries. It's also possible to locate records based on the numbers that they contain. For example, if you erase the criterion from cell B2 and enter the number *12,000* as a criterion in cell D2, the /Data Query Find command will highlight only the records that contain the value 12,000 in the Quantity field.

be able to move the highlight in the database to any of the Rubber flange records.

Edit Found Records

As long as you're looking at records with the /Data Query Find command, let's explore one more feature that you may apply often as you work with databases. That's the ability to edit found records while 1-2-3 is in FIND mode.

To see how this works, use the UpArrow and DownArrow keys to move the highlight to the February 5th Black inflation record—that's the one in row 12. Now, press the RightArrow key until the cursor within the highlight falls on cell D12. The entry there (*4,300*), is 200 units too low. Correct it by typing 4,500 and pressing Enter. Alternatively, you can press the EDIT key (function key F2) and change the contents of the cell as you would were you working in the spreadsheet without the /Data Query commands.

In either case, when you press Enter, the database highlight remains in place. You can highlight other records to make further changes, or end the find operation by pressing Enter or Escape. Then select Quit to return to READY mode.

Having completed this chapter, you:

- *Know how to prepare a Criteria range*

- *Are familiar with database-matching criteria*

- *Understand how to set Data and Criteria ranges on the /Data Query menu*

- *Can perform a Query Find to locate and edit records in a database*

24

Copy Selected Records from a Database

1-2-3's ability to find and edit database records is quite useful, especially when your database is very large. However, sometimes finding information isn't enough. Quite often you need to copy records from the database as you prepare reports. For example, you might need to consolidate the records from the Northern plant when you report on the plant's monthly output. Or, you might need to consolidate the Black inflation records to gauge inventory as you fulfill customer orders.

Whatever the case, 1-2-3 can copy records out of a database as easily as it can find records. The only trick beyond what you already know is that you must establish an Output range that will receive the records you select. Then you can apply the /Data Query Extract command.

The Output Range Receives Records

The /Data Query Find command highlights information within the database Input range. To copy selected records from the database, you must identify to 1-2-3 an area of the spreadsheet that should receive the copies. That area is the Output range. The Output range, like the Criteria range, has field headers that match the database field headers. Also, the Output range must span

In this chapter, you'll:

- *Learn how to copy selected records from a database with the /Data Query Extract command*

- *Establish an Output range that will hold selected records*

- *Create criterion formulas to select a collection of database records* enough spreadsheet rows to contain all of the records that your selection criteria will pull from the database.

Retrieve the Practice Worksheet

To see the Query Extract command in action, first retrieve the worksheet named PDBASE that you created in Chapter 22 and later modified in Chapter 23. If you saved as instructed in the previous chapters, your practice database worksheet should match the one shown in Figure 24.1.

	A	B	C	D	E	F	G
1	Date	Product	Site	Quantity			
2							
3							
4							
5	Date	Product	Site	Quantity			
6	03–Feb–92	Rubber flange	West St.	4200			
7	03–Feb–92	Black Inflation	N. Plant	4100			
8	03–Feb–92	02 Ring Gasket	West St.	12000			
9	04–Feb–92	Rubber flange	West St.	1200			
10	04–Feb–92	Black Inflation	N. Plant	4300			
11	04–Feb–92	02 Ring Gasket	West St.	12000			
12	05–Feb–92	Black Inflation	N. Plant	4500			
13	05–Feb–92	02 Ring Gasket	West St.	12000			
14	05–Feb–92	Rubber flange	West St.	3000			
15							

FIGURE 24.1: You've already set the database Input (A5..D14) and Criteria (A1..D2) ranges in the practice database worksheet that you saved in Chapter 23.

Establish an Output range by copying the database field headers off to one side of the database. Select /Copy, indicate range A5..D5 as the source range, and indicate cell F1 as the target range. Now enter a criterion in the Criteria range.

Use a Criterion Label Formula

Rather than select records based on label entries as you did in Chapter 23, try a new approach. This time, extract each of the records in which fewer than 4,000 units were produced in a day. To do this, you'll use a criterion that's a cross between a label and a formula.

Move the cell pointer to cell D2, and enter the characters '<4000. This creates a label that looks like a formula fragment meaning "less than 4,000." When 1-2-3 is performing a Data Query operation, this means "match records for which the Quantity field amount is less than 4,000."

The Extract

As you might guess, before you issue the Extract command, you need to tell 1-2-3 where in the worksheet you've established the Output range. To do this, select /Data Query Output and indicate range F1..I10. Notice that the range includes nine blank rows under the field headers. There are nine records in the database, so it's certain that a 10-row Output range can handle any number of records that you might extract. Select Extract from the /Data Query menu, and the appropriate records appear in the Output range. Select Quit so that 1-2-3 returns to READY mode. Your worksheet should match the one shown in Figure 24.2.

	D	E	F	G	H	I	J	K	
1	Quantity		Date	Product	Site	Quantity			
2	<4000		************Rubber flan West St.			1200			
3			************Rubber flan West St.			3000			
4									
5	Quantity								
6	4200								
7	4100								
8	12000								

FIGURE 24.2: The extracted records appear in range F2..I3. You can adjust column widths and assign numeric display formats to make the records easier to read.

There are problems with the information you've extracted, but nothing serious. While 1-2-3 extracted the numeric display formats of the date cells, it didn't set the column widths to accommodate the copied records. It's a simple matter for you to adjust the widths to reveal all of the extracted information.

Accommodate Any Number of Records

If your database Output range is too small to hold the records that you extract, 1-2-3 displays an error message. You have to expand the Output range and then reissue the Extract command. But there is insurance against overfilling the database Output range. That is to assign the Output range to only the row that contains the field headers. In your practice worksheet that would be range F1..I1. With a one-row Output range, 1-2-3 uses as many rows as necessary to extract matching records from the database.

There is a danger with this technique. When you select /Data Query Extract, 1-2-3 erases everything from the Output range except the field headers. Then it copies matching records from the database. With a one-row Output range, 1-2-3 erases everything directly beneath the Output range field headers to the bottom of the spreadsheet before copying the matching records. If you choose to use a one-row Output range, store nothing in the columns beneath the Output range field headers.

Extract Selected Fields

It's not necessary to extract all the information from each record to the database Output range. You can, for example, extract only the product names along with their production totals. Or, you might prefer to extract the dates along with the production totals. Whatever the case, you choose which fields of data to extract by the field headers that you use in the Output range.

To see how this works, create a second Output range in your spreadsheet. Enter the labels *Product* in cell G12 and *Quantity* in cell H12. For variety, change the criterion to select different records. This time, enter *'>4200* into cell D2 so that the /Data Query Extract command will select all records where production exceeded 4,200 units in a day.

Select /Data Query Output and indicate range G12..H122 (the address H122 is arbitrary—it could just as well be H100, or H50) in place of the earlier Output range. Finally, select Extract and then Quit. Unless you've already changed the column widths, your new Output range should match the one shown in Figure 24.3.

	E	F	G	H	I	J	K	L
1		Date	Product	Site	Quantity			
2		************	Rubber flang	West St.	1200			
3		************	Rubber flang	West St.	3000			
4								
5								
6								
7								
8								
9								
10								
11								
12			Product	Quantity				
13			02 Ring Gas	12000				
14			Black Inflatic	4300				
15			02 Ring Gas	12000				
16			Black Inflatic	4500				
17			02 Ring Gas	12000				
18								

FIGURE 24.3: The field headings in the database Output range determine which data 1-2-3 extracts from the Input range.

Having completed this chapter, you:

- *Know how to prepare database Output ranges to receive extracted records*
- *Understand how the field headers in the Output range help select the information you extract*
- *Have some sense of how formula labels select database records*
- *Are aware of how 1-2-3 erases the Output range before copying records into it.*
- *Are prepared to handle most database querying tasks*

More on Database Management

With any luck, you're convinced that 1-2-3's database facility is quite useful. You haven't seen half of what it can do. For one thing, there is a collection of @functions designed to let you perform statistical analyses on selected records in a database—we explore those functions in Chapter 26. There are also database querying commands that help you to remove unwanted records from a database and to get a sense of the types of information that your database contains. These are the commands we'll apply in this chapter.

What's in the Database?

One question that you might ask about a database is, "What information does the database contain?" Sure, you know that the database is production data from two plants, but perhaps you're not sure what products the plants produce. Perhaps the factories rotate production so that they manufacture one or two products for several days, then switch to another set of products, and so on. Several month's worth of data might represent many tens of products. The /Data Query Unique command can tell you what products are represented in the database.

In this chapter, you'll:

- *Learn to narrow a database selection*

- *Explore the /Data Query Delete command to erase database records*

- *Use the /Data Query Unique command to get an overview of your data*

- *Discover how the QUERY key can speed database tasks*

Retrieve the Practice Worksheet

As you did at the beginning of the last chapter, once again retrieve the worksheet named PDBASE. You created the sheet when you worked through Chapter 22 and made some additions to it if you followed the instructions in Chapter 23. It should match the sheet shown in Figure 25.1 once you've retrieved it from disk. Use this practice database to try out the /Data Query Unique command.

	A	B	C	D	E	F	G
1	Date	Product	Site	Quantity			
2							
3							
4							
5	Date	Product	Site	Quantity			
6	03–Feb–92	Rubber flange	West St.	4200			
7	03–Feb–92	Black Inflation	N. Plant	4100			
8	03–Feb–92	02 Ring Gasket	West St.	12000			
9	04–Feb–92	Rubber flange	West St.	1200			
10	04–Feb–92	Black Inflation	N. Plant	4300			
11	04–Feb–92	02 Ring Gasket	West St.	12000			
12	05–Feb–92	Black Inflation	N. Plant	4500			
13	05–Feb–92	02 Ring Gasket	West St.	12000			
14	05–Feb–92	Rubber flange	West St.	3000			
15							

FIGURE 25.1: The practice database worksheet stands unchanged from when you used it in Chapter 23—you shouldn't have saved any of the changes you made in Chapter 24.

Output Ranges for Unique Extracts

The /Data Query Unique command copies records from the database, eliminating duplicates from the selected records. 1-2-3 uses the fields in the Output range to determine which records are duplicates. For example, if you take all the fields into account in the practice database, there are no dupli-

Match Several Criteria
Suppose that you want to select all the records for products made at the West Street plant whose production units are greater than 4,300. In other words, it's not enough that the record is from the West Street plant: Its production total must also exceed a specified limit. A record must meet two criteria to fit this profile. In that case, enter both of the criteria directly beneath the field headers of the Criteria range. In our practice worksheet, you could enter *W** into cell C2, and *'>4300* into cell D2.

cate entries—an Output range that included all of the field headers would cause the /Data Query Unique command to extract all the records.

However, if you consider only the Product field, there are quite a few duplicates. In fact, each entry in the Product field matches two other entries in the field—there are only three *unique* entries. This is the answer to the question that we raised in the first place: What products are represented in the database?

Prepare to Be Unique

Understanding how the /Data Query Unique command works makes it clear how to set up an Output range to answer the question. Move the cell pointer to cell F1 and enter the label *Product*. This is the only field header needed to get a listing of the products that the company manufactures.

You're looking for a listing of all the products that the company manufactures—not of the products manufactured on a certain day or at a certain factory. In other words, there is no criterion to delimit which records 1-2-3 should consider in looking for product names—you want it to look at all the records and to return every product name in the database. Leave the second row of the Criteria range blank. You're ready to try the command.

Select /Data Query Output and indicate Range F1..F10 as the Output range. Then select Unique from the menu and Quit to return 1-2-3 to READY mode. The three product names—Rubber flange, Black Inflation, and 02 Ring Gasket—appear in the Output range. Your worksheet should match the one shown in Figure 25.2.

	A	B	C	D	E	F	G	
1	Date	Product	Site	Quantity		Product		◄
2						Rubber flange		►
3						Black Inflation		▲
4						02 Ring Gasket		▼
5	Date	Product	Site	Quantity				?
6	03−Feb−92	Rubber flange	West St.	4200				
7	03−Feb−92	Black Inflation	N. Plant	4100				
8	03−Feb−92	02 Ring Gasket	West St.	12000				
9	04−Feb−92	Rubber flange	West St.	1200				
10	04−Feb−92	Black Inflation	N. Plant	4300				
11	04−Feb−92	02 Ring Gasket	West St.	12000				
12	05−Feb−92	Black Inflation	N. Plant	4500				
13	05−Feb−92	02 Ring Gasket	West St.	12000				
14	05−Feb−92	Rubber flange	West St.	3000				
15								

FIGURE 25.2: The /Data Query Unique command reveals that the manufacturing plants produced three distinct products during the period represented in the database.

Query Again Without Menus

You've established the database-related settings and you've issued a /Data Query command, such as Extract or Unique. Now you want to change the criteria and reissue the Query command. You don't need to use the menus.

Try it in your practice database after you've extracted records to match Figure 25.2. In ready mode, enter the criterion *West** into cell C2. This selects the records for products manufactured in the West Street plant. Now,

instead of selecting /Data Query Unique and Quit, press the QUERY key—that's the function key labeled F7. 1-2-3 immediately lists the products manufactured at West Street.

Pressing the QUERY key automatically re-issues the last Data Query command to you issued via the menus. Learning to use this key can reduce your efforts when you wish to perform a rapid sequence of Find, Extract, Unique, or Delete database operations.

Delete Unwanted Records

One database chore that arises from time to time is the need to eliminate records from an existing database. For example, you might maintain a database of employee names in a department with regular turnover, so you often need to remove the records of departing employees. Or, perhaps you maintain an inventory database and your company drops a product so you need to erase it from the database. The /Data Query Delete command handles the work for you.

Four Steps to Data Deletion

Sure, you can delete records from a database in only two steps, but save yourself some agony and follow the four-step approach:

1. Save the database on disk.

2. Set a criterion.

3. Make sure you've set the right criterion.

4. Issue the Delete command.

Use the four-step approach to erase the database records for which production was greater than 4,000 units, but less than 10,000. OK, there's probably no good reason that you'd do this in this type of database, but the technique will apply some day to your work with other databases.

1. Save the Database on Disk

Perhaps you're being overly careful. After all, you're going to test your criterion before you use it to delete database records. But what if you forget to test the criterion? Or what if you test it, make the deletion, and then realize that you overlooked something? The point is, be safe and save.

You've already saved the practice database, so don't bother saving it again. Do remember to preserve a disk copy of your own database before you apply the /Data Query Delete command.

2. Set a Criterion

We've made this criterion a bit different from earlier ones. You're trying to select records whose units are between 4,000 and 10,000. To do that you need to create a criterion formula.

A criterion formula is a formula in the Criteria range that equates the first data cell in the corresponding database field to some target value or values. In other words, you need to write a formula in cell D2 that compares cell D6 with the target values 4,000 and 10,000. When you issue a query command, 1-2-3 scans the database record by record, substituting cell addresses for

A criterion formula must refer to a cell in the first database record.

What's #AND#?

The expression #AND# is one of 1-2-3's "logical operators." You can use it in formulas to tie one Boolean (conditional) statement to another. For example, the expression +D6>4000 is true when the value in cell D6 is greater than 4,000. Likewise, the expression +D6<10000 is true when the value in D6 is less than 10,000. To test whether the value in cell D6 is both greater than 4,000 and less than 10,000, use the #AND# operator to combine the expressions so they read +D6>4000#AND#D6<10000.

1-2-3 also offers an "or" operator that can return a true result when one of two conditions is met. For example, the expression +D6<4000#OR#D6>10000 is true when the value in cell D6 isn't between 4,000 and 10,000. That is, it's true when D6 is less than 4,000 or when D6 is greater than 10,000.

each successive database record into the criterion formula. When a field entry causes the formula to return a true result (1), the record is a match. When an entry causes a false result (0), the record isn't a match.

This might make more sense when you write the formula. First, make sure there is no other criterion in the Criteria range. Then enter the formula *+D6>4000#AND#D6<10000* into cell D2. The box titled What's #AND#? sheds some light on the formula's structure. In the meantime, notice that the formula returns 1. That's because the entry in cell D6 falls between 4,000 and 10,000—it meets the criterion.

3. Make Sure You've Set the Right Criterion

This step can be life-saving. To test the criterion, issue either the /Data Query Find command or /Data Query Extract. For this exercise, select /Data Query Find and examine the records selected by the criterion. In find mode, 1-2-3 restricts movement of the database highlight to rows 6, 7, 10, and 12. All of the records meet the stated criterion, so it's OK to delete them. Press Enter to end the Find operation.

4. Issue the Delete Command

Select Delete from the /Data Query menu. 1-2-3 displays a cautionary menu asking whether you really want to delete the records. Select Delete and then

```
D2: +D6>4000#AND#D6<10000                                         READY

          A              B           C           D          E      F      G     ◄
  1  Date          Product         Site        Quantity                         ►
  2                                                        0                     ▲
  3                                                                              ▼
  4                                                                              ?
  5  Date          Product         Site        Quantity
  6  03-Feb-92 02 Ring Gasket      West St.        12000
  7  04-Feb-92 Rubber flange       West St.         1200
  8  04-Feb-92 02 Ring Gasket      West St.        12000
  9  05-Feb-92 02 Ring Gasket      West St.        12000
 10  05-Feb-92 Rubber flange       West St.         3000
 11
```

FIGURE 25.3: The /Data Query Delete command removes the records whose production levels were between 4,000 and 10,000 units.

Quit. Your spreadsheet should match the one in Figure 25.3. Note that 1-2-3 automatically adjusts the database Input range to account for the deleted records. If you were to check, you'd find the Input range is now A5..D10.

Having completed this chapter, you:

- *Know how to learn what items are represented in a database*

- *Have a sense of how to work with multiple criteria*

- *Are aware of the #AND# and #OR# logical operators*

- *Can write criterion formulas to narrow down a database search*

- *Know how to delete records from a database*

Database @Functions

P erhaps you know enough about databases. Sorting records, finding selected items, extracting them, deleting, and modifying—that's about all anyone ever does with these powerful data structures. Still, many 1-2-3 users hit a point in their careers when they ask, "How can I calculate subtotals for the departments listed in my database?" Or, more generally, "How can I calculate statistics on selected database records?"

Functions to Calculate Statistics

Given the database shown in Figure 26.1, you might ask, how many Black Inflations were produced in the three days that the data represent? Or, what was the average daily production of Inflations? One obvious way to answer these questions is to extract the records of the data in question and then write formulas to sum the appropriate field. A much more efficient way to get the answers is to apply @D (pronounced "at-dee") functions.

Retrieve the Practice Worksheet

We promise this is the last time we'll ask you to do it, so please retrieve the database worksheet that you created and saved according to instructions in Chapter 22 and later modified when you worked through Chapter 23. If you've worked through the other chapters in Part IV, you've made further changes to that worksheet, but have not saved them. The file's name is PDBASE, and when you retrieve it your display should match the one in Figure 26.1.

In this chapter, you'll:

- *Learn how to calculate the statistics of selected database records*

- *Discover how the database @functions help to summarize data*

- *Calculate the sums and averages of several categories of data*

	A	B	C	D	E	F	G
1	Date	Product	Site	Quantity			
2							
3							
4							
5	Date	Product	Site	Quantity			
6	03−Feb−92	Rubber flange	West St.	4200			
7	03−Feb−92	Black Inflation	N. Plant	4100			
8	03−Feb−92	02 Ring Gasket	West St.	12000			
9	04−Feb−92	Rubber flange	West St.	1200			
10	04−Feb−92	Black Inflation	N. Plant	4300			
11	04−Feb−92	02 Ring Gasket	West St.	12000			
12	05−Feb−92	Black Inflation	N. Plant	4500			
13	05−Feb−92	02 Ring Gasket	West St.	12000			
14	05−Feb−92	Rubber flange	West St.	3000			
15							

FIGURE 26.1: Use the practice database that you created and saved in Chapter 22 to learn how to generate subtotals.

Calculate Subtotals

This may seem anticlimactic after all the other work you've done with databases, but your first task is to calculate the total production of Black Inflations for the three-day period recorded in the database. The procedure involves the use of the @DSUM function, the database Input range, and the Criteria range.

Enter the @DSUM Function

The @DSUM function calculates the sum of the values in a selected database field for all the records that meet a criterion. The function's syntax is @DSUM(*input,offset,criteria*). The *input* argument identifies the database Input range; the *offset* argument identifies the field that contains the entries

How's That Offset?
The *offset* argument in an @D function identifies which database field the function should use when it performs its calculations. The argument describes the field's location in the Input range in terms of how many columns the field lies to the right of the database's first field. For example, an offset argument of 1 means that the target field is one column to the right of the first field. An offset argument of 0 identifies the first field; that is, the field that is zero columns to the right of the first one.

to sum; and the *criteria* argument identifies a Criteria range that identifies the records to use in the calculation.

To see the @DSUM function at work, first enter the appropriate criterion in the existing Criteria range. To do this, move the cell pointer to cell B2 and enter *Black Inflation*. Now, enter the label *Sum* into cell F1 and enter the formula *@DSUM(A5..D14,3,A1..D2)* into cell G1. The result is 12,900—that's how many Black Inflations were produced.

Want to know the average daily production of Black Inflations? Enter the label *Avg* into cell F2, and enter the formula *@DAVG(A5..D14,3,A1..D2)* into cell G2. The average daily production of Inflations was 4,300 units.

You don't have to stop there, but we will. There are several more @D functions, each of which uses the same syntax as the @DSUM and the @DAVG functions. Tables 26.1 and 26.2 list the standard @D functions and the calculations they perform for all releases of 1-2-3 and for Release 3.1, respectively.

@D function	Calculation
@DAVG	Average of matching records
@DCOUNT	Total quantity of matching records
@DMAX	Value of maximum matching record
@DMIN	Value of minimum matching record
@DSUM	Sum of matching records
@DSTD	Population standard deviation of matching records
@DVAR	Population variance of matching records

Table 26.1: Standard @D functions for all releases of 1-2-3.

@D function	Calculation
@DGET	If there is only one matching record, this function returns the item stored in the offset column.
@DSTDS	Sample standard deviation of matching records
@DVARS	Sample variance of matching records

Table 26.2: Standard @D functions for Release 3.1.

@D Functions: No Menus Needed

You might notice as you're working through the main text that you don't need to access menus to apply these powerhouses. Although the functions refer to both database Input and Criteria ranges, you don't need to establish these ranges on the /Data Query menus for the functions to work. In fact, you can enter several tens of @D functions in a worksheet, each using the same database yet having its own Criteria range. This way, you might, for example, simultaneously calculate the total production output for all three products in your database.

Change Criteria to Change Calculations

Right now the @DSUM and the @DAVG functions you've entered perform calculations based on the records for Black Inflations. It's a simple matter to apply the same formulas in calculating statistics for Rubber flanges. All you need to do is to change the criterion that the functions use to select records.

Try it. Move the cell pointer to cell B2 and enter *R**. 1-2-3 reacts to the change and immediately displays new values in cells G1 and G2. There were 8,400 rubber flanges manufactured at an average rate of 2,800 per day.

A Final Note about Criteria Ranges

It's possible that we've given the impression that a Criteria range must contain headers for every field in the database Input range. If that's the case, please dispense with the notion. A Criteria range can be quite effective when it has only the header of the field for which you're writing a criterion.

For example, suppose that you wanted to calculate the total number of units produced by the West Street factory. Rather than use the existing Criteria range, create a new one in column F. This Criteria range will have a single field header.

Enter the label *Site* into cell F5 and then enter the criterion *West** into cell F6. Now, move the cell pointer to cell G3 and enter the formula *@DSUM(A5..D14,3,F5..F6)*. The formula reveals that the West Street plant produced 44,400 units in the three-day period.

Having completed this chapter, you:

- *Understand how to apply the @D functions*

- *Know what @D functions are available to calculate database statistics*

- *Are aware that a Criteria range can have as many or as few field headers as needed to identify the correct database fields*

- *Have considerable expertise with 1-2-3's database facility*

Part V
Graph Spreadsheet Data

Numbers and words are fine for many of us, but not for everyone. Quite a few people prefer to derive vital information from pictures. In truth, most of us learn best from a combination of numbers, words, and pictures. When the words and numbers make comparisons feel a bit grey, a good graph can illuminate differences in a flash. Alternatively, when a graph's contents are a bit confusing, some descriptive text can clarify the image.

If you had to break out the colored pencils, the drafting table, and a compass, you might choose not to prepare graphs and charts to illustrate your financial or experimental data. Even if your reports demanded illustration, you might keep the figures to a minimum.

Fortunately, you don't need the drafting equipment. The "3" in 1-2-3 represents your software's powerful graphing facility. By issuing a few menu commands, you can convert numerical spreadsheet data into bar charts, line graphs, pie charts, and more in moments. You can add titles to these graphs to clarify their content and soup them up with lines, arrows, and other freehand drawings. What's more, you can have 1-2-3 display the graphs wherever you want in the spreadsheet.

Part V starts you out creating a small practice worksheet with data that you eventually convert into a graphic image. Then, it shows how to clarify the graph with titles and legends and how to convert the graph from one graph type to another. The section concludes by showing how you can insert graphs in the spreadsheet and then use Wysiwyg's graph editing tools to add special features such as lines, arrows, and highlighted text.

27

Say It with Pictures

Creating a bar chart, a line graph, or a pie chart, is a walk in the park for 1-2-3. In fact, the task is so easy that it hardly deserves its own chapter. Still, you gotta start somewhere. Once you learn how to create one type of graph, you pretty much know how to create any type that 1-2-3 can draw. This chapter shows you how to convert the data from a simple sales model into a bar graph.

A Simple Model

The model that you'll create appears in Figure 27.1. It shows the revenue generated by a mail order company that sells products to cave explorers (cavers). The worksheet tracks sales of four products over a three-month period—the first quarter of 1992. It also uses a few Wysiwyg features that we haven't applied in previous chapters.

Tricks to Building the Model

There are a few tricks to creating this spreadsheet. For one, in spite of the fact that the titles in rows 1 and 2 appear centered in the sheet, they reside in column A. We used one of Wysiwyg's commands to center them after we altered their sizes and styles. This technique is quicker than trying to center titles by entering them in columns near the middle of the display. You might also notice that the spreadsheet data and calculations in this sheet are within a box that appears slightly elevated above the worksheet—it seems to cast a shadow be-

In this chapter, you'll:

- Draw on your spreadsheet expertise to build a small practice model

- Apply Wysiwyg to alter fonts and font styles, draw lines, and create a shadowed box

- Convert the data in your model into a bar chart

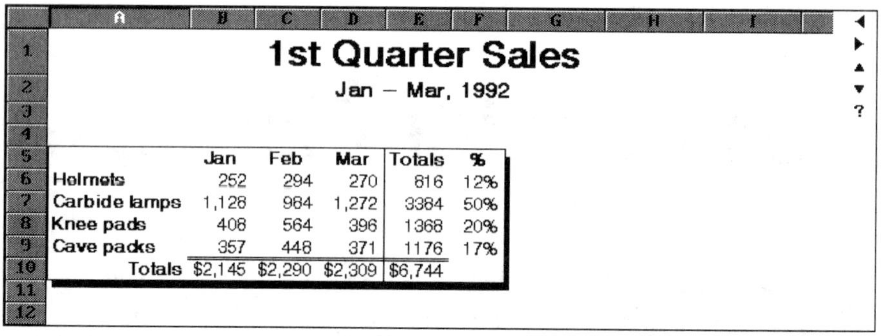

1st Quarter Sales

Jan – Mar, 1992

	Jan	Feb	Mar	Totals	%
Helmets	252	294	270	816	12%
Carbide lamps	1,128	984	1,272	3384	50%
Knee pads	408	564	396	1368	20%
Cave packs	357	448	371	1176	17%
Totals	$2,145	$2,290	$2,309	$6,744	

FIGURE 27.1: Build a model to match this spreadsheet so you can create graphs based on the data it contains.

hind it. Follow our directions for building the sheet, and we'll explain when and how to apply the special effects.

Labels Start by entering the titles in cells A1 and A2. Remember to start with an apostrophe label prefix when you type the label in cell A1. Leave the titles alone once you've entered them. Next, enter the labels in range A6..A10 and in range B5..F5. Start the label in cell A10 with a quotation mark (") label prefix and start each of the labels in row 5 by typing a caret (^) prefix.

Column Widths Use the /Worksheet Column Set-Width command to set the width of column A to 13 characters. Use the /Worksheet Column Column-Range Set-Width command to set the widths of columns B–E to 6. Then set the width of column F to 5.

Values and Formulas Enter the values shown in range B6..D9. Then enter the formula *@SUM(B6..B9)* into cell B10 and copy it to range C10..E10. Enter the formula *@SUM(B6..D6)* into cell E6 and enter *+E6/$E$10* into cell F6. Use the /Range Copy command to copy the formulas from range E6..F6 to range E7..F9.

Wysiwyg's :Format Text Align Center command will center labels (from left to right) within a specified worksheet range.

Numeric Display Formats Select /Range Format , (comma), enter *0,* and indicate range B6..E9 as the range to format. Select /Range Format Percent, enter *0,* and indicate range F6..F9. Finally, select /Range Format Currency, enter *0,* and indicate range B10..E10.

Wysiwyg Formats Start with the titles. Move the cell pointer to cell A1, select :Format Bold Set, and indicate range A1..A2. Select :Format Font 3 and indicate cell A1. Then select :Format Font 2 and indicate cell A2. Center the labels by applying commands from Wysiwyg's Text menu: Select :Format Text Align Center and indicate range A1..I2. Wysiwyg centers the labels within the range specified.

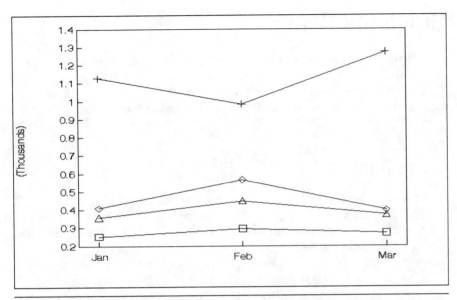

FIGURE 27.2: It takes a few moments to get 1-2-3 to produce this admittedly unattractive graph.

Doctor up the titles in row 5 and in column A by issuing the :Format Bold Set command twice. The first time, indicate range B5..F5 as the target range; the second time, indicate range A6..A10.

Add the Lines   To draw lines that match the ones in our worksheet, start with the cell pointer in cell A5. Select :Format Lines Outline and indicate range A5..F10. This places a line around the entire range. Select :Format Lines a second time, but this time select Shadow. Indicate the same range—A5..F10. Wysiwyg casts a shadow onto the spreadsheet.

Create the dividing line above the bottom line totals by selecting :Format Lines Double Top and indicating range B10..E10. Then, create the vertical dividing line by selecting :Format Line Left and indicating range E5..E10.

Save the Worksheet   It was a lot of work. But the presentation is impressive, and you did almost all of it using familiar commands. Save the worksheet under the name PGRAPH before you continue with this chapter. We'll come back to the practice graph worksheet in Chapters 28–30.

Graph the Data

For all the work you've done to get here, graphing the revenue data may seem trifling. Using the menus, you can establish just a few settings to get 1-2-3 to draw the graph that you want. For this exercise, you'll plot the monthly revenue for each of the listed products as shown in Figure 27.2.

Graph Ranges

Select /Graph. Release 2.3 users, as always, may elect to work with the dialog box that appears superimposed on the spreadsheet. In any case, you need to tell 1-2-3 where to find the data that you want to graph. To do this, you identify various "Graph ranges."

The X graph range identifies labels that 1-2-3 should display along the x-axis of the graph. The A range identifies values in the worksheet that 1-2-3 should plot as data points on the graph. The B–F ranges also identify data points—presumably from alternative sets of data. This will make more sense when you assign the Graph ranges and view the resulting graph.

Set Five Graph Ranges

Select X from the menu and indicate range B5..D5 as the X Graph range. This tells 1-2-3 to use the labels *Jan, Feb,* and *Mar* along the x-axis to identify the data points in the graph.

Select A, indicate range B6..D6, then select B, and indicate range B7..D7. Select C, indicate range B8..D8, and, finally, indicate range B9..D9 as the graph's D Graph range. Now select View from the menu. The graph appears, matching the one shown in Figure 27.2.

One-to-One Correspondence

OK, it's an ugly graph. We'll deal with that in a moment. Right now, take a look at the graph's structure. The x-axis has the labels that we promised. Above each of the labels is a tick mark, and above each tick mark are four data points. Each of the points above a tick mark originates from a separate graph range. You'd have to refer back to the spreadsheet to be sure of which data point represents which product, but we'll solve that problem in the next chapter.

Information along the graph's y-axis tells you that the data represent thousands—1-2-3 scaled the axis automatically to fit the data in the spreadsheet. As convenient as this may be, the data in this graph would be much clearer portrayed as a bar chart. It's a simple matter to make the change.

Change to a Bar Chart

When you've finished viewing a graph, press any key—except for the shift key, the Control key, or the Alt key. The graph vanishes, and you return to whatever you were doing when you chose to view the graph. So, press a key to clear the graph and then select Type from the graph menu.

There is a handy list of graph types from which to choose. The graph you just viewed was a line graph. To create a bar graph, choose Bar from the menu and then select View. The resulting graph appears in Figure 27.3.

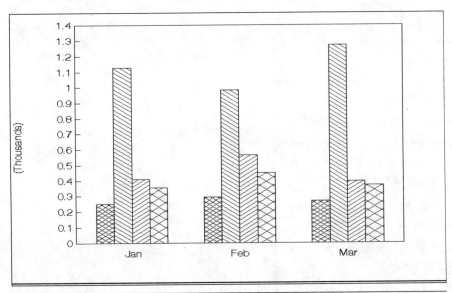

FIGURE 27.3: With only a few keystrokes you can change a graph's type from Line to Bar, or to any of the other types listed on the /Graph Type menu.

Enough for Openers

That's enough for one chapter. You've created a few graphs. And, while those graphs wouldn't win wall space in the Louvre, at least they've introduced the /Graph menu and the one-to-one nature of the data points established in Graph ranges. In the next chapter we'll retrieve the practice graph worksheet, create a few more graphs, and enter some titles and legends to give the graphs clarity. Don't save the worksheet with the graph settings—we'll use a special technique to reestablish those settings all at once when we get going in Chapter 28.

Having completed this chapter, you:

- *Understand the nature of Graph ranges and how they map to the points in a graph image*

- *Can assign Graph ranges to create line graphs and bar charts*

- *Are familiar with Wysiwyg's Line Shadow command*

- *Know how to center titles within a worksheet range*

- *Are prepared to explore more graph types and soup up the images with titles and legends*

Titles and Legends Clarify a Graph

In Chapter 27, you built a practice worksheet and used its data as the basis for creating a line graph and then a bar chart. The graphic images were a bit crude, lacking details that could reveal the meaning of the various graph elements. In other words, it was hard to tell from the graphs just what the lines and bars meant.

In this chapter, we'll revisit that practice worksheet and use it to recreate the bar chart. Then, we'll add some titles and legends to the graph so anyone looking at it will know that it illustrates sales revenue recorded in the worksheet. Finally, we'll apply a few other graphing options and create another type of graph.

Recreate the Bar Chart . . . Quickly

At the end of the last chapter, you had established the settings to display a bar chart based on the revenue data in the practice worksheet. To get to that point, you had indicated five worksheet ranges to correspond with the Graph ranges X, A, B, C, and D. There's a faster way to establish Graph ranges. Before you can apply the alternate technique, you'll need some data to graph.

In this chapter, you'll:

- *Learn how to create graph titles and legends*

- *Establish several Graph data ranges at once*

- *Use the GRAPH key to view a graph at any time in a work session*

- *Explore another of 1-2-3's graph types*

- *Name a graph so you can return to it later*

Retrieve the Practice Worksheet

Retrieve the practice worksheet named PGRAPH that you created when you worked through Chapter 27. It contains sales revenue data for a small company that sells supplies to cave explorers (cavers) through the mail. If you haven't created the practice sheet, jump back to Chapter 27 and build the model before you continue with the material in this chapter. The finished worksheet appears in Figure 28.1.

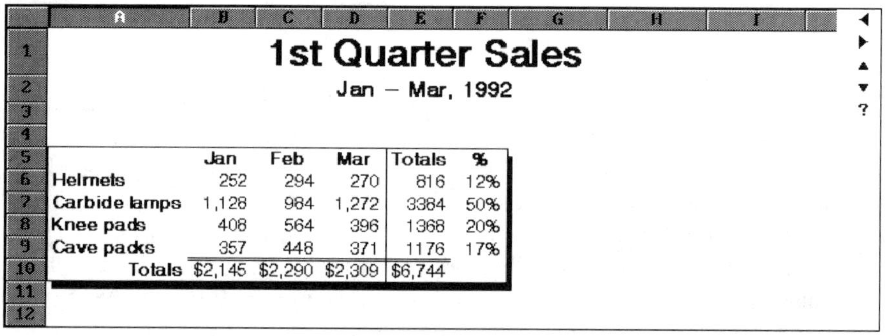

1st Quarter Sales

Jan – Mar, 1992

	Jan	Feb	Mar	Totals	%
Helmets	252	294	270	816	12%
Carbide lamps	1,128	984	1,272	3384	50%
Knee pads	408	564	396	1368	20%
Cave packs	357	448	371	1176	17%
Totals	$2,145	$2,290	$2,309	$6,744	

FIGURE 28.1: The sales revenue worksheet that you created when you worked through Chapter 27 serves as the basis for the graphs in this chapter.

Establish the Graph Ranges

For you to establish a collection of graph ranges all at once, the ranges must be in adjacent rows or columns. In many worksheets, as in the practice worksheet, that's how spreadsheet users tend to lay out their data. The X, A, B, C, and D Graph ranges that we need to establish are ranges B5..D5, B6..D6, B7..D7, B8..D8, and B9..D9, respectively. Proceed as follows.

Select /Graph Group and indicate range B5..D9. 1-2-3 displays a menu with two options: Columnwise and Rowwise. You want 1-2-3 to use each row of the Group range as a Graph range, so select Rowwise from the menu. 1-2-3 assigns each row in the Group range a separate Graph range, beginning with the first row as the X range, the second row as the A range, and so on. Select Type Bar and then View to see the result. The resulting graph, shown in Figure 28.2, should look familiar.

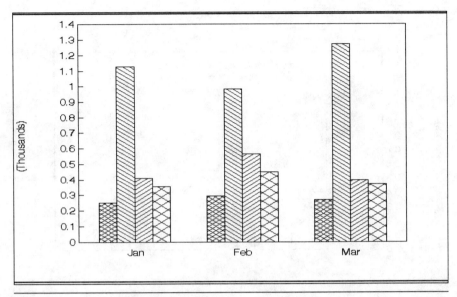

FIGURE 28.2: Using the /Graph Group command, you can establish five Graph ranges at once to create this bar chart.

Titles and Legends for Clarity

While the bar chart you just created is attractive, it isn't at all useful. All you can tell from looking at it is that it has something to do with January, February, and March and that it measures something in thousands. For the graph to take on any meaning, you should establish some titles and a legend. You accomplish both of these tasks by issuing commands from the /Graph menus.

The Main Graph Titles

The information that appears in the first two rows of your spreadsheet would help to clarify the graph's meaning—if that information were visible on the graph. Enter those labels as graph titles.

Press any key (except Shift, Control, Alt, Print Screen, Num Lock, and Scroll Lock) to clear the graph from your display. Then, select Options from

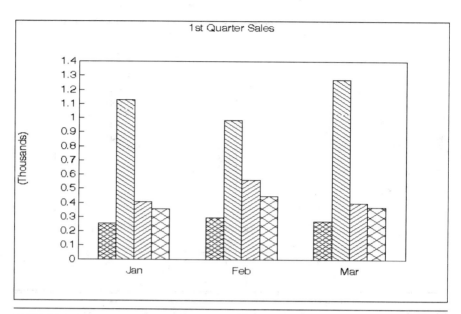

FIGURE 28.3: Adding a single title helps to clarify your graph's meaning.

the /Graph menu and select Titles. Select First and then enter *1st Quarter Sales*. Release 2.3 mouse users, feel free to work with the dialog box instead of the menus—click the First entry blank in the Titles box and then enter the title. In any case, press the GRAPH key—that's function key F10—to see the result of your addition. Your display should match the graph in Figure 28.3.

Press a key to clear the graph image and then select Titles Second. The title that you'd like to enter here, *Jan - Mar, 1992,* already exists in the worksheet. You can retype the entry as the second title setting in the same way that you typed the first title, but it seems a shame to retype things when you work on the computer—if the information is there, why not reuse it?

You can have 1-2-3 use an entry from the worksheet as a graph title by creating a reference to the cell holding the entry. To do this, enter a backslash (\) followed by the address of the appropriate cell. So, enter \A2 as the second graph title and then press the GRAPH key (F10) to see the result. Your graph should match the one in Figure 28.4.

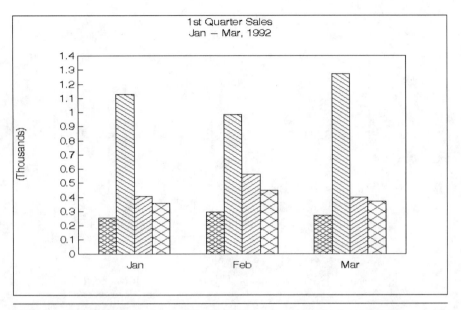

FIGURE 28.4: The Second Title graph setting \A2 pulls the title from the worksheet into the graph image.

An Axis Title and a Legend

The graph still needs some clarification. For example, what does each bar represent? For that matter, what do the units on the y-axis measure? Press a key to clear the graph display and then select Titles Y-Axis. The graph represents the number of dollars generated by each of the items represented, so enter *revenue in dollars* as the y-axis title. Press GRAPH to see the result.

Press a key to clear the display and then select Legend. With the Legend options, you can establish a listing that tells what each of the graph's bars represents. You can, if you wish, select A from the Legend menu and enter a word or words to identify the meaning of the Graph A range. Then, you can repeat the procedure for each of the Graph ranges in use. Alternatively, you can establish all of the legends at once by applying the Range command.

Select Range from the Legend menu and indicate range A6..A9 as the worksheet range that contains legend labels. Press the GRAPH key to see the result of your handiwork. It should be similar to the graph in Figure 28.5. Your results may vary depending on which release of 1-2-3 you're using.

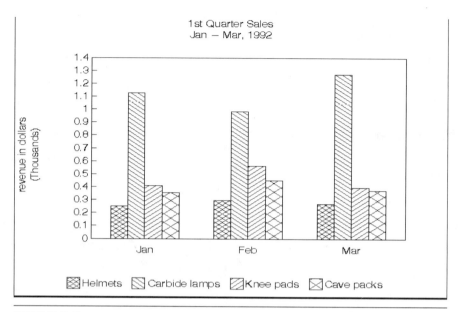

FIGURE 28.5: The completed bar chart has main titles and a title along the y-axis. It also has a legend to reveal what each bar represents.

Preserve the Graph

It's rare that a collection of data suggests only one useful graph to create. Quite often you want to view several graphs of a single data set. For example, you might want to plot the bar graph data with revenues grouped by product instead of by month. Then, each cluster of bars would represent three months' worth of data. Or, you might want to create a pie chart that shows the percentage of total revenue generated by each product.

In any case, it wouldn't do to abandon the existing graph settings in place of new settings. Instead, you can preserve the current settings under their own name. Then, you're free to create new graphs, each with its own name, and flip from one graph to another to get a detailed graphical overview of your spreadsheet data.

Name the Settings

To save a graph's settings, you must return to the main Graph menu. Press a key to clear the graph from the display and then select Quit from the menu. To preserve a graph's settings, select Name Create and enter a name—use the name *bar* for this exercise.

To prove that you've saved the settings and can return to the graph as needed, let's create a graph with another name. This will be a pie chart that shows what percentage of sales revenue each product generates.

Don't confuse the /Graph Save command with /Graph Name. /Graph Save doesn't preserve a graph's settings.

A Quick Pie Chart

Start by clearing out some settings that you won't want in the pie chart—specifically, the Graph ranges. A pie chart requires only two Graph ranges. The X range identifies labels that apply to each of the slices of the pie, and the A range identifies the values on which to base the pie slices. To clear the ranges, select Reset Ranges Quit. Users of 1-2-3 Release 3.1 should also consult the *Release 3 Graphs Are Different* box for further instructions.

Select X from the graph menu and indicate range A6..A9 as the X Graph range. Select A and indicate range E6..E9. Finally, select Type Pie, and press the GRAPH key. The resulting graph shows quite clearly that carbide lamps account for 50% of the mail order company's revenues.

Press a key to clear the display, and then save the graph's settings. Remember, to do this, select Name Create, and enter a name. In this case, use the name *pie*.

Release 3 Graphs Are Different

1-2-3 Release 3.1 puts more detail into a pie chart than Release 2.3 does. We used Release 2.3 when we prepared the Figures for this book. So, if you're using Release 3.1, your displays won't match ours exactly. More importantly, you'll need to reset the graph legends setting before you create the pie chart described in the main text. Unfortunately, to do that you also must reset the titles settings—there aren't separate reset commands to remove legends and titles.

To reset the legends, press Escape several times to back out of the graph menus. Then select /Graph Reset Options Quit. Reestablish the First and Second titles as follows: Select Options Titles First, and enter \a1; select Titles Options Second, and enter \a2. There's no need to reestablish the y-axis title because a pie chart has no axes.

Want to get back to the bar chart? Select Name Use and either enter the name *bar* or select it from the resulting menu. Return to the pie chart by selecting /Graph Name Use and indicating *pie* as the graph that you want to view. Pressing the GRAPH key causes 1-2-3 to display whichever graph you last activated via the /Graph Name Use command.

Save before Stopping

Please save the spreadsheet—once again use the name PGRAPH. You've done a lot of work to establish graph ranges, titles, and legends, and they all save along with the rest of the worksheet. We'll use the established graphs when we work with some of Wysiwyg's graph-related commands in Chapters 29 and 30.

Having completed this chapter, you:

- *Have considerable experience with 1-2-3's graph-related commands*

- *Are familiar with three popular graph types*

- *Know how to establish several Graph ranges in a single operation*

- *Can clarify your graphs by adding titles and legends*

- *Are aware the GRAPH key can activate the most currently viewed graph*

- *Know how to preserve a graph's settings and establish several graphs in a single worksheet*

29

Add a Graph to the Spreadsheet

Y ou probably noticed as you worked through Chapters 27 and 28 that when a graph appeared on the display the spreadsheet vanished. Then, to return to the spreadsheet, you had to press a key to clear away the graph. This behavior of graphs and spreadsheets is, in part, residue from the early days of spreadsheet computing. 1-2-3's original design let you use two monitors at once—one whole monitor to display the spreadsheet and text and a second to display graphs. In lieu of two monitors, users settled for flipping back and forth between the sheet and graph.

One of the by-products of the old approach to graphs is that you could print either the spreadsheet or a graph, but you couldn't print one along with the other. Nowadays, you can place graphs directly into the spreadsheet so that they appear side by side with the data that they represent. You can do this in 1-2-3 thanks to the Wysiwyg add-in. Then, when you print the spreadsheet, the graph prints right along with the data, as if the graph were simply another cell entry.

Graphs in the Sheet

If a picture helps you convey your point, then it's crucial for you to include graphs among the numbers and labels in your printouts. That's the whole point behind spreadsheet publishing: It lets you create presentation quality printouts directly from the spreadsheet. Let's work a bit in the PGRAPH sheet and see how to create a finished report.

In this chapter, you'll:

- *Place a graph in the sheet alongside spreadsheet data*

- *Discover the effect on a graph of altering data in the spreadsheet*

- *Learn to insert rows in a spreadsheet*

- *Enter text using Wysiwyg's rudimentary word processor*

	Jan	Feb	Mar	Totals	%
Helmets	252	294	270	816	12%
Carbide lamps	1,128	984	1,272	3384	50%
Knee pads	408	564	396	1368	20%
Cave packs	357	448	371	1176	17%
Totals	$2,145	$2,290	$2,309	$6,744	

1st Quarter Sales
Jan — Mar, 1992

FIGURE 29.1: Retrieve the practice worksheet that you last modified and saved in Chapter 29.

Retrieve the Practice File

Retrieve the file named PGRAPH that you first created in Chapter 27 and later modified and saved in Chapter 29. That worksheet shows three months of sales revenue generated by four products handled by a small mail-order company. If you haven't created that file, please jump back to Chapter 27 and work your way up to this point. The practice worksheet should match the

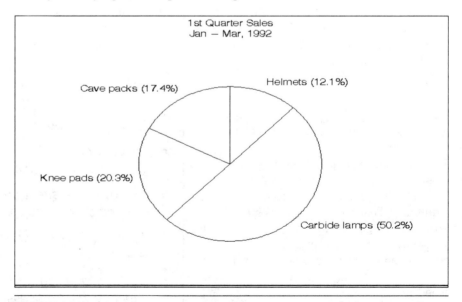

FIGURE 29.2: The graph named *pie* reveals what percent of revenues each product generated in a three-month period.

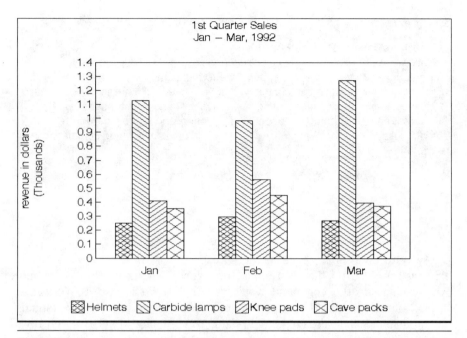

FIGURE 29.3: The graph named *bar* shows the monthly revenue generated by each of four products.

one shown in Figure 29.1, and it should have two graphs created from it named *pie* and *bar*.

By way of review, make sure the two graphs exist after you retrieve the worksheet. First select /Graph Name Use, and enter *pie*. The graph shown in Figure 29.2 should appear. Press a key and select Name Use a second time. This time enter *bar* to produce the graph shown in Figure 29.3. If one or the other of the graphs is absent, press Escape to return to READY mode and then jump back to Chapter 28 for instructions on creating the graphs.

Make Way for a Graph

A graph that you insert into the spreadsheet can be of any size. You're going to squeeze a graph in between the spreadsheet's title and the data that now resides in range A5..F10. Don't worry. You won't be doing it by scrunching the graph into a tiny space. Rather, open up a gap in the spreadsheet to make way for the graph insertion.

Inserting Doesn't Disrupt Formulas
Notice that after you insert seven rows in the sheet the values of the formulas in the boxed range haven't changed. The formulas themselves have changed to reflect their new positions in the worksheet—they still refer to the data that moved along with them. Inserting rows and columns in the sheet can have different effects on formulas depending on where the formulas are in relation to the inserted space. We examine the row and column insertion commands in depth in Part VI.

Make a Gap?

One way to open up a space in the spreadsheet is to insert rows between existing rows. To do that you apply the /Worksheet Insert Row command. When you issue the command, you'll see that there is also a /Worksheet Insert Column command that you might guess lets you insert new columns among columns that already contain data. You're going to insert seven rows into the spreadsheet.

Start with the cell pointer in row 5 and select /Worksheet Insert Row. Indicate a seven-cell range within whatever column holds the cell pointer. You can do this by pressing DownArrow six times. Then press Enter. The spreadsheet data move downward in the sheet, leaving room to insert a graph.

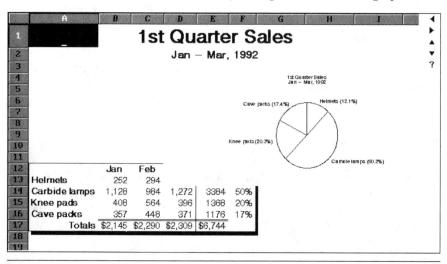

FIGURE 29.4: The newly inserted graph fills a range that extends beyond the right edge of the display and overlaps with some spreadsheet data.

Insert the Pie Chart

There's really not much room for a graph in the space we created, but we'll use a little trick to squeeze in the pie chart. Select :Graph Add Named and select the name *pie* from the resulting menu of graph names. 1-2-3 asks you to identify the range to hold the graph. Indicate range D4..J13. Yes, the range extends beyond the edge of the visible worksheet and overlaps the spreadsheet data. But you'll see in a minute that these things are OK. The resulting worksheet should match the one in Figure 29.4.

You can read the text of the graph if you squint, so the only real problem is that it blocks out some data. Change that in a jiffy by making the graph transparent. Right now the graph's display range is opaque. Select :Graph Settings Opaque No and either indicate any cell within the graph range or enter the graph's name, *pie*. In either case, the data reappear from under the graph as shown in Figure 29.5.

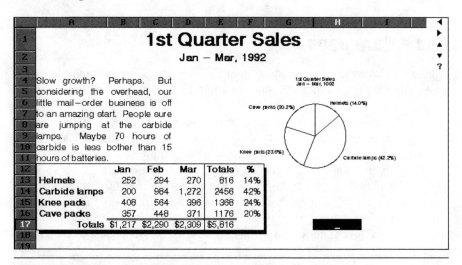

FIGURE 29.5: A translucent graph reveals the cell entries that reside in the sheet behind it.

The Graph Is Alive

The graph that you just added to the sheet is "alive." That means that while it reflects the current values in the spreadsheet, it will change automatically to reflect any alterations you make to those values. Try it and see how it works.

Enter the value *200* in place of the current entry in cell B14. This dramatically reduces the percentage of carbide lamps sold in proportion to other items. Both the formulas and the graph immediately reflect the altered value.

Spreadsheet Word Processing

Here's a little bonus that comes with a spreadsheet publishing add-in. Wysiwyg contains a rudimentary word processor. You invoke the word processor by issuing commands from the Wysiwyg menus, and then you work as you would in the typical stand-alone package. Wysiwyg automatically wraps text as you fill each line. It even lets you move an edit cursor around in the text range to fix mistakes that you make while you're typing.

Add a Paragraph

A lesson in word processing alone could fill a book. We're not going that far. Just follow along so you get a sense of what it's like to do word processing in the spreadsheet.

Start by selecting :Text Edit and indicating range A4..E11. The image of the graph goes blank, and a vertical bar cursor appears against the left border of the spreadsheet in cell A4. You're word processing.

To get a feel for it, type the following paragraph exactly as it appears. Don't press Enter as you type—1-2-3 will make the text fit automatically. If you make a mistake, simply press the Backspace key to erase it and then continue typing. If you see a mistake that you made several words or lines earlier, use the arrow keys to move the cursor back. Use the Backspace or the Delete

Spreadsheet Publishing Overkill

Beware the allure of a spreadsheet publisher. Before there were spreadsheet publishers, spreadsheet printouts were all very similar. With a spreadsheet publisher, you can add so many pyrotechnics to a worksheet that the data gets lost. Our little practice worksheet already looks busy, and we've hardly strained Wysiwyg's capabilities.

The message is, be judicious in your use of special effects. You want your pages to grab a reader's attention and get a point across clearly with minimal effort on the reader's part. If the page is too grey—all text and no figures — a reader may yawn and pass it up. However, if the page is too busy, it might also scare people away.

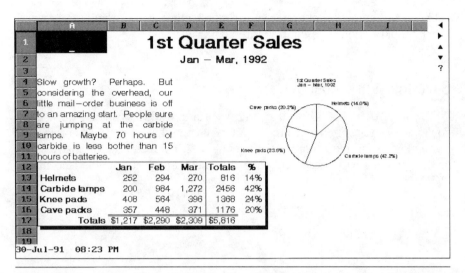

FIGURE 29.6: The practice worksheet with a pie chart and some text added is starting to look like a finished report—albeit a bit busy.

key to erase mistakes as you would in 1-2-3's EDIT mode—and retype them as usual. Then, use the Arrow keys to return to where you left off. When you've typed the entire paragraph, press the Escape key to end the word processing session. Here's the paragraph to type:

> Slow growth? Perhaps. But considering the overhead, our little mail-order business is off to an amazing start. People sure are jumping at the carbide lamps. Maybe 70 hours of carbide is less bother than 15 hours of batteries.

You might have noticed as you typed that Wysiwyg let the text extend only to column D. Remember that column D is the first column of the inserted graph. The Wysiwyg word processor automatically keeps your text ranges from overlapping with established graph ranges. When you finished typing and pressed Escape, the graph reappeared in the sheet.

Text with Square Corners: Even Justification

One more quick detail to tidy up the report. Realign the text that you just entered so it has straight edges. To do this, select :Text Align Even and indicate range A4..D11. Wysiwyg uses proportional spacing to make the text fit between the spreadsheet frame and the left edge of the graph. Your worksheet should match the one in Figure 29.6.

Save the Worksheet

We promise that this is the last time we'll ask you to save this worksheet. You've made a lot of changes to it, and we'll come back to it in Chapter 30. If those changes aren't in place, you may be a bit confused by the instructions in that chapter. Go ahead and save the sheet under its original file name, PGRAPH.

Having completed this chapter, you:

- *Know how to insert blank rows into the spreadsheet*

- *Can insert named graphs into the sheet*

- *Understand how to make a graph reveal what lies under it in the worksheet*

- *Are aware of how 1-2-3 updates a graph in the sheet when you change values on which the graph is based*

- *Know how to perform rudimentary word processing in the spreadsheet*

- *Are capable of creating fairly complete reports*

30

Spruce up a Graph in the Sheet

Once you've told 1-2-3 to create a graph, and you've added titles and legends to clarify the graph's meaning, you still might not be satisfied with the presentation. The graph might contain particularly interesting data that you wish to highlight, or there might be some message that you want to superimpose on the image to add to a reader's understanding.

Wysiwyg's graph editing tools let you fine-tune a graphic image. With Wysiwyg, you can add lines and arrows to a graph image, draw boxes and circles, superimpose text, and even create freehand drawings. The items that you add to a graph are resizable, rotatable, and otherwise rearrangeable, meaning that even after you place them in a graph, you can fiddle as needed to create the perfect presentation.

Wysiwyg's Graph Editor

A graph editor is a software program that helps you create graphical images. You might be familiar with a paint program of the type that became popular shortly after the Macintosh computer hit the market— those programs are graph editors. Wysiwyg has its own built-in graph editing utility.

When you activate the graph editor, a selected graph expands to fill the display, and a special menu of editing tools appears. Working in the graph editor can feel as though you've detached from 1-2-3 and

---

In this chapter, you'll:

- *Learn how to spruce up a graph in the spreadsheet*

- *Gain an understanding of graphical "objects"*

- *Apply some of Wysiwyg's graph editing tools to modify a graph*

- *Add an oval, some text, and arrows to highlight bars in a graph*

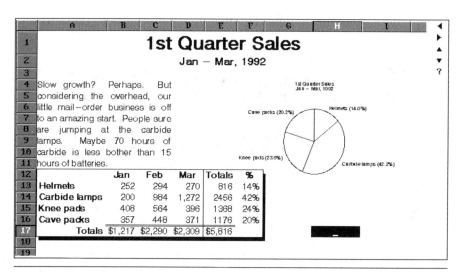

FIGURE 30.1: The file named PGRAPH holds a slick-looking worksheet that you'll use as you explore the Wysiwyg graph editor.

somehow headed off into another realm of computing. Still, the techniques you apply in the editor aren't tricky and can be applied to almost any graph editor you'll ever encounter.

Retrieve the Practice Worksheet

You might be getting sick of this instruction, but please retrieve the worksheet named PGRAPH that you created in Chapter 27 and modified in Chapters 28 and 29. If you haven't created and updated the worksheet, please skip back to Chapter 27 and work forward to this point before you tackle this material.

The PGRAPH worksheet contains a title, a range of text, a highlighted range of data and calculations, and the image of a pie chart as shown in Figure 30.1. The worksheet also contains settings for a bar chart—you're going to use the bar chart as you explore the graphics editor. If your worksheet doesn't match ours, again, please work through the preceding chapters in this section until you've caught up with us.

Place the Graph in the Sheet

Before you can use the graph editor to dress up an image, you must add the image to the spreadsheet. You're going to dress up the bar graph that you created in Chapter 28, so start by placing it in the sheet below the high-lighted range of data and formulas.

Remember, to place a named graph in the sheet, select :Graph Add Named, select the graph name from the menu—in this case, select *bar*—and then indicate the range to hold the graph. Indicate range B20..H31 for this graph. Fiddle with the arrow keys a bit until you've adjusted your display to match the one shown in Figure 30.2. While you're at it, check out the legend across the bottom of the graph image—as you can see from the illustration, something about the legend is obviously wrong. The *Interesting Consequences of Row Insertions* box explains what's wrong and how to fix it.

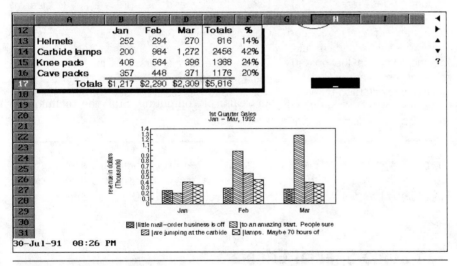

FIGURE 30.2: After you insert the bar chart, move the cell pointer around until your display matches this. Notice that the graph's legend is decidedly screwed up.

Activate the Graph Editor

Be prepared for a change of pace. To modify the bar chart that you've just added to the sheet, you first activate Wysiwyg's graph editor. When you do this, the worksheet will fall away, and the graph will expand so you can more easily see what you're doing as you work with the editing tools. Activate the

---

Interesting Consequences of Row Insertions

As you'll learn in Part VI, inserting rows and columns prudently in the sheet doesn't usually disturb range settings. In fact, consider that after you inserted rows and moved your revenue data down in the spreadsheet, 1-2-3 still knew how to draw the pie and bar charts whose settings you had established earlier. Still, somehow inserting rows threw the graph legends out of kilter.

Most of the ranges that you establish as settings—such as database Input and Criteria ranges, or Graph data ranges—are "live" references just like cell references. In other words, 1-2-3 keeps track of the referenced ranges as long as you follow certain rules when you change the layout of the spreadsheet (we'll examine those rules in Part VI). Any graph settings that you establish by entering a backslash followed by a cell reference are not live (the /Graph Options Legend

Range command enters references in this way). Rather, they refer absolutely to the original cells no matter how you alter the sheet.

When you followed instructions in Chapter 29 to insert rows, you moved the cells that contain the graph legend right out from under the recorded settings. The graph legends settings continue to refer to cells A6, A7, A8, and A9 even though the appropriate labels are now in range A13..A16. Reestablish the appropriate legends as follows: Select /Graph Name Use, enter *bar,* and then press a key to clear the resulting graph from the display. Select Options Legend Range and indicate range A13..A16. Select Quit and then select Name Create. Enter *bar* to preserve the new graph settings under the old name and then select Quit to return to ready mode. You've restored the proper legend.

Mouse users can activate the graph editor by double-clicking anywhere within a graph in the spreadsheet—there's no need to use the Wysiwyg menu.

. . . .
. . . .
. . . .

graph editor by selecting :Graph Edit and entering the graph's name, *bar.* Your display will be similar to the one shown in Figure 30.3—the graph's exact layout varies depending on which release of 1-2-3 you're using.

Add Some Special Effects

You're going to place an oval in the graph. Then you'll add three arrows, each pointing from the oval to one of the bars that represents sales of carbide lamps. Finally, you'll enter the word *Phenomenal* inside the oval. Start by adding the oval.

To add an object to the graph, select Add from the menu. There's quite a list of objects that you can add; select Ellipse. Now check out Figure 30.4 and its accompanying text to get an idea of what's going on the display. If you're a mouse user, also read the *Use the Mouse to Place Objects* box. Then continue with this text.

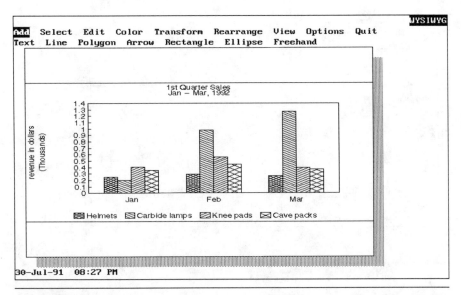

FIGURE 30.3: When the graph appears in the graph editor, you'll notice that the editor's menu is active and awaiting your instructions.

Maneuver the cross hairs that appear somewhere on your display so that they fall at coordinates x=890 and y=751. If you're using the keyboard, press Enter and then use the Arrow keys to expand a highlight over to coordinates x=2,044 and y=1,273. If you're using a mouse, drag from x=890 and y=751 to x=2,044 and y=1,273. In either case, an oval appears in the graphic.

Use the Mouse to Place Objects

The mouse is in its element when you're working in a graphics editor. You can point and click with the mouse to indicate where you want to place objects, and typically you need only drag from one point to another to determine an object's size. Once you've established a graphic object, you can reselect it with a mouse by clicking the object directly within the graph. This will make a bit more sense as you proceed with the chapter.

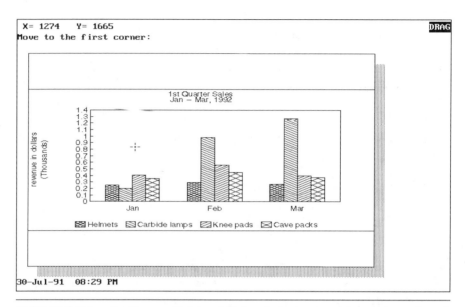

FIGURE 30.4: While you're adding a graphical element, Wysiwyg displays large cross hairs somewhere on the graph image. In this figure, the cross hairs are just above the third bar in the graph. The coordinates in the top left of the display tell you the cross hairs' offset from the top left corner of the graphic. Our cross hairs are at the x coordinate 1,274 and the y coordinate 1,665. Use the Arrow keys or a mouse to move the cross hairs as you determine the placement of a graphical object.

Add Text to the Graphic

To place the word *Phenomenal* inside the oval, you must add the word to the graphic. Select Add Text. The graph editor prompts you to enter the text that you wish to add. Enter *Phenomenal.* The word appears in about the middle of the graphic, complete with cross hairs embedded in it. Use Arrow

Get a Grip on an Object
When the ellipse appears in your graphic, it has a tiny square on top, at the bottom, and at each end. These squares are "handles." Handles appear on any selected graph object. The significance of selecting an object is that commands that move objects, alter their sizes, delete them from the graphic, and so on, affect only currently selected objects. If you were to select Rearrange and then Delete from the graph editor's menus, the oval would vanish because it's the only currently selected object. We'll see how to select established objects in a moment.

keys or a mouse to center the word in the oval—press Enter or click with the mouse when you're satisfied with the placement. You'll notice that the handles vanish from the ellipse, and a new collection of handles appears around the text—the handles won't show in the finished graphic.

Add Some Arrows

By now you're getting the hang of this. Select Add Arrow. Wysiwyg prompts you to indicate a first point—that's the end of the arrow opposite the arrowhead. Select a point in about the center bottom of the ellipse—near coordinates x=1,403 and y=1,273. If you're using the keyboard, move the cross hairs there and press Enter. Then, move the cross hairs to the top of the highest bar in the January cluster and press Enter again. If you're using a mouse, click at the first point, move the cross hairs to the top of the highest bar in the January cluster, and then double-click.

Use the same technique—that is, select Add Arrow and draw arrows from somewhere on the ellipse to each of the highest bars in the clusters—to add two more arrows so that your graphic is similar to the one shown in Figure 30.5.

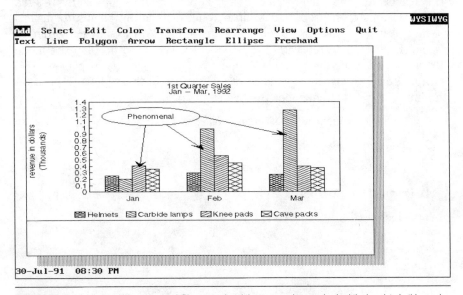

FIGURE 30.5: Adding an ellipse, the word *Phenomenal,* and three arrows has emphasized the key data in this graph.

Select and Modify an Object

Try one last task before you finish your graph editing adventure: Make the word *Phenomenal* stand out a bit more. To do this, change the font in which Wysiwyg renders the word.

Start by selecting the text object. Mouse users can simply click anywhere in the word *Phenomenal* to select the object—handles appear around it instantly. Keyboard users select objects by choosing the word Select from the menu and then One. Wysiwyg prompts you to point to the object you want to select. Move the cross hairs to the word *Phenomenal* inside the oval and press Enter—that's when the handles appear.

Change the selected object's font by choosing Edit Font. Font 2 is slightly larger than font 1, but small enough that the text will still fit inside the oval, so select 2. Choose Select None to clear the handles from the graphic. Then choose Quit to return to the spreadsheet.

That's It for Graphics

This has been a long chapter, and you've applied a lot of your software's features. Obviously, the report is a little rough—it hardly begins to make a point. But it would be hard to consider any more effort as staying within the realm of "getting started with 1-2-3." You're welcome to develop the model further if you want the practice—remember to save it if you plan to work with it later. The logical conclusion of an exercise of this type is to print out the finished report. Remember the five steps for printing:

1. Make sure your printer is on and ready.

2. Align the paper in the printer.

3. Tell 1-2-3 what range to print.

4. Preview the printout.

5. Select Go.

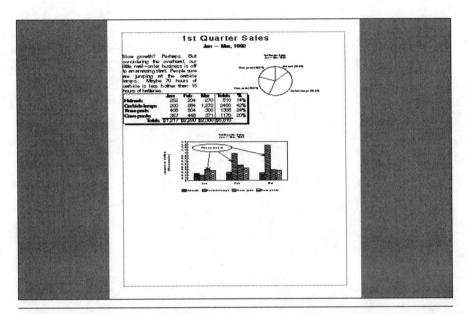

FIGURE 30.6: Wysiwyg's :Print Preview command reveals on screen how your printed page will look.

If you want to try it, select :Print Range Set and indicate range A1..I32 as the print range. Select Preview from the print menu—your preview screen should look something like the one in Figure 30.6. Press any key to clear the preview display when you're satisfied. If you want to waste the paper, select Go to send a copy of the print range to your printer.

Having completed this chapter, you:

- *Are aware that inserting rows and columns can have undesired results*

- *Have a basic understanding of Wysiwyg's graph editor*

- *Are familiar with the graphics cross hairs cursor*

- *Know how to add objects to a graph*

- *Can recognize the handles that identify selected objects*

Part VI
On the Way to Mastery

There's a lot to learn about spreadsheet computing. You're off to a good start. Having completed Part V, you're capable of producing slick reports based on fairly complex calculations. Oh, yes, we skipped a lot of material—you should continue your exploration of 1-2-3 by fiddling more on your own, by digging around in the on-line Help facility, and by reading other books and periodicals about computing.

Before you leave this book, there are a few key concepts that you should carry with you into your further adventures. Most important is to develop some sense of how to modify a spreadsheet's structure after you've already created a model, or part of a model. You learned in Part V that you can insert rows and columns in a spreadsheet to make way for more data. However, if you're going to use such a technique you should understand its possible ramifications.

While 1-2-3 lets you insert rows and columns, it also lets you delete them. The idea is simple enough, but deleting a column can lead to some serious problems if you don't do it correctly.

The rules that apply to inserting and deleting rows and columns apply similarly to moving cells and ranges of data. That's right, it's possible to rip a cell or a range out of the spreadsheet and drop it back in at a new location. Again, the rules that apply to this procedure can be confusing, but understanding them is important to any serious spreadsheet user.

This final part of the book deals with such concepts as moving spreadsheet data and inserting and deleting columns and rows. While we're at it, we'll explore a few commands that you can use to get around quickly in large spreadsheets. Finally, we'll take a cursory look at spreadsheet macros—a special feature of 1-2-3 that lets you automate some of the tasks that you perform repeatedly.

Move It!

Rearranging a spreadsheet. It sounds simple enough—and it is simple. You select /Move, indicate the cell or range to move, and then indicate the top left corner cell of the destination range. You'll find reasons to move data repeatedly during a session with 1-2-3. Should the headers be in row 1 where you entered them or in row 5? Could you fit some more information in a table if you moved its last column of data to the right? Wouldn't the latest label you entered make more sense if it were one cell higher in the sheet?

As simple as all of this is, you can get into trouble when you move things in the spreadsheet. You must be cautious. When you understand the effects of moving data, you'll be able to avoid the pitfalls and emerge from each move with your spreadsheet models intact.

A Moving Experience

The easiest way to develop an understanding of the /Move command is to put it to use. This chapter presents a series of simple exercises that you can perform to illustrate the rules of moving cells and ranges.

Tear the Spreadsheet Fabric

When you copy a single cell, the /Copy command records an image of the cell's contents and recreates the image in a second cell—leaving both cells in place. In contrast, the /Move command rips a cell out

In this chapter, you'll:

- *Learn how to move data in the spreadsheet*

- *Explore the differences between the /Move and the /Copy commands*

- *Discover some pitfalls that can arise when you move cells and ranges*

- *Learn how to protect against making serious errors*

of the spreadsheet and drops it at the destination. The hole created by ripping out a cell heals over immediately with a new, blank cell. But whatever cell was at the target destination before you issued the /Move command gets obliterated.

Do a quick experiment to see the /Move command in action. Enter your name into cell A1. Then select /Move, indicate cell A1 as the range to move, and indicate cell A2 as the destination range. 1-2-3 rips the cell from its location at A1 and drops it back at cell A2. As you'd expect, the moved cell assumes its new address, but subtle things take place that this little experiment failed to reveal. Try a different experiment.

The Effect on Cell References

This matter of ripping cells out and dropping them back has its greatest effect on cell and range references. When you move a cell, 1-2-3 tries to keep track of any formulaic references or worksheet settings that involve the cell. To better understand what this means, enter the formula $+B1*2$ into cell A1 and enter the value 8 into cell B1.

After entering the formula and the value, select /Move, indicate cell A1 as the range to move, and indicate cell A3 as the target. The moved formula continues to refer to cell B1! 1-2-3 assumes that you want to preserve the

---

Undo Can Guard You

How would you like to guard against mistakes that you make with the /Move command? You can if you want, by activating 1-2-3's Undo capability. It's best to be in a blank worksheet when you activate Undo. Then select, /Worksheet Global Default Other Undo Enable. If you want Undo to be active during all future work sessions, select Update from the resulting menu. If you'll be using Undo only from time to time, activate it at the beginning of a work session.

With Undo active, you can instantly reverse the effects of whatever you've done since 1-2-3 was last in READY mode. For example, the spreadsheet starts in READY mode when you move a range and ends up there afterward. Here's how to undo a /Move command: While holding down the key marked Alt, press function key F4. Select Yes from the resulting menu. If you had damaged any formulas or trashed some data in the move, pressing Alt-F4 restores the damaged formulas or data.

You may not always be able to use Undo. Especially in Release 2.3, the Undo facility eats up a lot of RAM. This can seriously limit the size of a spreadsheet—particularly when you're working with the Wysiwyg add-in attached as we recommended near the beginning of this book. You'll have to experiment in your own spreadsheets to discover when you can and cannot use Undo.

integrity of the relationships that your formulas describe—even when you dramatically alter the locations of the formulas and the data cells.

Formulaic Integrity Goes Both Ways

You just moved a formula away from the cell it references, and the reference remained intact. Likewise, you can move referenced cells around, and formulas that you don't move won't lose track of the data to which they refer. Try it.

Select /Move, indicate cell B1 as the range to move and indicate cell C1 as the destination. The result of the formula in cell A3 doesn't change. If you check it out, you'll find that it reads +C1*2.

Don't Destroy Key Cells

The dangers of the /Move command arise from the way it destroys cells at a target location. When you copy information into a cell referenced by a formula, the formula uses the new information to determine its result. If you drop a moved cell or range onto a cell referenced in a formula, you invalidate the formula—the reference to the obliterated cell becomes ERR.

Don't move cells or ranges onto values referenced by formulas.

An Experimental Obliteration

Here's an experiment to contrast the effects of copying and moving cells onto referenced cells. Enter the value *4* into cell C2. Now copy the value from C2 to cell C1. The value of the formula in cell A3 immediately changes to reflect the new entry in cell C1—the referenced cell remain intact, only its contents change.

Enter the value *8* into cell C2 and then move cell C2 onto cell C1. The formula in cell A3 returns ERR. After the move operation, the original cell C1 no longer exists; the formula recognizes the change and alerts you to it. Scoot on over to cell A3, and you'll see that ERR has replaced the original cell reference within the formula. It now reads +*ERR*2*. If you really mean it to read +C1*2, you must recreate the formula.

A Range Moving Model

The /Move command can have its most bizarre effects when you apply it to moving worksheet ranges. Set up a scenario to see how this works.

Start by erasing the worksheet (/Worksheet Erase Yes Yes). Then, enter values as shown in Figure 31.1.

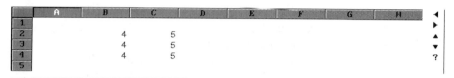

FIGURE 31.1: Use these values in formulas to see the effects of moving spreadsheet ranges.

Enter the formula @SUM(B2..B4) into cell B5 and copy it to cell C5. Each of the formulas refers to a range of cells.

Predict the Move Effects

The first test is to move both of the formulas down two rows. Guess the outcome of moving range B5..C5 to cell B7 and then move it by selecting /Move, indicating range B5..C5 as the source range and cell B7 as the destination. The formulas continue to refer to ranges B2..B4 and C2..C4, respectively.

Here's a trickier move: What will happen if you move cell B4 onto cell B6? Think about it. Remember that 1-2-3 thinks of a range in terms of its top left corner cell and its bottom right cell. Cell B4 is the bottom right cell in range B2..B4—the range referenced by the formula in B7. Move the cell and see what happens: Select /Move, indicate B4 as the source cell and indicate B6 as the target.

Move Affects Settings as Well
Everything we say in the main text about moving cells involved in formulaic references applies as well to cells used in worksheet settings. For example, suppose that you've established a database Input range as A1..D10. If you move a range that includes cell D10, you'll alter the dimensions of the range recorded under the /Data Query Input setting. Likewise, dropping a cell or a range on the top left or bottom right corner of the Input range would invalidate its setting—1-2-3 would no longer know what to use as the Input range.

The value of the formula in B7 doesn't change, but move the cell pointer to B7 and check out the formula's range reference. It now reads @SUM(B2..B6). Moving the corner cell of the range transformed the formulaic reference to the range. The new formula is perfectly valid—it simply references two more cells than before. Prove it by entering 4 into cell B4 and again into cell B5. The formula's result reflects the additions.

Destroy a Range Reference

Just as the /Move command can destroy a formulaic reference to a single cell, so can it wipe out an entire range reference. It's interesting, however, that you can wipe out cells within a range as long as you don't wipe out the range's all-important corner cells.

To see how this works, move cell B3 to cell C3. This leaves a blank where the original B3 started out and places the value 4 into the range summed by the formula in cell C5. That formula's result reflects the change—the formula continues to refer to range C2..C4. What do you figure will happen when you move cell B4 onto cell C4? Try it and see. As you should expect, the formula in C5 suddenly returns ERR because you trashed the range it referenced.

Use /Move, but Use It Cautiously

The message in all of this isn't, "Don't use the /Move command." On the contrary, you should capitalize on it. The ability to rearrange a spreadsheet so easily lets you create and recreate a model until it perfectly meets your needs. The message, then, is be careful when you use the /Move command. Make sure when you move a large range, that there is room for the range to fit at its target destination. Since you need to indicate only the top left corner of the destination, you might not notice data below and to the right that will be obliterated by a large incoming range.

Having completed this chapter, you:

- *Understand the difference between the /Copy and the /Move command*

- *Are aware of the destructive aspect of moving cells and ranges*

- *Know how moving cells can affect range references in formulas and worksheet settings*

- *Can activate the Undo feature to protect against blundering*

- *Are prepared to explore the /Worksheet Insert and /Worksheet Delete commands*

Make Way for Data-lings

This chapter shouldn't keep you tied up for long. You already learned about inserting rows and columns when you worked through Part V. There, you created a small sales revenue model and then used the /Worksheet Insert Rows command to make room in the sheet for some text and a graph. That's what inserting rows and columns is about: Opening up space between existing entries to accommodate further entries.

The problems you need to watch for when you insert and delete rows and columns are quite similar to the ones that can arise when you move data. If you understand what we covered in Chapter 31, then this chapter will be a walk in the park.

Try Some Insertions

You'll most easily understand how to insert and delete rows if you do it a few times. However, inserting or deleting rows in a blank worksheet isn't very meaningful. It's only after there's data in the sheet that fiddling with the rows and columns begins to matter.

A Crack in the Sheet

If moving a cell or a range tears a piece out of the spreadsheet, then inserting rows or columns rips the spreadsheet from end to

> *In this chapter, you'll:*
>
> - *Review how to insert rows and columns in the spreadsheet and make room for added data*
>
> - *Learn how to delete rows and columns from the sheet*
>
> - *Discover the similarities between the /Worksheet Insert commands and the /Move command*

end. Create a simple spreadsheet to match the one in Figure 32.1, and we'll use it to illustrate the effects of cracking apart the spreadsheet.

FIGURE 32.1: Enter numbers in an otherwise blank worksheet so you can use them to illustrate the effects of inserting rows and columns.

After you enter the numbers, enter $@SUM(B2..B4)$ into cell B5 and copy the formula to cell C5. Now make some guesses as to how the /Worksheet Insert Row command will affect your entries.

A Few Puzzlers

Suppose that you insert a row at row 2 in the sheet? Remember, inserting a rows displaces everything at and below the topmost row of the insertion range. To see how this works, insert two rows at row 2. Select /Worksheet Insert Row and indicate any range that spans rows 2 and 3. B2..B3 will do nicely. 1-2-3 moves all of the data and formulas down.

What if you insert a single row at the new row 7? That's the row that now contains formulas. The insert would move the formulas down in the sheet, but would it change the formulaic references? Inserting at row 7 would be equivalent to using the /Move command to modify the sheet. The formulas would continue to refer to the values in range B4..C6. Try it. Select /Worksheet Insert Row and indicate cell B7. Then check out the formulas to confirm the results of the insertion.

Finally, what if you insert rows in the middle of the data ranges to which the summary formulas refer? The range references within the formulas will "stretch" to include the newly inserted rows. Try it. Select /Worksheet Insert Row and indicate range B5..B6 as the insertion range. The formulas end up in row 10. The one in B10 ends up referring to range B4..B8, and the one in C9 refers to C4..C8.

Actually, the risk involved in inserting rows is small. It has the effect of making space without destroying existing cells. But keep in mind that inserting rows displaces everything in the spreadsheet downward—across the entire width of the sheet. Herein lies the danger. When you insert rows, you can disrupt tables, databases, or reports that the rows intercept off to one side or the other of the visible sheet.

An inserted row or column runs the entire length or depth of the spreadsheet.

About Inserting Columns

All the rules that apply to inserting rows apply as well to inserting columns—only transposed 90 degrees. To insert columns, select /Worksheet Insert Column and indicate a range that spans as many columns as you want to insert. 1-2-3 makes the insertion at the leftmost column of the insertion range.

Close the Cracks

If you want danger, then delete rows or columns from a spreadsheet. Deleting a row removes it, all of its data, and any references to the row from the spreadsheet. When you delete a row, you destroy it completely, with all the effects you get from moving one range onto another.

For example, suppose there's a formula in cell A1 that reads +A2*8. If you delete row 2, the formula becomes invalid—row 2 no longer exists in the spreadsheet. Try deleting a few rows in your practice sheet.

First, select /Worksheet Delete Row and indicate range B5..B6. As you might expect, the worksheet closes up—the formulas in row 10 move up to row 8, and their range references "shrink" to include only rows 4, 5, and 6. That was a safe bet. Now try deleting row 4—that row is critical to the formulaic references in cells B8 and C8. Select /Worksheet Delete Row and indicate cell B4. As you must expect by now, the formulas return ERR.

And Column Deletions?

What can we say? The rules for deleting columns are the same as the rules for deleting rows—flipped 90 degrees.

On Your Own

We promised up front that inserting and deleting rows and columns isn't very tricky. The important caution is to be aware of your spreadsheet's layout when you apply any of these commands. While inserting rows or columns won't destroy data, doing so may disrupt tables or databases off to the sides of the currently visible worksheet area.

On the other hand, deleting columns and rows literally rips them out of the spreadsheet. Any data in those rows or columns vanishes forever. Likewise, formulaic references to deleted rows or columns and worksheet settings that include them, can evaporate in a flash. Be cautious of how you apply these commands.

Having completed this chapter, you:

- *Know how to insert and delete spreadsheet rows and columns*

- *Are aware of the dangers of making insertions and deletions*

- *Have a fairly complete understanding of methods for reorganizing spreadsheet models*

Shrink the Sheet

I f you use 1-2-3 a lot in your job, then you've probably built at least one fairly large spreadsheet. Large spreadsheets mean effort. Effort to get from one part of the model to another, effort to create formulas whose referenced cells are at opposite ends of the sheet, effort to know what the bottom line shows while you're changing variables near the top.

A lot of the effort you expend in a large spreadsheet goes to a lack of familiarity with all the tools available to you. For example, when you use the End key in conjunction with the Arrow keys, you can reduce 5, 10, and even 100 keystrokes to 2. The GOTO key can send the cell pointer directly to any cell or named range in the worksheet. If that's not enough, the /Worksheet Window commands let you divide the display into two views of the spreadsheet so you can look at both the top row and the bottom line at one time.

Keys to Efficiency

There are hundreds of ways to increase your efficiency with the spreadsheet. Trying to cover all of them would go way beyond the scope of this book. Still, you shouldn't finish your introduction to 1-2-3 without learning a few of the dynamite shortcuts. One technique that can save you hours over the course of a month is especially helpful to people who use the cursor control keys to navigate in the sheet.

In this chapter, you'll:

- *Discover techniques that help you to work efficiently in large models*
- *Apply the End key to jump from place to place*
- *Use the GOTO key to get to a cell or range in a hurry*
- *Learn how to split the display into two or more windows on the sheet*
- *Control spreadsheet recalculation*

The End Key

When you press RightArrow, the cell pointer moves one cell to the right. Quite often you want to move the pointer several cells—perhaps to the end of a row of data or to the first data cell in a row. Using the End key can get you there in a jiffy.

To see how the End key works, start by entering the label *Test* into cell C1. Use the /Copy command to replicate the label in each cell of range C1..E6 and again in each cell of range C10..E14. When you've finished copying labels, your spreadsheet should match the one in Figure 33.1.

Copy a Cell onto Itself
Here's a handy shortcut. Sometimes you need to enter a value, a label, or a formula and copy it to every cell in a range—for example, when you follow the instructions in the main text of this chapter. Making the entry in a cell within the target range can save a few keystrokes. For example, to enter the label *Test* in every cell of range C1..E6, enter the label first into cell C1. Then select /Copy, indicate C1 as the cell to copy, and indicate range C1..E6 as the destination range. Copying a cell onto itself always recreates the cell's contents exactly.

	A	B	C	D	E	F	G	H	
1			Test	Test	Test				◀
2			Test	Test	Test				▶
3			Test	Test	Test				▲
4			Test	Test	Test				▼
5			Test	Test	Test				?
6			Test	Test	Test				
7									
8									
9									
10			Test	Test	Test				
11			Test	Test	Test				
12			Test	Test	Test				
13			Test	Test	Test				
14			Test	Test	Test				
15									

FIGURE 33.1: Set up this array of entries so you can try out the End key.

Apply the End Key for Quick Hops

When you press End and then an Arrow key, the cell pointer slides across the spreadsheet very rapidly. If there are no cell entries to interfere, the cell pointer will slide all the way to the end of the sheet in whatever direction you've selected. Try it. Press Home so that the cell pointer starts in cell A1. Then press the End key. An indicator with the word *END* in it appears in the bottom right corner of the display.

With the END indicator on, press DownArrow. The cell pointer slides immediately to cell A8192. Press End and then RightArrow. The pointer slides to IV8192—the bottom right corner of the spreadsheet. Press End and then UpArrow to get to cell IV1 and, finally, press End LeftArrow.

Details about the End Key

You've almost circumnavigated the spreadsheet—but the data in range C1..E6 got in the way. You see, when the cell pointer is in a blank cell, pressing End and then an Arrow key slides the pointer to the first data cell in the direction the Arrow key points. Press End and then LeftArrow a second time. Now the cell pointer stops in cell C1. This is one of two behaviors the pointer will exhibit when it starts in a data cell and you press End followed by an Arrow key.

If there are entries in cells contiguous to the starting data cell, the pointer slides to the last data cell in the sequence. If there are no contiguous entries in the direction of the selected Arrow key, the cell pointer slides until it meets an obstruction—either another data cell or the end of the spreadsheet.

Press End DownArrow to move the pointer to cell C6. Press End Down-Arrow again to move the pointer to cell C10. Fiddle a bit more with the End and Arrow keys until you're clear about their effects on the cell pointer. You can see that pressing End DownArrow could send the pointer from the top of a column of 3,000 entries to its bottom instantaneously. That's a lot faster than using the DownArrow key alone.

Go Directly to It

No matter how large or small the spreadsheet, you sometimes know where you want the pointer to be but any sequence of Arrow key presses will take a while to get you there. If the pointer is in cell G79 and you want it to be in F22, then apply the GOTO key.

The GOTO key is function key F5. When you press it, 1-2-3 prompts you to identify the desired destination. Type a cell address, or a range name, and press Enter. Try it. Press function key F5 and enter *IV8192*. The pointer jumps directly to the bottom right corner of the sheet—and orients the sheet so that the destination cell is in the top left corner of the display. Don't be alarmed that there are no letters or numbers in the frame to the right and below the final cell. Press GOTO and enter *C10* to return to the labels you entered earlier.

Worksheet Windows Provide Alternative Viewpoints

When your spreadsheets get really big, it can be hard to keep track of the details of one section while working in another section. For example, you may be writing a summary formula in cell A795 that refers to several cells in row 90. You know vaguely which cells to include in the formula, but the whole process would be easier if you could see the cells while you're writing the formula. You can see the cells.

1-2-3 lets you divide the display into more than one window. If you think of your view through the worksheet frame as a window onto the sheet, then you can imagine splitting the display so that there are several windows each looking at its own selected area. Release 2.3 of 1-2-3 allows up to two windows at a time, and Release 3.1 allows up to three windows.

Create a Second Window

To split the display into two windows, start by positioning the cell pointer where you'd like the split to occur. For a vertical split, there must be at least one column visible on each side of the cell pointer. For a horizontal split, rows must be visible both above and below the pointer.

In your practice worksheet, press Home, and then press the RightArrow key four times so that the cell pointer is in column E. Now select /Worksheet Window Vertical. A second frame appears on the display, and the cell pointer ends up in cell D1 of the right-hand window. Your spreadsheet should match the one shown in Figure 33.2.

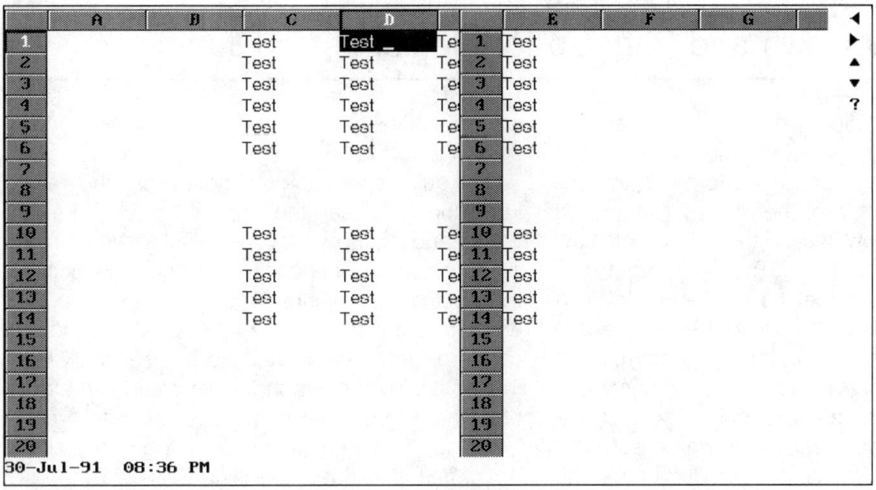

	A	B	C	D			E	F	G	
1			Test	Test _	Te	1	Test			◄
2			Test	Test	Te	2	Test			►
3			Test	Test	Te	3	Test			▲
4			Test	Test	Te	4	Test			▼
5			Test	Test	Te	5	Test			?
6			Test	Test	Te	6	Test			
7						7				
8						8				
9						9				
10			Test	Test	Te	10	Test			
11			Test	Test	Te	11	Test			
12			Test	Test	Te	12	Test			
13			Test	Test	Te	13	Test			
14			Test	Test	Te	14	Test			
15						15				
16						16				
17						17				
18						18				
19						19				
20						20				

30-Jul-91   08:36 PM

FIGURE 33.2: Split the display vertically to create two windows in the sheet.

Window Synchronization

At the moment, the windows are synchronized. This means that any vertical movement the cell pointer makes in one window causes a corresponding vertical movement in the other window. Try pressing the DownArrow key repeatedly until the spreadsheet begins to scroll in the left-hand window. The right-hand window scrolls as well.

You can override window synchronization if you want to be able to navigate within one window without changing your view in the other. To do this, select /Worksheet Window Unsynch. When two horizontal windows are synchronized, horizontal movement in one translates as well to horizontal movement in the other. You can experiment on your own to see how this works.

In the meantime, try an experiment to see how you can take advantage of having two views on the sheet. Start by disabling synchronized window scrolling. Select /Worksheet Window Unsynch. Now press the PageDown key four times (usually marked PgDn on the cursor control keypad.) This moves the cell pointer into the neighborhood of row 90. You'll enter a formula in cell A90, so find that cell and move the cell pointer to it.

PageDown and PageUp for Medium-sized Jumps

We've been holding out on you. There's a simple way to make short jumps within the spreadsheet. When you need to move the cell pointer from the top of the display to the cells near or just below the bottom of the display, press the PageDown key. Pressing PageDown jumps the spreadsheet up in the window exactly as many rows as are visible on the display at the moment. Because the cell pointer remains stationary in the window, a new cell moves in underneath the pointer—as if the pointer itself had jumped down a screen's worth of rows. Pressing PageUp jumps the worksheet down in the window in the same way, effectively moving the cell pointer up one screen's worth of rows.

For quick side-to-side jumps, press the Tab key—located near the top left of your keyboard and often marked by two Arrows pointing in opposite directions. Pressing Tab alone moves the cell pointer one screenful of columns to the right. Holding down the Shift key and pressing Tab moves the pointer back to the left. Holding down the key marked Ctrl and pressing RightArrow has the same effect as pressing Tab. Likewise, pressing Ctrl-Left-Arrow is equivalent to pressing Shift-Tab.

Use Windows to Build Formulas

The trick here is that you're going to build a formula that concatenates strings from several cells near the top of the spreadsheet. It's hard to remember which cells you're going to use, but with two windows, you can access both parts of the sheet at once.

Start by typing a plus sign (+) and then press the WINDOW key—that's function key F6. The cell pointer hops to the right-hand window, and the status indicator reveals that 1-2-3 is in POINT mode. Use the cursor keys to move the cell pointer to C1—the first of the cells to use in your formula. Type an ampersand (&) as the concatenation operator, and the cell pointer jumps back to the cell A90 in the left-hand window.

Pressing the WINDOW key (F6) while 1-2-3 is in READY mode with two windows opened moves the cell pointer from one window to the other.

Type " " (a quotation mark, a space, and a quotation mark), and then press the WINDOW key (F6) a second time. With the cell pointer in the right-hand window, point to cell D1, and press Enter to complete the formula in cell A90. The cell pointer finishes in cell A90 of the left-hand window.

Even if you prefer not to use POINT mode when you create formulas, your formula building can benefit from using two windows. You might simply divide the display, unsynchronize the windows, and then arrange one of the windows to reveal cells your formulas will reference. Then as you type the formulas, you can read the needed cell addresses from the frame of the second window.

Windows for Release 3.1 Users

The /Worksheet Window command in Release 3.1 leads to more options than it does in Release 2.3. For example, the /Worksheet Window Map command temporarily displays the worksheet as a map of codes that identify the types of entries and the ranges that you've named throughout the sheet. Pressing Escape clears the map display and returns you to a normal window display.

The /Worksheet Window Perspective command causes 1-2-3 to show three layers of the spreadsheet at once, stacked one on top of another. Working in three-dimensional worksheets is beyond the scope of this book, so we'll leave you to explore the Perspective command on your own.

Release 3.1's /Worksheet Window Graph command is nearly obsolete—it divides the display at the cell pointer to show the worksheet on the left and the current graph on the right. The feature was an early method offered to let users view data and graphs side by side. It has two advantages over Wysiwyg's ability to place graphs in the sheet. First, you can view a graph and the sheet simultaneously no matter where in the sheet the cell pointer happens to be. Second, you can view a graph and the sheet simultaneously even without Wysiwyg attached. Again, explore the /Worksheet Window Graph command on your own to gain a better understanding of how it works.

Close the Window

It's important to understand that both of the windows look at the same spreadsheet. Data and formulas you enter through one window also appear in the second. Also, anything you delete through either window is gone from the spreadsheet—it won't be there if you switch windows and go looking for it.

A few of the things you do in a spreadsheet will apply to one window and not to the other. For example, the default numeric display format that you assign via the /Worksheet Global Format command can be different in one window from that of the other. Also, column widths that you change in one window don't change in the other.

When you've finished your work with two windows, return to the normal spreadsheet display by selecting /Worksheet Windows Clear. The single window that remains on the display retains the default numeric display format and the column widths of the leftmost or uppermost of the two windows.

Less Sluggish Performance

Quite often a large spreadsheet contains lots of formulas. The formulas can really slow you down. This is because 1-2-3 reevaluates a spreadsheet's formulas every time you make a new entry or change an existing entry in the sheet. Fortunately, 1-2-3 doesn't recalculate every formula just because it's a formula. 1-2-3 recalculates only the formulas whose calculations could be affected by the changes you've made.

For example, if the spreadsheet contains two formulas, +A1 in cell A2 and +B1 in cell B2, then changing the entry in cell A1 causes 1-2-3 to recalculate only the formula in cell A2. Release 2.3 can take awhile to figure out which formulas to recalculate. Release 3.1 figures out immediately which formulas to calculate. In either case, depending on the relationships among the formulas, and on how many formulas there are, it can take several seconds or even minutes for 1-2-3 to be ready after you make an alteration. You can speed up your work in a sluggish spreadsheet by setting worksheet recalculation to manual.

Manual versus Automatic

If your large models are slow, select /Worksheet Global Recalculation Manual. From then on, 1-2-3 won't update formulas each time you change the sheet. In fact 1-2-3 won't update formulas until you press the CALC key (function key F9).

With recalculation set to manual, changing a cell's contents produces an indicator in the bottom of the display that reads *CALC*. This tells you that some of the formulas in your sheet may not be aware of any new values—they may be returning incorrect results. If the CALC indicator is on in your spreadsheet, assume that the formulas aren't current, and trust them only after you press the CALC key.

Try a small experiment to see how this works. Select /Worksheet Erase Yes Yes to clear the sheet. Then enter the formula +A1*2 into cell A2. Enter *8* into cell A1. Now select /Worksheet Global Recalculation Manual.

Change the 8 in cell A1 to read *7*. The CALC indicator appears at the bottom of the display, and the formula in A2 continues to return 16—that's the result of the calculation from before you entered 7 into A1. Press the CALC key (F9), and 1-2-3 updates the formula. You can reactivate automatic recalculation by selecting /Worksheet Global Recalculation Automatic.

Having completed this chapter, you:

- *Are familiar with several strategies for working efficiently in the spreadsheet*

- *Can apply the End key to make quick hops among data cells*

- *Are aware of how to make the cell pointer jump one screen's worth of rows or columns*

- *Know how to use the GOTO key to move the pointer directly to a cell or a range*

- *Understand how to create a second window on the worksheet*

- *Can unsynchronize window scrolling and use windows as you build formulas in POINT mode*

- *Have a sense of how 1-2-3 recalculates formulas and can control recalculation manually*

34

Work across Files

When spreadsheet files start proliferating on your hard disk, you'll notice certain information arises repeatedly from one sheet to another. A table that you create in one set of sales commission calculations could apply as well in many other calculations. Or, the two quarterly reports from the first half of a year might be useful if consolidated into a single report.

Once you've saved a spreadsheet on disk, you may want to retrieve it into another spreadsheet alongside other data. 1-2-3's /File Combine commands let you do just that. You can copy labels, values, and formulas from a disk file into the current spreadsheet, you can bring only the values from disk into the sheet, and you can even subtract the values on disk from the values in the current sheet.

The File Combine Commands

Perhaps the greatest use of the /File Combine commands is in consolidating information from several sheets into one. There are several ways to go about

doing this, and looking at the various ways will reveal a bit about how the commands work. Before you can apply the /File Combine commands, you'll need to create a simple model and save a copy of it on disk.

A Model to Combine

We tried to keep the practice worksheet for this discussion simple. It appears in Figure 34.1. To create it, start in a blank worksheet, and enter the labels shown in range A1..B1. Then, enter the values in range

In this chapter, you'll:

- *Learn how to move data from one spreadsheet into another*

- *Explore one technique for consolidating several worksheets into one*

- *Examine some of the rules that apply to combining spreadsheet files*

	A	B	C	D	E	F	G	H
1	June	July						
2	4	5						
3	4	5						
4	4	5						
5	4	5						
6	4	5						
7	20	25						
8								

FIGURE 34.1: This simple spreadsheet will help as you explore the effects of the /File Combine commands.

A2..B6. Finally, enter the formula @SUM(A2..A6) into cell A7 and copy it to cell B7. Select /File Save and enter the name PCOMB to create a disk copy of the model.

Now, change the entries in range A2..B6 so that each of the values in column A of the range is 7 and each of the entries in column B is 8. The resulting worksheet should match the one in Figure 34.2.

	A	B	C	D	E	F	G	H
1	June	July						
2	7	8						
3	7	8						
4	7	8						
5	7	8						
6	7	8						
7	35	40						
8								

FIGURE 34.2: By modifying the worksheet currently in RAM, you distinguish it from the copy that you just saved on disk.

Combine a Copy

The simplest way to combine one file into another is to bring an exact copy of a disk file into the current spreadsheet. Before you do this, you should be certain of the dimensions of the model in the disk file and bring it into the current worksheet at a point where it won't disrupt existing entries.

You know that the disk file you're about to combine contains two columns of entries running from cell A1 to cell B7. The current worksheet contains data in the same range, so it wouldn't be prudent to bring the disk file in starting in cell A1—that would wipe out the existing information in range A1..B7 and replace it with incoming information. Move the cell pointer to cell D1 before you combine files.

	A	B	C	D	E	F	G	H
1	June	July		June	July			
2	7	8		4	5			
3	7	8		4	5			
4	7	8		4	5			
5	7	8		4	5			
6	7	8		4	5			
7	35	40		20	25			
8								

FIGURE 34.3: The /File Combine Copy command places the incoming spreadsheet beginning at the location of the cell pointer.

Bring the disk model into the current worksheet by selecting /File Combine Copy Entire-File, and entering the file name *PCOMB*. The disk data appear starting in cell D1. Examine the formulas so you see that the incoming formulas retain their relationships with the cells they referenced in the disk file—the formulas still sum the information in the cells directly above them. Your worksheet should match the one in Figure 34.3.

Some File Combine Rules

The /File Combine Copy command brings an exact copy of a disk file into the current worksheet—replacing any entries in the sheet with corresponding incoming entries. So, if there were an entry in cell G1, and you combined a file in which an entry coincided with cell G1, the incoming entry would supercede the original one. On the other hand, if there is no corresponding entry to replace one in the current sheet, the /File Combine Copy command leaves the current entry intact.

That's a mouthful. Try an experiment to see how it works. Select /File Save and enter the name *PCOMB2* in place of the existing file name. Now your disk holds a copy of the worksheet currently on your display. Use the /Range Erase command to erase range B1..D7, leaving the entries in columns A and E. Now, enter your name into cells B4, C4, and D4.

Here's the scenario: You'll combine the PCOMB2 file into the current worksheet starting at cell A1. The entries in columns A and E will seem not to change because they are identical in both worksheets. The incoming file will replace the entries you erased from columns B and C—and incoming entries will supercede your name in both cell B4 and D4. However, because the incoming file has no entry in cell C4, your name in that cell will survive the combine operation. Try it.

Press Home so the pointer is in cell A1. Then select /File Combine Copy Entire-File and enter the name *PCOMB2*.

File Combine Consolidations

The /File Combine Copy command brings a lot of information into the spreadsheet. When you combine a file this way, you bring in values, labels, and formulas, doubling in some cases the total cell entries. One of the reasons you might combine files in the first place is so you can summarize the data that the files contain.

Consider the original spreadsheet that you created in this chapter. It contains some labels, values, and summary formulas. Such a spreadsheet might represent the revenues generated by a particular sales office during a two-month period. If you have 10 sales offices, you might want to combine the data from 10 office-specific spreadsheets into one summary sheet. As long as the sheets have identical structures, you need not bring 10 copies into the current sheet. Rather, you can use the /File Combine Add command to bring one copy in on top of the next.

Try Adding Files

Try a simple consolidation to see how 1-2-3 can total up a series of similar files. Start by erasing the entries from range C1..E7 of the practice worksheet. Then position the cell pointer in cell A1 and select /File Combine Add Entire-File. Enter *PCOMB* as the name of the file to combine. The values in range A2..B6 increase—they now reflect the sums of the preexisting values and the incoming values. The formulas in cells A7 and B7 return new sums based on the updated entries.

The /File Combine Add command adds any incoming values to corresponding values in the spreadsheet. The command also places incoming values that correspond to blank cells into the blank cells. The /File Combine Add command doesn't change cells in the current worksheet that already contain formulas or labels nor does it bring formulas from disk into the sheet—rather, it brings in the current values of formulas from disk.

So, to tally up similar revenue reports from 10 sales offices, you could begin in a blank worksheet and use the /File Combine Copy command to bring in the first file. Bring in the remaining nine files by leaving the cell pointer in place and issuing the /File Combine Add command. After you complete the file combining process, be sure to save the consolidation file under its own name or you'll lose the summary of your data.

Having completed this chapter, you:

- *Know how to bring a copy of a disk file into the current spread-sheet*

- *Understand how 1-2-3 consolidates values when you apply the /File Combine Add command*

- *Have a good idea of how to create a spreadsheet that summarizes the data in several identically formatted sheets*

Macros Made Easy

Repetition is dull. Repetition is dull. Repetition is dull. Repetition is dull. Repetition is dull. Repetition is dull. Repetition is dull. Repetition is dull. Repetition is dull. Repetition is dull. Repetition is dull. Repetition is dull.

Convinced? This being the case, a lot of what you do when you work in the spreadsheet is dull.

Depending on the model you're building, you may enter a particular label —your company's name, for example—again and again. Or, you may edit a sequence of cell entries, changing each one identically. Perhaps you need to insert row after row into the sheet or continually set and reset column widths. Maybe there's a particular collection of Wysiwyg cell formats that you want to assign repeatedly throughout the sheet. All these tasks become less dull when you apply spreadsheet macros.

Macros Defined

A macro is no more than a label or a collection of labels in the spreadsheet. The labels represent whatever keys you would press to perform a given task.

When you activate a macro, you tell 1-2-3 to read the characters in the labels and "press" the corresponding keys automatically—as if the software is replacing you at the keyboard. Create a simple macro so you get an idea of how this works.

Write Your First Macro

The first macro you write will type your name automatically. Start in an otherwise

---

In this chapter, you'll:

- *Learn how to automate tasks in the spreadsheet*

- *Write your first spreadsheet macro*

- *Create a few simple macros that can speed your work in the sheet*

FIGURE 35.1: The entry in cell A1 isn't part of the macro. It serves only to remind you of the macro's name.

blank worksheet and enter your name into cell B1. Then enter the characters \n into cell A1. If you were the author of this book, your worksheet would match the one in Figure 35.1.

Your macro resides in cell B1, and the label in cell A1 represents the name that you'll assign to the macro. Assign the name by selecting /Range Name Create, typing \n, and pressing Enter. Then indicate cell B1 as the range to name. Your macro is ready for a test run.

Try the Macro

Test the macro with the cell pointer in a blank cell—cell A5 will do. Start the macro running by holding down the Alt key and pressing *N*. Your name appears on the edit line in the control panel! Press Enter to store your name in cell A5, or press Escape to clear it from the edit line.

Any macro whose name consists of a backslash followed by a single letter is this easy to run—while holding down the Alt key, you press the letter in the macro's name. 1-2-3 simply repeats each of the characters listed in your macro as if typing them in your place. This raises a question: How do you include instructions in a macro to press such keys as Enter, Escape, Right-Arrow, and so on? Pressing these keys doesn't produce characters that you can record as labels. Is there any way to make a macro press them?

Special Key Indicators

The answer is yes, your macros can tell 1-2-3 to press such keys as Enter, RightArrow, and Delete. In fact, the macro that you just created and tested might feel more complete if it pressed Enter after typing your name. That would enter your name in the current cell rather than simply type it in the control panel.

To make a macro press keys other than the alphanumeric keys, include special key indicators in the macro instructions. The special key indicator that means "Press Enter" is a single tilde (~). Try adding one to your macro so you can see how it works.

Move the cell pointer to cell B1 and press the EDIT key (F1). Now type a tilde and press Enter. Your macro's instructions mean "Type the name and press Enter." Try running it. Move the cell pointer to cell A6 and then hold down the Alt key and press N. The macro enters your name in the cell.

Other Key Indicators

The special key indicator for the Enter key is unique. It's the only key indicator that doesn't share the standard format for key indicators. Most key indicators consist of a key name enclosed in braces. For example, the indicator that means "Press the RightArrow key" is {RIGHT}, and the indicator that represents the Home key is {HOME}.

Sometimes you want a macro to move the cell pointer down immediately after it enters a label in the worksheet. Modify your macro by adding the key indicator for the DownArrow key. That indicator is {DOWN}, so enter the label {DOWN} into cell B2. Then, move the cell pointer to cell A7 and press Alt-N. Press Alt-N several times in succession to enter your name repeatedly in column A. Pretty cool, huh?

Macro Flow of Control

You've just demonstrated an important point about macros: 1-2-3 reads macro instructions from left to right across a cell. When it has read and followed the last command in a cell, your software looks for further commands in the next cell. 1-2-3 continues reading instructions from left to right and down the column until it encounters a blank cell or one that contains a nonlabel entry. This means you can enter several tens or hundreds of macro commands down a column and create some very involved automated programs.

Further Macro Concepts

A macro can "press" just about any key that you can. This means your macros can contain characters that issue menu commands along with other instructions. For example, you might write a macro that selects /Range Format Currency, enters 2, and presses Enter to assign a currency format to the current cell. Such a macro appears in Figure 35.2. Again, the label that appears

FIGURE 35.2: The macro in cell B1 of this figure assigns a currency format to the current cell when you press Alt-F.

in cell A1 isn't part of the macro. It identifies the name that you'd assign the macro so you could trigger it by pressing Alt-F.

Notice that the macro makes menu selections by typing the first letter of the appropriate menu item. This convention is important—it helps you to recognize a macro's meaning when you see it in the worksheet days or weeks after you create it. Don't have a macro select menu items by moving the menu pointer with {LEFT} and {RIGHT} commands.

Macros on Your Own

The little you've done with macros is a solid introduction for a spreadsheet user moving into the intermediate category. Actually, if you worked through this entire book, you're quite a bit more knowledgeable about 1-2-3 than the average intermediate user.

Having an awareness of macros puts you at the hazy boundary between intermediate and advanced user. You may not yet be able to apply these tools in a significant way, but you're prepared to deal with them as your expertise increases.

Having completed this chapter, you:

- *Understand the concept of automating spreadsheet tasks*

- *Know what a macro is and how to create one*

- *Know how to name a macro so you can start it running with a few keystrokes*

- *Are familiar with macro key names*

- *Have a sense of how macros can issue menu commands as if you were pressing the keys instead*

- *Are a crack 1-2-3 spreadsheet computerist*

1-2-3 At Work

Every lesson about 1-2-3 should include an example or two of 1-2-3 solving real world problems. This appendix offers three examples. The first spreadsheet presented in this appendix lets you calculate your net worth. That is, given all of your debts and assets, what is your total financial value? The second spreadsheet helps you to balance your bank account and compare your bookkeeping to that of your bank. The third spreadsheet helps to relieve you of boredom. It lets you create some snazzy graphs reminiscent of the designs you might have created using a Spirograph set as a child (or with a child)—or whenever.

Each example begins with a short discussion of what the spreadsheet you're about to build does. It includes an illustration of the spreadsheet and gives step-by-step instructions for entering the labels, values, and formulas and for making appropriate settings. The discussions finish with instructions for using the finished spreadsheets, so you'll be able to use them with your own data.

What Are You Worth?

The question of your net worth might never concern you. However, should you wish to borrow money or buy things on credit, a bank or a lending institution is likely to be very interested in your financial worth. 1-2-3 is the perfect tool for keeping track of that information.

The worksheet shown in Figure A.1 contains labels and formulas that together define a net worth model. Once you've created the model by following the instructions in this text, you'll be able to enter your financial data into the blank cells of columns B and D and then see your net worth displayed on the worksheet's bottom line. You'll be able to print the spreadsheet and take a copy with you when you need to discuss finances with a lender or credit company.

	A	B	C	D
1	**Personal Balance Sheet**			
2	**Your Name Here**			
3				
4	**Assets**		**Liabilities**	
5				
6	**Accessible cash**		**Unpaid bills**	
7	Cash		Rent	
8	Savings account(s)		Condo fees	
9	Checking account(s)		Utilities	
10	Pay owed to date		Credit card balances	
11	Other (lottery, sweepstakes, etc.)		Insurance premiums	
12	Total accessible cash	$0	Services (diaper, yard, etc.)	
13			Support (alimony, child support...)	
14	**Property**		Total of unpaid bills	$0
15	Car(s)			
16	Recreational vehicles		**Long-term debt**	
17	Furniture and appliances		Auto loan(s)	
18	Tools		Student loan(s)	
19	Clothing		Personal loan(s)	
20	Jewelry		Business loan(s)	
21	Miscellaneous		Home improvement loans	
22	Total value of property	$0	Other long-term debt	
23			Total of long-term debt	$0
24	**Real estate**			
25	Primary residence		**Real estate loans**	
26	Secondary personal residences		Primary residence	
27	Time shares (value of your share)		Secondary personal residences	
28	Commercial properties		Time shares	
29	Parking spaces		Commercial mortgages	
30	Other real estate		Parking spaces	
31	Total value of real estate	$0	Other real estate loans	
32			Total of real estate loans	$0
33	**Financial Investments**			
34	Life insurance (cash value)		**Taxes now due**	
35	Certificates of Deposit		Local	
36	Retirement account(s)		State	
37	Stock portfolio (current value)		Federal	
38	Equity in businesses		Property	
39	Money loaned		Inheritance	
40	Pension (amount vested)		Other taxes	
41	Vested unexercised stock options		Total of taxes now due	$0
42	Other financial holdings			
43	Total financial investments	$0		
44				
45	**Assets**	$0	**Liabilities**	$0
46				
47			**Net Worth**	$0
48				

FIGURE A.1: When you fill in the blanks in this spreadsheet, you'll have an attractive net worth document to present to a lending institution.

Set Column Widths and Enter Labels

Start with the cell pointer in cell A1 of a blank worksheet. Select /Worksheet Column Set-Width and adjust column A to a width of 26 characters. Move the pointer to column B and set the width there to 10 characters. Set the width of column C to 26 and the width of column D to 10.

Enter all of the labels that you see in column A of the worksheet in Figure A.1—including the titles in cells A1 and A2 (of course, you should replace the label in cell A2 with your own name). Your entries won't appear in the same type faces and styles that you see in the figure. Enter all of them anyway, and you'll change the fonts as appropriate in a moment. Most of the labels in column A are left aligned, but the label *Assets* in cell A4 is centered, and you must begin with a caret label prefix when you enter it. Also, each of the labels in cells A12, A22, A31, and A43 is right aligned. Begin with quotation mark label prefixes when you enter them. Begin with a quotation mark when you enter the label *Assets* in cell A45 as well.

Enter the labels in column C just as you did the ones in column A. Again, the label *Liabilities* in cell C4 is centered, and the labels in cells C14, C23, C32, C41, C45, and C47 are right aligned.

Enter Formulas

You enter the formulas in this spreadsheet even before you enter values for the formulas to use in calculations. Later, when you enter your personal financial information, the formulas will automatically calculate your total assets and liabilities.

Move the cell pointer to cell B12 and enter the formula *@SUM(B7..B11)*. Remember, there are two methods you can use to create the formula. Either type the characters *@SUM(B7..B11)* and press Enter or type *@SUM(*, highlight range B7..B11, type a closing parenthesis, and press Enter. Either type or use POINT mode to enter other formulas as listed in Table A.1.

Cell	Formula
B12	@SUM(B7..B11)
D14	@SUM(D7..D13)
B22	@SUM(B15..B21)
D23	@SUM(D17..D22)
B31	@SUM(B25..B30)
D32	@SUM(D26..D31)
B43	@SUM(B34..B42)
D41	@SUM(D35..D40)
B45	+B12+B22+B31+B43
D45	+D14+D23+D32+D41
D47	+B45-D45

TABLE A.1: Enter these formulas in your worksheet.

Each of the formulas should return 0 when you enter it.

Spruce Up the Presentation

The essential parts of your spreadsheet are in place. You could enter your financial information, and the model would calculate your net worth. However, with your knowledge of Wysiwyg's spreadsheet publishing features, you might as well polish the worksheet so your financial statement is a pleasure to look at even if the bottom line isn't such a pleasure.

Set the Global Numeric Display Format

All of the numbers that you'll enter in the net worth model are dollar amounts. It makes sense, then, to set the global numeric display format to show currency. Select /Worksheet Global Format Currency and enter *0*.

Change the Available Fonts

Start by adjusting the fonts and font styles as you see in Figure A.1. First, select :Format Font Replace. The fonts currently available aren't quite what you need to make your spreadsheet match ours. You make the correct fonts available by replacing some of the original eight options with new options.

Font 1 is probably 12-point Swiss. That's OK, but we prefer the Dutch font, so we changed to 12-point Dutch. To do this, select 1 and then select Dutch. When prompted, enter *12* as the font size. Remember that font 1 is the one that Wysiwyg uses automatically for all your spreadsheet entries—you may notice the characters on the underlying spreadsheet change to reflect your modification.

Replace font 2 by selecting Replace 2 and then Dutch. Enter 16 as the point size for this font. Use the same procedure to replace font 3 with 18-point Dutch. Select Quit and return to READY mode. You're ready to go to work.

Accentuate the Titles

Now that the appropriate fonts are available, you can assign them to the titles in your model. Start with the cell pointer in A1 and select :Format Font 3. Indicate range A1..A2 as the range to format. Select :Format Bold Set and indicate range A1..A2 a second time to add emphasis to the titles. Drop down to cell A4, select :Format Font 2, and indicate A4..C4 as the range to format. Select :Format Bold Set and indicate the same range.

Except for the one in cell C47, you don't need to change the font of the remaining titles, only the font style. To change the title in cell A6, select :Format Bold Set and indicate cell A6. Repeat this procedure to set boldface for the entries in cells C6, A14, C16, A24, C25, A33, C34, A45, and C45.

Finally, dress up the entry in cell C47 by selecting :Format Bold Set and indicating the cell. Select :Format Font 2 and once again indicate cell C47. You're ready to add the lines that help guide a reader's eyes among the entries in the completed financial statement.

Add Lines and Shading

There are lines all over the net worth worksheet. Perhaps the trickiest to create are the lines and shading that surround the title at the top of the page. Start with the cell pointer in A1 and select :Format Lines Outline. Indicate range A1..B2, and Wysiwyg draws a box around the titles. Now select :Format Lines Shadow Set and indicate range A1..B2 a second time. The box with the titles appears to jump off of the page.

You'll create the lines associated with each subsection of the spreadsheet in turn. The procedures for each subsection are similar, only the ranges differ. Start with the section titled *Accessible cash*.

Move the pointer to cell A6 and select :Format Lines Bottom. Indicate range A6..B10. Move the pointer to cell B12, select :Format Lines Outline, and press Enter to indicate B12 as the cell to format. Select :Format Lines Double Top and indicate range A12..B12.

That's the drill. Try it again for the *Unpaid Bills* section of the model. Move the pointer to C6, select :Format Lines Bottom, and indicate range C6..D12. Drop the pointer to cell D14, select :Format Lines Outline, and press Enter. Finally, select :Format Lines Double Top and indicate range D14..C14. Follow this pattern starting with the cell pointer in A14, again with the pointer in C16, with the pointer in A24, C25, A33, and finally starting with the pointer in C34.

Select :Format Lines Outline and indicate cell B45. Then issue the command again and indicate cell D45. Select :Format Lines Double Outline and indicate cell D47. Select :Format Lines Double Bottom and indicate cell C47. All that's left to finish the model is to add some vertical lines.

Select :Format Lines Left and indicate range A6..A42. Select :Format Lines Right and indicate range D6..D40. Finally, select :Format Lines Double Left and indicate range C6..C43. The net worth model is ready to run! But before you start using it, save a copy of it on disk.

Select /File Save and enter an appropriate file name—*NETWORTH* should do nicely. You'll be able to start with this unused copy of the net worth model should you want to help out friends or family members with their net worth calculations. After you've filled in your own numbers, you'll save the model under a different file name so that you don't disturb the original unused version of the file.

Use the Net Worth Model

There are no tricks to using the net worth template. You need only to fill in the cells in columns B and D with the data suggested by the labels in columns A and C. There are a few things to keep in mind.

The *Accessible cash* section of the assets column should include your liquid assets, as well as money that is absolutely yours—outstanding pay (including accounts receivable if you're a consultant and you've billed or will be billing for work that you've already completed) goes in cell B10, and other incoming cash such as lottery winnings, outstanding cash refunds from your income tax filings, and inheritances goes in cell B11. Only enter values in cells B10 and B11 for cash that you can prove you'll be receiving at any point in the future.

Under *Property*, enter your best guess at the resale values of each of the items you include. For example, if you could sell your car for $3,500, enter that amount in cell B15. Add up the resale values of all your possessions and enter the totals in the appropriate cells. Enter the full market value of your real estate holdings in the *Real estate* section, even if you haven't fully paid for the properties. Make sure you enter the current values of your investments in the appropriate cells of the *Financial investments* section—don't use calculations of what your investments will be worth when they mature.

In the *Unpaid bills* section of the liabilities columns, enter only amounts for which you are absolutely in debt. If you paid all your bills yesterday, they shouldn't appear in this section. Of course, make sure the money that you've paid isn't included as an asset in one of your bank accounts—if you've written the check you've spent the money.

Enter the total outstanding principal for any loans in the *Long-term debt* section and for any mortgages and second mortgages that would fall in the *Real estate loan* section. Finally, enter appropriate amounts in the *Taxes now due* section. This section is most likely to affect people who are self-employed or who have a lot of income from sources other than a full time job.

When You Know Your Net Worth

When you finish entering your financial data, your net worth appears in cell D47. To print a copy of the spreadsheet, make sure your printer is on and ready and make sure you've selected the appropriate printer driver. Remember, to select a driver, choose :Print Configuration Printer and then pick from the resulting list. Select Quit to return to Wysiwyg's main print menu and then select Range Set. Indicate range A1..D47 as the range to print and then select Go.

To save a copy of your completed net worth statement on disk, select /File Save and type a file name—such as *MYNET*—to distinguish the finished copy from the original unused net worth worksheet.

Balance Your Checkbook

Balancing a checkbook is only as challenging as recording the amounts of the checks you write and saving and recording receipts from your various financial transactions. If you're careful about these things, then a few minutes with paper and pencil reveal that your bank keeps equally good records about how you use your checking account. On the other hand, if you lose one receipt or fail to record a single check amount, your monthly bank statement might take you by surprise.

More problematical than losing track of a checking account transaction is making a mistake in your calculations as you tally your monthly checking activity. If you're working with pencil and paper, you must track down numerical errors and add and subtract all of the transactions again and again until you resolve discrepancies. If you're working with a calculator, you might need to reenter all of your transactions repeatedly until your checkbook balances. Resolving errors is easiest when you use an electronic spreadsheet to balance your account.

A Simple Check Recorder

We're not about to offer a complete checkbook management system in 1-2-3. That's a project for an intermediate or advanced level book. Rather, the worksheet in Figure A.2 lets you enter your last month's account balance at the top of the sheet and then list your transactions starting in row 9. Formulas in column F reveal the account's running balance after each transaction clears.

Once you've built the model, you can retrieve it each month and enter your transactions to check your accounting against your bank statement. If you make a mistake entering transactions, you'll be able to correct it in a jiffy simply by replacing the erroneous entry in the spreadsheet. Here's how to proceed.

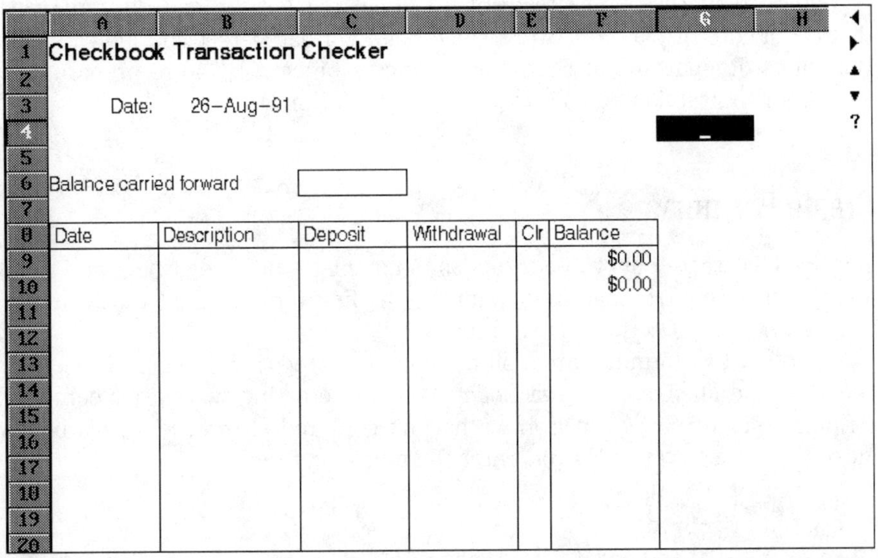

FIGURE A.2: This spreadsheet looks simple, but it uses some complex formulas to help you balance your checkbook against your monthly bank statement.

Set Widths

Start in a blank worksheet and select /Worksheet Column Column-Range Set-Width. Indicate range A1..F1 as the range of columns and enter *10* as the target width. Move the pointer to column B and select /Worksheet Column Set-Width. Press Enter to set the width of the current column and then enter *13*. Use the /Worksheet Column Set-Width command to establish a width of 3 characters for column E.

Enter Labels and Set the Display Formats

Enter labels as they appear in the illustration. Be aware that the title *Checkbook Transaction Checker* is a long label stored in cell A1. Also, the entry *Date:* is a right-aligned label in cell A3—begin with a quotation mark label prefix when you enter it.

Almost all of your entries in this worksheet will be dollar amounts, so set the global numeric display format to currency with two decimal places. Remember, to do this you select /Worksheet Global Format Currency and enter *2*.

Your worksheet is going to display the current date in cell B3, so assign that cell a date display format: Select /Range Format Date 1 and indicate cell B3. Select /Range Format Date 1 and indicate range A9..A40 to prepare column A for transaction dates that you'll enter later on.

Create Formulas

You need to create only three formulas to complete the spreadsheet and then add the lines that delineate the columns. The first formula is @NOW. Enter it into cell B3, and it returns today's date.

The other two formulas are a bit more complicated than the first. In fact, to complete the checkbook spreadsheet, you'll be creating two rather complex formulas that use an @function we haven't explored elsewhere in this book. Move the cell pointer to F9 and enter the following formula:

```
@IF(@CELL("type",E9)="b",C6,C9-D9+C6)
```

Move to cell F10 and enter the following:

```
@IF(@CELL("type",E10)="b",F9,C10-D10+F9)
```

The first of the two formulas is a conditional statement that returns the balance carried forward from last month (from cell C6) if there's no entry in cell E9. If there is an entry in cell E9, the formula adds the value from C9 to the value in cell C6 and subtracts the value from D9. This calculates your account balance subsequent to whatever transaction you record in row 9.

The second of the formulas looks for an entry in cell E10. If E10 is blank, the formula returns whatever value is in cell F9. If E10 contains an entry, the formula adds the value from cell C10 to the value in cell F9 and subtracts the value from cell D10—returning your account balance after whatever transaction you record in row 10.

If these explanations are a little confusing, rest assured that the formulas will do exactly what they need to do when you enter transactions according to the instructions that come later in this appendix. Rather than explain exactly how the formulas work, we'll leave you to examine them carefully and decipher their structures on your own. Press the HELP key and use 1-2-3's Help facility to find information on the @CELL function. All that's left to do is to add the special Wysiwyg formatting to make your spreadsheet match ours.

Add Some Lines and Boxes

There are only a few embellishments to the checkbook spreadsheet. The first is to the title in cell A1. It's boldfaced and a slightly larger point size than the other text in the sheet. To modify it in your worksheet, move the pointer to A1, select :Format Font 2, and press Enter. Then, select :Format Bold Set and press Enter once more.

Move the cell pointer to C6, select :Format Lines Outline, and press Enter. Move to cell A8, select :Format Lines All, and indicate range A8..F8. Drop down to cell A9, select :Format Lines Left, and indicate range A9..F40. Finally, select :Format Lines Right and indicate range F9..F40. The length of the vertical lines that you've created is arbitrary. If you typically have more than 30 checking account transactions a month, extend the lines downward as needed.

In any case, the model is ready to use. But, before you try it out, save a copy of it to disk. To save the spreadsheet, select /File Save and enter a file-name such as *CHECKS*. You'll be able to retrieve this spreadsheet whenever you need help balancing your checkbook at the end of a month.

Does It Balance?

Using the checkbook worksheet is pretty easy. Start by entering your account's balance from the previous month into cell C6. Then drop down to cell A9 and use the @DATE function to enter the date of your first checking transaction for the month you're balancing. Enter a description in cell B9 of the transaction that you're recording and then enter the transaction amount in either column C or D, depending on whether you're recording a deposit or a withdrawal.

When you make an entry in column C or D, the formulas in column F continue to return the balance from the previous month. However, when you make an entry in cell E9, the formulas will be updated to reveal a new balance. We recommend using an "*X*" in cell E9, to mark the transaction as having cleared the bank. So, for every transaction that has an amount in column C or D, you must enter *X* in column E if the transaction appears on your bank statement. If the transaction isn't on your bank statement, then leave a blank cell in column E so that the formulas don't include the transaction when calculating your account balance. This approach lets you record all of your bank transactions in the spreadsheet, but still obtain a correct balance should some of your checks not clear by the time the bank prepares your statement.

Enter a second transaction in row 10 of the worksheet, marking it with an X in column E if it has cleared, and then enter a third transaction in row 11. Once you've recorded a transaction in row 11, copy the formula from cell F10 to F11 to calculate your account's balance after the new transaction. Continue to enter transactions in this manner, putting a date, a description, a deposit or withdrawal amount, and an X in each row and then copying the formula from the preceding row of column F to calculate a new account balance.

Of course, when you've entered all of your transactions for the month and marked each with an X, your spreadsheet's balance formula should return the same amount that appears on your bank statement. If that's not the case, make sure you haven't checked as cleared any transactions that aren't in the statement. It's also possible that you haven't checked off a transaction that has cleared. If this type of error doesn't account for the discrepancy between your spreadsheet and your bank statement, then look for numbers in your spreadsheet that simply aren't correct. If you find a mistake in a deposit or a withdrawal amount, simply enter a new value to replace the erroneous one and the formulas instantly reflect the change. Finally, look for transactions recorded on your bank statement that you haven't entered in the spreadsheet, and vice versa.

Once you've balanced your checkbook, save the spreadsheet under a new file name if you wish. Don't save under the name CHECKS as that will replace the unused checkbook transaction checker model. Rather, use a file name that identifies the month recorded in the spreadsheet. For example, after balancing your checkbook in June of '82, save the spreadsheet as CKJUN82. Or, simply erase the spreadsheet from RAM—once your checkbook balances, you may have no need for a computer record of the month's checking activity.

Recreational Computing

The emphasis in spreadsheet computing is on work. But work can become boring. One way to alleviate boredom at work is to come up with ways to "play" with whatever tools you use during the day. The tool that you happen to be using is a wonderful plaything. 1-2-3 offers some wonderful diversions.

One fascinating way to pass some time with the spreadsheet is to use it to generate exotic graphs. All you do is supply some interesting data. Then 1-2-3 can draw complex pictures that represent the data and that look as if you spent hours mapping out intricate patterns. Consider, for example, the image in Figure A.3. It took about 15 seconds to create. Once you see how easy it is to vary the look of one of these "spirographics," you'll be able to

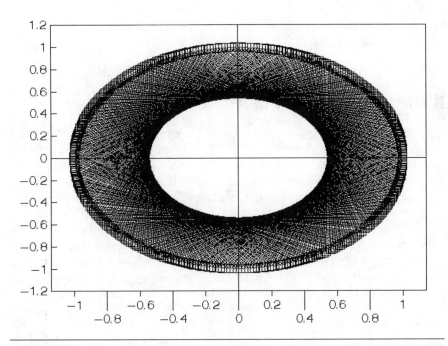

FIGURE A.3: With very little effort, even an inexperienced spreadsheet user can create complex geometrical patterns.

design several unique images in a matter of minutes simply by manipulating values in the spreadsheet.

Instant Graphification: A Spirographic

Enough talk. Let's get down to some fun. Start in a blank worksheet and use the Data Fill command to enter a sequence of values in column A. To do this, select /Data Fill and indicate range A1..A350 as the range to fill. Enter *0* as the Start value, *2* as the Step value, and press Enter to accept 8191 as the Stop value.

Now skip over to cell B1 and enter the formula *@SIN(A1)*. Enter *@COS(A1)* into cell C1. Copy both of these formulas down the worksheet by selecting /Copy, indicating range B1..C1 as the range to copy from, and indicating range B1..B350 as the range to copy to. All that's left is to graph the data.

Select /Graph Type XY—you're creating a scatter plot. Then select X and indicate range B1..B350 as the X graph range. Select A and indicate range C1..C350 as the A graph range. Now select View.

It's Pretty, but What Is It?

The graph, as you might surmise, is the sines of a list of values plotted against the cosines of the same values. The cosine of a number paired with the sine of the number describes a location on the circumference of a circle. The first location, associated with the number 0 in cell A1, is at the coordinates (0,1)—that's the very top of the circle. The second location, associated with the number 2 in cell A2, is at coordinates (.909297,-0.41614)—a bit less than a third of the way around the circle. When you graph the two points, 1-2-3 draws a straight line from the first coordinate to the second. Each pair of numbers in columns B and C describes a point that is a little less than a third of the way around the circle from the preceding point. Connecting the points with straight lines results in the snazzy pattern of lines.

Fiddle Further for Fun

OK, understanding what makes the graph look the way it does isn't important to being able to play with it. Try a few variations on the spirographic theme.

Press a key to clear the graph from the display and then select Quit from the graph menu. Now change the intervals between the values in column A. Instead of going a third of the way around the circle for each point, go about a quarter of the way.

Here's how to figure out what a quarter of the way around a circle is: Once around the circle is 2 times π—about 6.28. A quarter of that is about 1.5. So, select /Data Fill and press Enter to accept range A1..A350 as the range to fill. Press Enter to accept 0 as the Start value and enter *1.5* as the Step value. Press Enter to accept 8191 as the Stop value.

The formulas in columns B and C are updated instantly to reflect the changes in column A. And, since the graph settings are already established, you need only to press the GRAPH key (function key F10) to see the results of your handiwork. Do that now.

What happens when each data point is almost halfway around the circle from the preceding point? Press any key to clear the graph display and then select /Data Fill. Press Enter to accept the range to fill, enter *0* as the Start value, *3* as the Step value, and press Enter to accept the existing Stop value.

Press GRAPH (F10) to see the effect of your changes. You may be getting the idea by now that watching 1-2-3 draw the graphs is a big part of the fun of creating them.

Beyond the Basic Circles

The spirographic designs you've created so far are quite simple. With a little effort, you can come up with some pretty wild figures based on the same basic principal. For example, clear the graph from the display and then reset the intervals in column A to 1. Remember to do this, select /Data Fill, press Enter twice, type *1*, and then press Enter twice more. Now change the formula in column C.

Start by moving the pointer to cell C1 and pressing the EDIT key (function key F2). Type *@SIN(A1)* and press Enter. Now copy the new formula down column C by selecting /Copy, indicating cell C1 as the range to copy from, and indicating range C1..C350 as the target range. Press the GRAPH key.

Press a key to clear the graph and use the Data Fill command to fill column A with values separated by intervals of 3. See the result by pressing the GRAPH key. Try the graph again using intervals of 2 for the values in column A.

That's all we're telling you. Part of the fun with these spirographics is in coming up with your own combinations of sines and cosines that when plotted together create attractive patterns. Use your experiences here as a starting point and, then whenever you get bored on the job, experiment to create your own spirographic designs.

Index